CLINICAL APPROACH TO PROMOTION OF ENTREPRENEURSHIP AMONG WOMEN

Important Books by the Same Author

- *Community Development and Extension in India*, Gandhigram Rural Institute, Gandhigram, 1970.
- *Agricultural Extension in Thailand: A Study of the Training & Visit System*, HSD Monograph No. 15, Division of Human Settlements Development, Asian Institute of Technology, Bangkok, Thailand (co-author), 1988.
- *Small-Scale & Cottage Industries in Bangladesh: Prospects & Potential for Rural Development*, HSD Monograph No. 16, Division of Human Settlements Development, Asian Institute of Technology, Bangkok, Thailand (co-author), 1988.
- *The Valayar of South India*, Volume I, "Society and Religion" (Foreword by Prof. Yogesh Atal, UNESCO, Regional Advisor for Social and Human Sciences), 1990.
- *The Valayar of South India*, Volume II, "Culture and Economy" (Foreword by Prof. K.N. Sahay of Ranchi University), 1990.
- *The Valayar of South India*, Volume III, "Sex and Divorce" (Foreword by Prof. R. Subramanian of Gandhigram Rural Institute), 1990.
- *Rural Industrialization, Small-Scale and Cottage Industries in Asia*, United Nations Centre for Regional Development (UNCRD), Nagoya, Japan, July, 1991.
- *Rural Development: Problems and Prospects*, Inter-India Publications, New Delhi, 1991.
- *Participatory Rural Development in Asia: A Critical Analysis*, Inter-India Publications, New Delhi, 1994.
- *A Model for Securing People's Participation in Janmabhoomi – Rural Development*, with a Foreword by Nara Chandrababu Naidu, Dr. MCR HRD Institute of AP, Govt. of Andhra Pradesh, Hyderabad, 2001.
- *Reflections on People, Places, Events and Books – A Journey Through Time*, Inter-India Publications, New Delhi, 2001.
- *Neeru-Meeru – A Massive Popular Action for Water Conservation in Andhra Pradesh*, with a Foreword by Nara Chandrababu Naidu, Dr. MCR HRD Institute of AP, Govt. of Andhra Pradesh, Hyderabad, 2001.
- *New Approaches to Rural Development* with a Foreword by Sri P.V.R.K. Prasad, IAS, Anmol Publications Pvt. Ltd., New Delhi, 2002.
- *A Practical Handbook on Training* with a Foreword by Sri P.V.R.K. Prasad, IAS, Anmol Publications Pvt. Ltd., New Delhi, 2003.
- *The Unforgettable Characters* – (Under Publication).

CLINICAL APPROACH TO PROMOTION OF ENTREPRENEURSHIP AMONG WOMEN

[*In Reference to Asia*]

By

E.D. Setty

Ph.D.

ANMOL PUBLICATIONS PVT. LTD.

NEW DELHI - 110 002 (INDIA)

ANMOL PUBLICATIONS PVT. LTD.
4374/4B, Ansari Road, Daryaganj
New Delhi - 110 002
Ph.: 23261597, 23278000
Visit us at: www.anmolpublications.com

Clinical Approach to Promotion of Entrepreneurship Among Women

First Published, 2004

ISBN 81-261-1885-7

PRINTED IN INDIA

Published by J.L. Kumar for Anmol Publications Pvt. Ltd., New Delhi - 110 002 and Printed at Mehra Offset Press, Delhi.

Contents

Preface *vii*

Acknowledgement *xiii*

1. Introduction 1
2. Women in Society 4
3. A Model for Developing Agro-Enterprises Among Farm Women in Asia 19
4. Empowerment and Development of the Poor through their Participation – A Case Study from Bangladesh 38
5. Role of Banks in Entrepreneurship Development 58
6. Extension Education in Aid of Agricultural Marketing 65
7. Small-Scale Industrial Development in the Asian Context 88
8. Rural Industrialization in India 109
9. Field Approach to Development of Entrepreneurship 161
10. Role of Women in Socio-economic Development 201
11. Entrepreneurial Initiatives by Women Self-Help Groups in Andhra Pradesh 213
12. Efforts of NGOs in Promoting Mini-enterprises among women 244

Appendices 267

Index 405

Preface

In the process of planned and balanced rural-regional development in the developing countries in Asia, the set of challenging and vital questions faced by most of them is how to generate fuller employment for the labour force, how to increase the income levels of the people and how to reduce the regional and rural-urban disparities in the standards of living. Naturally, the action response to this challenge has been diverse, but with one common factor, that is, the emphasis on industrialization, especially rural industrialization. We cannot think of geometrical leaps in industrial development in the predominantly agrarian economies. One realistic and practical mechanism in meeting the challenge to development appears to be the promotion of small-scale and cottage industries that will accord with the existing human talent, infrastructure and material resources.

In the whole gamut of small industry promotion, entrepreneurship development, which may be called human resource development, is a pivotal factor. Its nature being such, it can grow and be developed only over a period of time. It needs organization, motivation, training and sustained institutional support.

Three principal factors which are vital for economic development in terms of employment-generation, utilization of human and physical and material resources and empowerment of women are stressed in the present volume. Developing entrepreneurship among women cannot be achieved in a vacuum and conditions in general are to be created and environment should be made conducive and preparedness and willingness on the part of the society in general are essential to promote entrepreneurship among women which would lead to their empowerment.

In socio-economic development of people, harnessing natural and human resources adopting ever-advancing and relevant technologies, entrepreneurship development as an instrument plays a very significant role. The Concept of entrepreneurship is of diverse and massive nature relating to micro to macro level enterprises. The development of entrepreneurship has not been even and there has been a very slow growth of it as an economic productive activity. Only certain segments of traditional occupational and ethnic groups and predominantly menfolk take to new enterprises. The present volume mainly focuses on the way to go about encouraging women to venture into entrepreneurial activities.

Since EDP has been a dependable means to generate entrepreneurial activity, there are a number of publications dealing with this concept and approach. Here is a modest attempt focusing on development of entrepreneurship among women.

The Introductory chapter, in brief, highlights the importance of developing entrepreneurship among women especially among the poor. It emphasizes that the surest and dependable means of empowerment of women is through economic-entrepreneurial pursuits.

Chapter-2 highlights the relevance and importance of developing entrepreneurship among women, briefly touching upon the significance and the history of creating a respectable place and status for women folk. It briefly points out the potential woman clientele who are to be encouraged to move into entrepreneurial activity.

Chapter 3, in general, presents a model for developing agro enterprises among farmwomen.

Chapter 4 is an illustrative and comparative model from

Bangladesh in organizing poor women into groups and helping them to become self-reliant. The Bangladesh Rural Advancement Committee (BRAC) has been for the past several years mobilizing and organizing poor women into groups helping them financially, training and guiding them in starting small-scale enterprises and facilitating the marketing of the products produced by the groups. It is similar to the activities of the Grameen Bank. The BRAC efforts serve as an effective model in organizing the poor women motivating and assisting them to operate as mini-entrepreneurs.

Chapter 5 briefly speaks of the role of banks in entrepreneurship development.

Chapter 6 though the title speaks of extension in aid of agricultural marketing, it could be taken as the marketing strategies for the products of small-scale enterprises. It illustrates the extension methods that are to be employed in generating awareness and securing the means to venture into entrepreneurial activities. Entrepreneurship development in a larger sense is an educational process. The chapter explains the ways to market agricultural products. Of several problems which may be called factors in the entire field of entrepreneurship development, marketing of products in a competitive world appears to be really a challenging one.

Chapter 7 which is rather comprehensive focuses on the ways in which small-scale and cottage industries are being promoted in Asia. Further, it lays emphasis on the need for rural industrialization and on the economy related to cottage and small-scale industries. It highlights the fact that the future prosperity of agricultural countries in the Asian region lies in the working hands of the villagers who are a hidden resource which needs to be mobilized. The chapter further focuses and brings out the advantages and disadvantages in respect to the large-scale and small-scale industries and highlights the role of industry in integrated rural development.

Chapter 8 which is rather elaborate briefly covers the industrial development policies promulgated by the Government of India during the past six decades in promoting small-scale enterprises providing incentives to the neo-entrepreneurs and making reservation of items for manufacture in the small-scale sector. In order to translate the industrial policies, issued periodically, the chapter lists out the institutional framework that has been established both at the national and state level.

Chapter 9 may be considered as a key chapter which details the approaches to development of entrepreneurship highlighting the sociological aspects, physical conditions, cultural patterns and human resources in promoting entrepreneurship in a given community. It speaks of the kind of barriers and stimulants in promoting entrepreneurship. It spells out four principal factors that matter in EDP namely, organization, infrastructure, resources and entrepreneur himself. It draws the attention of EDP promoters to the need for a successful utilization and blending of these factors which promote entrepreneurship. The different phases that one has to go through in promoting entrepreneurship are detailed in this chapter.

Chapter 10 is of a general nature describing women in society and their participation in development activities. It lays emphasis on empowering women enabling and facilitating them to participate in all development programmes which of course, is a stupendous task.

Chapter 11, in brief, details the manner in which the DWCRA programmes are being helped by different institutions and the way in which the self-help groups carry on the mini-enterprises and the kind of products they make and the way they go about improving their standard of life. This chapter concludes with an illustrative case study from the district of Warangal in Andhra Pradesh, entitled "Empowering Women through Self-Help Groups".

Chapter 12 in brief speaks of the efforts made by Non-Governmental Organizations (NGOs) such as Hindustan Lever Limited (HLL), Padmavathy Sangam, Rashtriya Seva Samithi (RASS) and Swayam Krushi Mutually Aided Cooperative Thrift Society in encouraging and helping women below poverty line to get self-employed. The Hindustan Lever Limited under its Project Shakti helps marketing of its products by the women, thus paving the way for individual and group entrepreneurial venture on the part of the poor women. It only indicates that not only the government but also the NGOs in their own self-interest and also to help the society could pave the way and lead the poor segments of population towards better way of life through economic pursuits.

It may be mentioned here that the volume contains relevant appendices which are of reference value. Appendix-I provides a detailed training design of entrepreneurship development. Appendix-II (A) deals with the industrial policies promulgated by the Government of India right from 1948 down to 1991. Appendix-II(B) details the activities of Khadi and Village Industries Commission. Appendix-III(A) indicates some important resources and their industrial uses. Appendix-IV provides information about the schemes for women entrepreneurs offered by the Govt. of India and State Governments and other governmental agencies.

The volume, in brief, covers the need, the way to go about developing entrepreneurship, in general, and specifically among women of diverse socio-economic background. It may be mentioned here that each chapter in the volume stands as an independent unit at the same time interrelated with the main focus on entrepreneurship development. As mentioned earlier, it is a trifocal study primarily focusing on developing entrepreneurship among women, secondly the need to go in for entrepreneurship development in general, and finally and rather importantly going in for rural industrialization. It is believed that the book will be of interest and use for the people engaged in promoting entrepreneurship in general and particularly among women, trainers and teachers in the field of EDP and the students pursuing courses in entrepreneurship development. The book in a word describes the course of action one may have to take in promoting entrepreneurship, emphasising Clinical Approach.

—**E.D. SETTY**

Acknowledgement

The idea and encouragement behind this book on Clinical Approach to Promotion of Entrepreneurship Among Women is Sri P.V.R.K. Prasad, IAS, Director General, Dr. MCR HRD Institute of AP & Ex-Officio Special Chief Secretary to Govt. of Andhra Pradesh. I took it as an opportunity and attempted this volume. I am deeply indebted to him. I am thankful to Sri M. Yanadaiah, Senior Steno, Dr. MCR HRD Institute of AP for his help as usual in preparing the manuscript. I would like to record here my grateful thanks to the sources named and unnamed from which I have adopted some material. I express my grateful thanks to M/s. Anmol Publications Pvt. Ltd., New Delhi for undertaking publication of this volume as they did, in an excellent way, my earlier two books: 1) New Approaches to Rural Development and 2) A Practical Handbook on Training.

AUTHOR

1

Introduction

For the past several centuries, there have been attempts to ameliorate the status of women in the society. The privileges or the status accorded to and enjoyed by women differ from culture to culture and from age to age. Sporadic political, social and religious attempts have been there to elevate or treat women as equal to man. We have not so far succeeded in bringing about the equality of sexes. One may write volumes and speak at length on the need for empowerment of women, but in reality and practice it may end as a wishful thinking. The importance that she enjoys at home is different from the way in which she is treated outside. Whether it is political emancipation or ensuring of social equality, it has been in the process for several centuries. One significant and potent factor that would empower women is through their economic contribution. We find a very close relationship between women empowerment and women taking to self-employment or some entrepreneurial activity. Here we emphasize entrepreneurial activity exclusively in the domain of women and managed by women. It could be one of the surest ways of bringing about equality between man and woman.

One can think of several approaches to remedy the gender inequality and imbalances in development, but one substantive approach could be promoting entrepreneurship among women. The usefulness of this approach depends on how seriously and faithfully it is translated into action. Unless there is something exclusive answering the cause and improving the economic conditions of women, any grand designs, formulation of policies and diluted approaches in the name of women development will hardly bear fruits.

Various conferences and seminars have brought out the point forcefully that integration of women in all sectors of economic and social development is necessary for national development. One could see some kind of reluctance, hesitation and unwillingness and prejudices in respect to encouraging women going in for entrepreneurial activity. There is a need to bring about a change in the attitude of people and the state has to make special efforts to create a facilitating situation to gradually encourage women to move into entrepreneurial field. These approaches are to be from several angles political, economic, social and religious but one solid effort could be motivating and facilitating women to take up some enterprises. One may speak volumes on why women are to be brought into the entrepreneurial activity. There is a need. If you are to treat them and make them equal to man the more effective means is through economic pursuits. Entrepreneurship is not only an economic and business endeavour, but also it is a blend of economic, social and political elements. Developing entrepreneurship among certain segments of women is not an easy task. Different societies and cultures are deeply rooted in discriminatory values and prejudices in respect to women. To cross these social attitudinal barriers is a very difficult task. But we have to make a beginning. Elsewhere and even in the context of India, we had made some beginning in respect to encouraging entrepreneurship among women. This effort is to be multi-pronged, serious and systematic, so that we create a non-discriminatory social condition of equal opportunity for both the sexes.

In view of the importance accorded to and restricted freedom enjoyed by women folk, there is a need to adopt clinical approach in promoting entrepreneurship among them. Here we may just mention that the freedom enjoyed or the importance accorded to women varies from group to group, influenced by racial, ethnic, religious and socio-cultural factors. There is no universal standard instrument in promoting entrepreneurship among women. Approaches differ depending on the diversity of categories of women in view of as mentioned above ethnic background, educational level, size of the family, tradition, aptitude and affordability on the part of the prospective individual woman entrepreneurs. Different and appropriate strategies are to be adopted to bring the women on to the threshold of entrepreneurial activity. As one could realise, this kind of promotion of entrepreneurship among women cannot be spontaneous, we cannot think of working wonders in a short span of time. Here one may liken developing entrepreneurship among women to that of various stages of schooling of children i.e., from nursery, kindergarten, primary, secondary, college and university. One has to apply different approaches, strategies keeping in view the differential categories of prospective woman entrepreneurs. Irrespective of the economic, ethnic and social status of women in different groups, what appears to be essential is clinical approach, where you pay attention to the individual, to the family and move on to the community preparing the ground for the emergence of women as entrepreneurs. It is just a kind of a social, cultural clearing all the way and establishing the track for the women to move on to taking to some entrepreneurial activity.

We can expect emergence of women entrepreneurship when conditions are created by the government, both central and state in terms of policy measures and sustained support system. Keeping this in mind, the book provides a detailed picture of entrepreneurship development, rural industrialization pertaining to Asia and in particular India with a focus on developing entrepreneurship among women.

2

Women in Society

Women and Society

In the historical evolution of mankind, woman has been an economic partner to man, besides her biological and social roles. It is said that it was the woman who discovered the possibility of domesticating plants for food and beginning the rudiments of hoe-culture. It was so when man was in the hunting and gathering stage. Since then, through agricultural and industrial revolutions, she has been an economic partner in the family of man. She started the enterprise of food cultivation and later adopted bartering the food articles for other necessities of life.

Over a period of time, certain patterns of life and the division of labour changed. She worked on the farm, kept the house and reared the children. Further, in the Indian (Hindu) context, when social stratification (caste-system) and occupations became institutionalized, the womenfolk confined themselves to the chores assigned to them and assumed by themselves in their respective occupations or professions. Again over a period of time, class distinctions emerged, accompanied with restrictions, norms of time or social sanctions and certain freedom enjoyed by women. In the general society, high- and middle-class women tended to confine themselves to the biological and social roles of rearing children and keeping the house. But in the case of economically lower-class women, besides their biosocial roles, they had equal or more than equal share in the economic activities of the family.

In the recent past, as a result of increase in women's education, industrialization, urbanization, social and occupational mobility, the emergence of nuclear families, westernization, politico-social movements and changes in the value system, some educated women have taken to certain careers. Some, compelled by economic necessity, have taken to small business and trade.

Woman has been the economic partner of man in several fields, but when it comes to entrepreneurship, man seems, outwardly, at any rate, to dominate the entrepreneurial world. Entrepreneurship is not simply a masculine job as army or navy. She, too, is equally endowed with the psychological qualities and managerial abilities that matter in successful entrepreneurship. Sometimes, the environment and opportunities are the same both for man and woman. But interestingly, the entrepreneurial activity in the traditional developing societies has been restricted to man. Time has come when one starts thinking, exploring and working towards the woman entrepreneurship.

Women clientele could be categorized into several groups, based on residence, education, family occupation or profession, socio-economic level and employment. Based on the above criteria, we can think of the women in terms of: (a) rural, (b) urban, (c) educated employed, (d) educated unemployed, (e) land owning, (f) landless, (g) tenant farmer, (h) artisan groups, (i) supporting the family economically, (j) just keeping the house, (k) enjoying considerable leisure; and (l) just thinking of doing some small business or activity to supplement the family's income.

Two Objectives

The entrepreneur may be either an individual or a group; both are equally significant in less developed countries. Though choosing an enterprise is an individual's free-choice activity, in most cases, it is the decision of the family, the kin-group or the community. There is need to stimulate and influence the group so that the potential entrepreneur gets the kind of encouragement and support to start and run the chosen enterprise. Women constitute a significant lot in the group.

Women are to be reached and motivated, so that they extend a helping hand to men in their entrepreneurial venture and the women too, take to some enterprises.

The Clientele

Though the focus here is on entrepreneurship among women, the menfolk are not ignored in the approach; they are also to be influenced and worked with, so that the women secure the freedom and support to venture into some entrepreneurial activity with social and cultural sanctions and not hampering their familial roles. The development of entrepreneurship could be simultaneous among men and women, as the latter constitute fifty per cent of the population.

Now the question is: Who are the prospective woman entrepreneurs? We can think of three general groups of women, amongst whom we can attempt entrepreneurial activity. They are: (a) the rural, (b) urban, and (c) the tribal women with variables such as, education, skill, aptitude, abilities, economic level, employment and entrepreneurial opportunities distributed among the three groups in varying degrees.

A word here about the tribal women. Women in the tribal societies contribute as much as or more than men to the family income. In a relative sense, they enjoy greater social and economic freedom than the women in the caste society in India. For instance, the tribal women in Manipur, Mizoram, Meghalaya and Nagaland are in the forefront in running small business and trade. In Imphal, a market complex is exclusively run by women. A similar practice obtains in Aizwal (Mizoram), where one can see a large number of women carrying on business and trade in garments, textiles, cosmetics, electronic goods, etc. There is much scope to develop entrepreneurship among tribal women.

Potential Entrepreneur

In general, the potential woman entrepreneur may be a teacher, a nurse, a secretary, or any woman stuck in a job that does not fulfill her or which does not bring sufficient income. The entrepreneurial woman is simply the woman who wants to start her own business.

The personnel in the various agencies engaged in socio-economic developmental programmes, more especially, the extension functionaries of the entrepreneurial development agencies come into contact with and address mostly the tasks of the menfolk in the client community. Seldom are women contacted. The decision-making is not done by man alone though he is in the forefront in all business and commercial activities. The woman is there behind many decisions that concern social and economic issues of a family. It is a paradoxical situation that though woman is in the background, her understanding and choices influence the kind of decision a man takes and the course of action he pursues.

It may be said that women are the missing link in the chain of entrepreneurial development programmes. We may briefly look into the problems, and prospects of entrepreneurship and the approach towards entrepreneurship development among them. This situation leads us to a brief understanding of women and their socio-cultural milieu.[1]

Women entering the field of entrepreneurship is not altogether new and depending upon the family occupations, the services rendered by the family traditionally, women have been there as part contributors to the income of the family. This contribution may be in terms of their knowledge and skills and support to the enterprise of the family. However, statistically speaking their involvement especially in case of some ethnic groups and classes is rather very marginal. This marginality of their involvement or their association with the enterprises varies from community to community and from culture to culture.

There are several contributing factors and hurdles or barriers to promotion of entrepreneurship especially among the women in the rural areas. We may just mention the barriers or impediments in generating entrepreneurial activity among the women folk. First, it is the individual, then the family of the individual and the third dimension is the community wherein the individual lives. Within the community you have the kind of leadership, which may either facilitate or block the movement of women taking up entrepreneurial activity. One may approach the question of EDP among women either from the macro level or from the micro level. Both these approaches are essential to build a conducive entrepreneurial climate in the community. To begin with one has to identify the potential entrepreneurs and try to motivate them and at the same time prepare the family and the community for extending their support and encouraging the individual woman to move into some entrepreneurial activity. As mentioned above, the promoter of entrepreneurship amongst women may begin with the individual, identify the individual, find out the educational level, knowledge and skills and the level of motivation on the part of the individual woman, whether she has any idea, any inclination go get employed or shoulder some responsibility in initiating some entrepreneurial activity. Sometimes, the individual may not be ready to venture into action for it is something new that she is asked to enter, but at the same time she may have some interest and may be ready to take some risk in starting some enterprise. So long there is no objection from the family members and that she is prepared to venture into some enterprise then there will be no problem. In such a situation, it is up to the industrial development agency, or entrepreneurship promoters to provide her the support so that she can make a beginning. Sometimes, in rural tribal settings based on their tradition and value system especially in the case of women venturing into a new kind of economic activity they may not get the support or approval from the family and the community. Here comes the task of educating and mobilizing support to all the individual women, families and the communities, so that as mentioned above, over a period of time you build a climate which will facilitate the individuals and the families moving into activities which would generate employment and income for them.

One has to take into account the kind of leadership that obtains in the community, the influence of leaders on individuals. We may note that in several instances, though the individuals are ready to take to some entrepreneurial activity they look for a nominal formal approval from the opinion leaders in the community. In any community the leaders play a dual role support or obstruct. Some are positively oriented towards individual development. Some of them try to have a grip on the community, exercise their authority and command over them. They entertain some fear that once the individuals especially some entrepreneurs earn money, generate employment, become economically sound, the leaders may find that kind of a change in development threatening to them. The idea here is, that all the leaders are not positively disposed towards development among the members in the community. Therefore, whether the leaders are positive or negative, the industrial promotion agent has to prepare the leaders so that they do not discourage women taking to entrepreneurial activity. We speak of this kind of situation in traditional type of communities.

When it comes to educated woman members coming from liberal type of families who are looking for opportunities to better their economic status, one may not find social-cultural barriers preventing them taking up enterprises. One may think of several levels of potential entrepreneurs in the population. In some cases, one has to prepare assiduously in respect to the lowest layer of the potential entrepreneurs. In some cases, one has to start right from the beginning which will be mostly of motivational nature and in other cases it will be helping them in respect to location of a site, financial and technical assistance and in most of the cases in marketing of the products. Especially, in traditional type of communities, this is the way to motivate women and prepare the ground for their venture into entrepreneurial activity. It is empowering women through entrepreneurial activity. The employment they generate, the income they contribute strengthen their status in the family and in the society.

We may also think of the existing traditional occupations and services rendered by different communities that pave the way for entrepreneurial activity with improved technology, diversification of products and finding new markets. And at the same time going in for new kind of economic activities.

In the context of promoting entrepreneurship, one may think of the Hindu Jajmani System which has emerged and survived as an institution for centuries in India.

The Hindu Jajmani system which has gradually evolved and functioned as an institution for centuries in India has systematized distinctive occupations and activities among various groups of people. It has assured occupations to different groups which prevailed as a mechanism of interdependency amongst various communities in terms of goods and services. It has provided knowledge and skills for each occupational and servicing groups and each community was assured of occupation and service. These occupational and servicing groups for centuries never or seldom thought of moving out of their traditional prescribed occupations. But over a period of time, with the advent of industrialization and literacy and educational level on the part of the younger generation, some of the members in the family slowly moved out of the traditional occupations taking to other jobs and entering other services. Sometimes, inadequate means of survival within the traditional occupations or professions made people gradually go in for other kinds of livelihood pursuits. Here lies the encouraging climate among the traditional occupational and servicing castes for developing entrepreneurship.

Women's economic contribution more often has not been reckoned with. Their contribution in the family occupation or service has been rather invisible in many of the communities in agriculture, or in non-agricultural fields. But once they go in for some enterprises managed by them it brings some change in their status and behaviour. It is likely to bring a change in the attitude of male members towards women and change in their behaviour towards them. It builds confidence among women and their self-esteem is likely to increase. In a larger sense, it is utilization of human resources for productive purposes creating wealth in order to better the living standards of people. It is to generate entrepreneurship among the poor since most of them being landless. It will help them self-employed and also the enterprises they may take to would sustain them and better their living. Some of the enterprises may be based on the knowledge and skills they have at the moment. They are to be trained providing them knowledge and technical and managerial skills required in respect to the enterprises they have started.

As mentioned above, efforts are to be made modernizing or improving local community based enterprises wherein the new woman entrepreneurs may make use of their traditional knowledge and skills. To start with sometimes, one may think of enterprises based on the locally available resources to meet the local demands of certain articles or services.

We may have to sometimes assume that there is zero entrepreneurial activity in a particular community. With that kind of presumption we have to go in for educating and motivating the individual, the family and the community. Things were started only in this manner earlier also. One may have to think of all possible ways of earning or increasing income and creating wealth.

The suggestion here is clinical approach to EDP among women: Here it is a question of slowly bringing about change in the value system, attitude or disposition on the part of the prospective woman entrepreneurs and the members in the family concerned. It should also extend to the community from wherein the women are expected to emerge as small entrepreneurs.

Approach

Entrepreneurship is a function of certain socio-cultural setting. Though the focus in the book is on developing entrepreneurship among women, we cannot exclusively approach women and motivate them to take to some entrepreneurial activity. We can expect emergence of women entrepreneurship when conditions are created by the state in terms of policy measures and diverse type of assistance i.e., to b extended to the neo-woman entrepreneurs. Keeping this in mind, we have included a detailed picture of entrepreneurship development, rural industrialization pertaining to Asia and in particular in respect of India. These chapters could be taken as a kind of a general background or socio-economic environment which, it is believed, would facilitate emergence of women entrepreneurship.

In developing entrepreneurship, we need to take women into account, understand and motivate them gradually bringing about changes in the culture of the group.

The natural resources in a given area and the associated economic and industrial activities and the skills thereof provide a base, a starter for some enterprises, that may be taken up by the potential woman entrepreneurs. Further, based on the resources, skills and needs, some new enterprises and services can be listed and canvassed among the prospective woman entrepreneurs. While surveying, identifying and recommending enterprises, the location, qualifications, skill and market for the products and services may be borne in mind. There can be enterprises that suit rural, tribal and urban conditions. Some maybe rural-specific and some urban-specific and still some may be common to both rural and urban conditions. For instance, dairying, poultry, food products, hotel industry, vegetable-vending kitchen-gardening (on commercial lines), weaving and making incense sticks, may suit the rural clientele. Similarly, enterprises such as radio-repairing, dry-washing, watch repairing, running libraries on commercial lines, preparing ready-made garments, tailoring, toy making, hand-printing and running salons, can be the enterprises that the towns-folk can take up. Some activities, whether they are connected with manufacturing, processing, producing and servicing goods can be taken up both in the rural and urban areas.

It may be relevant here to mention that Small Industries Service Institute (SISI), Indore, Madhya Pradesh, India has been for some years now, organizing training programme for prospective woman entrepreneurs and helping them to start their enterprises. In the Silver Jubilee Commemorations publication *Small Industries for Woman Entrepreneurs*, 1979, the SISI has listed 114 enterprises that may be taken up by woman entrepreneurs. The suggested enterprises fall under: (a) chemical industries, (b) food industries, (c) paper-conversion industries, (d) hosiery and textile industries, (e) ceramic and glass industries, (f) leather industries, (g) engineering industries and (h) electrical/electronic industries. Most of the above industries are urban-oriented.

Institutional Support

The promotion of entrepreneurship among women depends very much upon organization, education, stimulation and motivation of the clientele through concerted and systematic approach, focusing on the individuals and groups. This objective can be accomplished gradually through working with people and demonstrating the possibilities of women venturing into entrepreneurial activities, accompanied with adequate rewards-economic development and social growth.

The existing official machinery can carry out this task of EDP among women. These agencies may lay emphasis on the clientele under discussion and also fix up some targets in their case and there can be sub-plans for EDP in the case of women.

With respect to EDP among women, the women development or welfare organizations can work towards creating an entrepreneurial climate among women and also can help the industrial personnel in stimulating, identifying, motivating and selecting prospective woman entrepreneurs.

At the district and sub-district levels, the women welfare workers who are supposed to be in the know of, and in close touch with the womenfolk, can play a significant role in creating awareness and can guide the potential woman entrepreneurs. The question that matters here is how best the existing development agencies work, mobilize, communicate and coordinate their activities in reaching the potential woman entrepreneurs and create a climate for entrepreneurial movement among them.

Women's Clubs

The women's clubs that have been organized in rural and urban areas during the past decades are under the purview of the district women welfare agencies. They are feeder institutions and are voluntary. However fragile or strong and enduring they may be, they serve as sources and internal agencies for entrepreneurial development among women. Some of the clubs organize and perform some economic activities, such as sewing, knitting, leaf-plate-making and food processing, besides their social, educational and cultural activities. The woman workers are in touch with these bodies. At the moment, the women's club can be a potential and a promising institution that can be utilized under the EDP among women.

Self-employment

One potential source for woman entrepreneurs is the educated women who plan and prepare themselves for some career. Till now, we have not made any significant effort in creating awareness of self-employment or entrepreneurial possibilities while the women are still on the campuses of educational institutions or universities. The entrepreneurial development agencies, along with the management of educational institutions, may organize training programmes for the senior students during summer holidays, exposing them to the feasible enterprises they can take up after completing their education. They should be acquainted with the scope available in the areas of their specialization and the kind of support they can expect from governmental agencies in starting and running their enterprises.

Role of Educational Institutions

It is not only the self-generated motivation on the part of the individual and encouraged by understanding the need and demand for a particular service and good and influenced by a conducive environment, the individual takes initiative towards some entrepreneurial activity. Besides this self-motivated initiative and action on the part of the individual, the educational institutions right from the high school and up to the university level could play a very positive and significant role in motivating the students of both the sexes to venture into self-employment, or go in for some enterprise. Today, entrepreneurship development as a regular course is being offered in some of the institutions both at the graduate and undergraduate level. One may even think of introducing a course on entrepreneurship development in schools of management, and in polytechnics. Even if it were not to be a regular course with some credits, the institutions may invite personnel from District Industries Centre, Directorate of Industries and Khadi and Village Industries Commission and several other organizations who deal with promoting entrepreneurship and arrange guest lectures to the students. When you look at the other developed countries in the world, the percentage of people going in for employment in government is far less and on the other hand, they take to self-employment or get into industrial and service sector. Therefore, there is a need to sow the seed of EDP right at the high school and college level, so that, the students prior to their graduation may plan to go in for some kind of entrepreneurship. In a systematic way this kind of awakening and motivating the individuals prior to their leaving the school or college to think of various potential alternatives for entering into some profitable kind of enterprises. Such an approach would bring in substantive change in the economic development generating young entrepreneurs.

Of several educational institutions, the women polytechnics are a rich and promising area where the development programme of entrepreneurial motivation can be organized as a regular extra-curricular activity. Further, the institutions which offer courses in agriculture and home sciences, horticulture, sericulture, sylviculture do offer innumerable possibilities of self-employment in the fields the students study and specialize.

Further, organizations such as Lions Club, Rotary and Jaycee can take up entrepreneurial development programme among women.

Social Infrastructure

The multiplicity of agencies that function in the field of entrepreneurial development can with comparative ease provide the physical and economic infrastructural facilities for starting enterprises. But the formidable problem that we face in promoting entrepreneurship among women is resistance, apathy, shyness, inhibition, conservatism, poor response, all governed by cultural traditions, value system and social sanctions. Interestingly, women, in general, share several traits. There is no denying the fact that it is an uphill task to develop entrepreneurship among women. But one encouraging feature is that there is no zero level of entrepreneurship and we are not operating in an entrepreneurial vacuum in the case of women.

What is required is a congenial entrepreneurial climate which motivates, encourages and facilitates individual and group movement conducive to entrepreneurial activities. Today, the entrepreneurial climate is rather lacking both among men and women. But there exists the potential and the prospect.

The entrepreneurial climate consists in creating positive attitudes among the people, developing new needs, increasing the level of aspiration, helping people to see the possibilities of alternative and remunerative avocations, preparing people to accept changes in the economic and social spheres and working through important persons, leaders and local institutions, all converging on entrepreneurial movement and activity. This aspect of building up the social infrastructure can be accomplished only through educating and organizing the community and ED Promotional agencies providing the requisite physical and economic infrastructural facilities.

Training

The training of personnel for promoting entrepreneurship among women is an essential part of the programme. The emphasis in the training programme is on understanding the culture and the styles of life and the kind of approach, skills and strategy required in promoting entrepreneurship among women, besides the other inputs that go into the general entrepreneurial development programme *(Please see Appendix-I for further details).*

Conclusion

The primary or the principal factor in developing entrepreneurship among women is not in terms of infrastructure or financial assistance or identifying an enterprise but it is a question of clearing the ground for their movement into entrepreneurship. For ages together they have been confined to a secondary role and confined to the homes and you have to bring them out so that they become self-reliant, self-respecting enterprising people. Though there are several factors contributing to the emergence of women as entrepreneurs, the sustained and coordinated effort from all dimensions would pave the way for the woman moving into entrepreneurial activity thus contributing to the social and economic development of the members of the family and thereby gaining equality and equal importance for themselves. In a word, one cannot think of empowerment of women minus the economic component. The main economic component should be in terms of women entering diverse fields of entrepreneurship.

In sum, we may say that the women constitute a significant segment in the population. Till now, they have not been the focus of entrepreneurial development. The need today to develop entrepreneurship among them is imperative, the development of entrepreneurship among men and women being simultaneous. The question of EDP among women is a question of choice, priority and organization.

REFERENCE

1. E. Desingu Setty, 'Developing Entrepreneurship Among Women' in *Man and Development*, Vol. II, No. 3 (Chandigarh: Centre for Research in Rural and Industrial Development, 1980).

3

A Model for Developing Agro-Enterprises among Farm Women in Asia

In the preceding chapters, we have briefly looked into the ways to go about establishing small-scale and cottage industries and development of entrepreneurship, here is a model which focuses on development of agro-enterprises among farmwomen.

Woman has been the economic partner of man in several fields, but when it comes to entrepreneurship man seems, outwardly, at any rate, to dominate the entrepreneurial world. Entrepreneurship is not simply a masculine job such as the army or navy. Woman too, is equally endowed with the psychological qualities and managerial abilities that matter in successful entrepreneurship. Sometimes, the environment and opportunities are the same both for men and women. But interestingly, the entrepreneurial activity in the traditional developing societies has been restricted to man (Setty, 1980).

Although women "hold up half the sky", as the Chinese saying goes, until recently they have remained invisible in most development plans. Where programmes have addressed women's productive capacity at all, they have tended to incorporate a welfare bias rather than promoting genuine opportunities for economic independence. As a consequence, rural women in many developing countries find themselves bypassed by the social and economic advantages accruing to men. Dixon (1978) attributes this neglect of women by the development planners mainly to the following four factors:

(1) Male dominance in decision making in international and national planning agencies, as well as the under-representation or non-representation of women of these bodies.
(2) The "invisibility" of rural women's productive activities because of their concentration in the informal sectors of the economy, in subsistence agriculture, and in the home.
(3) The primitive kind of technology used by women in domestic work and agriculture which requires solution in small-scale intermediate technology rather than the grand scheme so favoured by planners and
(4) The powerlessness of the women themselves, resulting both from their lack of economic leverage and from cultural restrictions that severely limit their ability to press for policy changes on their own behalf.

However, the picture has gradually changed. Increasingly, international agencies are turning their attention to the integration of women in development as a strategy for improving economic conditions and promoting the adoption of family planning. Attesting to this concern are numerous resolutions from the 1974 International Women's Year Conference in Mexico City, and from the voluminous background papers and UN agency reports preceding and following these conferences. Individual donor governments, too, are expressing interest in policies linking development with the status of women and population questions.

The Percy Amendment to the U.S. Foreign Assistance Act, for example, requires that the provisions of the Act "shall be administered so as to give attention to those programmes, projects, and activities which tend to integrate women into the national economies of foreign countries, thus, improving their status and assisting the total development effort". Thus it could be noted that the leverage of good intentions already exists at the international level and in many cases at the national level, and what is needed are concrete proposals for action and research.

With increasing attention recently being paid to rural women, the major bilateral and multilateral aid agencies are apparently looking for fundable projects that would promote the integration of women in development while simultaneously leading to a reduction of births. The World Bank in India for example, has funded smaller projects that employed rural women in the production of goods with export potential. The IRDP in Bangladesh has received a large World Bank loan to build a family planning component into the rural women's cooperative scheme.

The "Credit Scheme for a Training-cum-Production Centre: Income Generating Activities for Women", funded by FAO in India, in collaboration with non-governmental organizations, aims to develop centers accessible to rural women for promoting various types of small-scale cottage industries and agro-based industries. It hopes gradually to diversify the training to include other appropriate and profitable income generating activities e.g., machine embroidery, quilt making, woollen and cotton handloom weaving, processing of marketable food products and others. The immediate objectives were to provide employment for a specific group of 500 village women and to establish the main training-production centre so that the village women could be trained to produce goods of improved design with a traditional embroidery called "kasooh".

The findings of a comprehensive study on "Rural Women's Participation in Development" published by the UNDP (1980) propose that for rural women new initiatives are particularly urgent in matters of agricultural production, cottage and small-scale industry, credit, marketing, energy, technology, education and training.

Asian Women at work

Throughout Asia women have been making an important contribution to family income. The lower the socio-economic level of the family, the greater the proportion of total income contributed by women. More and more women are bringing cash to the family budget, either from the sale of grain received as payment for labour on large landholding, as cash pay, or small sums derived from a multiplicity of secondary pursuits such as weaving, sewing, mat making, and the preparation and sale of snacks.

Markets in Southeast Asia, from Myanmar to the Chinese border, are dominated by women selling small quantities of fruits and vegetables, grown by themselves or bought from others. In the Philippines, women are self-employed in low income, low prestige, traditionally feminine types of work which permit them to look after home and family. Filipino women also care for chicken and pigs, fetch water, perform household tasks and fish by traps. Petty trade is carried on mainly by women.

In Laos, petty trading in village shops is mostly in the hands of women: they purchase fruits and vegetables from middleman and sell in markets.

In Nepal, during the slack agricultural season, men may leave home on trading ventures or go to India for seasonal work; many men serve abroad in Gurkha regiments. Women brew beer, distill liquor and sell the products.

The Sri Lankan women are more important in economic activities in the dry zone than in the wet zone. As family income rises, women and girls are withdrawn from labour, working only on the family farm during seasonal peak times.

The head of the family decides who will do what work.

Women in the tribal societies of India contribute as much as or more than men to the family income. In a relative sense, they enjoy greater social and economic freedom than the women in the caste society in India. For instance, the tribal women in Manipur, Mizoram, Meghalaya and Nagaland are in the forefront in running small business and trade. In Imphal, a market complex is run exclusively by women. A similar practice obtains in Aizwal, Mizoram, where one can see a large number of women carrying on business and trade in garments, textiles, cosmetics, electronic goods etc. (Setty, 1980).

Thus it may be observed that most Asian women prefer work that can be carried out in or near the home, to avoid conflict between their roles as homemaker and wage-earner. A widespread source of income is the care of domestic livestock and the sale of their products. Women invariably look after scavenging chicken, milk and feed cattle in the Indian subcontinent, attend to poultry and often cattle in Indonesia and Thailand.

A recent study of six Asian countries by Campbell (1990) attempts to provide some insights into the complexities of rural economy and society in a comparative framework of Asia and highlights some of the social changes that may have occurred in rural communities that have transferred from traditional cultivation practices to mechanized farming. The case studies of India, Indonesia, Korea, Nepal, Philippines and Thailand find that finance and record keeping are largely in the hands of the senior women of rural households. Women have become less dependent upon agriculture and are used less in the cultivation of land. This has freed them for other occupations and allowed a greater diversification of the economic base.

Need for Developing Entrepreneurship among Farm Women

Most rural women's work remains outside the cash sector, which so far has debarred their economic activities from being quantified and included in national income statistics. Urban-based planners, according to Epstein and Watts (1981), should take the blame. These planners lack familiarity with village life, therefore, they hardly take into account women's economic importance not only in their indirectly productive activities as household managers and reproducers of labour, but also in their income-earning roles as farm workers, traders, etc. Female labour is thus still excluded from any concerns for increased rural productivity.

In the developing countries it is observed that unemployment and underemployment are greater for women than for men. Moreover, increasing the efficiency of agriculture has been widely shown to have adverse effects on the employment of women, due to the realignment of tasks in the sexual division of labour. Only now it is beginning to be realized that plans for development must have components aimed specifically at women, if women are to benefit from them. In this context, it has been suggested that the upgrading of women's productive activities by the provision of income-generating employment outside the home may break the cycle of rural poverty and high fertility characteristic of economically stagnant rural economies. The employment of women is expected to function as significant prong in strategies to increase productivity and alleviate poverty. Women's earnings raise total household income. Their earnings are of particular importance if they constitute one unit of an income-generating partnership.

To meet their survival requirements, households have practised division of labour, based on sex and age, long before Adam Smith ever propounded the advantages of specialization. Improved domestic technology is an aspect of rural development which has so far received far too little attention. It must precede any attempt to enable women to get more involved in direct productive activities. It is also an essential part of the improvement of the quality of rural life, and moreover it is likely to facilitate the formation of more active female pressure groups in rural Asia.

Efforts to promote small enterprise development in rural areas have, until now, been directed towards men only. Women are equally endowed with motivation and managerial capabilities in starting and running small enterprises located in their own homes or communities. Promoting and developing such entrepreneurship among rural women will require initiative, encouragement and support from the development agencies.

Experience has it that the new farm technologies often result in displacement of farm labor, increase in leisure time and surplus agricultural production. This opens up opportunities and incentives for developing alternative income-generating activities within the community. Potential areas are utilization of agro-products in small processing enterprises and the allocation of redundant female agricultural labour to off-farm employment. It must be recognized that as long as total income in most of the rural communities of Asia is inadequate to maintain acceptable standards of living for the family as a whole, attempts to improve the position specifically of women are not likely to proceed far beyond the realm of good intentions. This calls our attention to the urgent need for developing entrepreneurship among farmwomen.

Agro-enterprise for women

There are several issues involved when one thinks of the entrepreneurship development among women. One is widespread ignorance about the kind of work farm women do. It is intended that the collection, in one place, of this much detail about the work they do should help planners and programme implementers at all levels, as well as donors, to learn about the aspects of household and rural economy that women are in charge of. Such information not only establishes the fact of women's integration in the household and rural economy, but it indicates why they must be included in rural development efforts to increase production and provide equitable distribution. At a very practical level, it indicates which rural extension services must be directed to women in order to be effective in increasing food production.

Though choosing an enterprise is an individual's free-choice activity, in most cases, it is the decision of the family, the kin-group or the community. There is need to stimulate and influence the group so that the potential entrepreneur gets the kind of encouragement and support to start and run his enterprise. Women constitute a significant lot in the group (Setty, 1980).

The agro-enterprises to be promoted for such a client group constitute a special entity. The philosophy behind the modern concept of agro-enterprises is integrating industry with agriculture for planned, harmonious and balanced growth and development of the two, encompassing all the operations from primary production through processing to the marketing of ultimate products, including by-products.

Such agro-industrial development implies the growth of industries in rural areas through interdependence on agriculture under a system of mutual and complementary output. It is a process of simultaneous growth of industry and agriculture, in which the output of one serves as the input of the other and vice-versa. It signifies the proximity and affinity between agriculture and industry (Setty, 1991). In view of this, some important resources and their industrial uses where women could be self-employed are recommended (*For further details, please see Appendix-II (A)*)

The principal agricultural resources found commonly in

Asian countries are paddy, sugarcane, barley, corn and maize, cotton, coconut, cashew nut, tea, coffee, jute and other fibre crops. Such resources and their by-products permit many known and some less known industrial uses. The list of items appended here though not exhaustive, may form the basis for agro-industrial promotion (*For further details please see Appendix – II (B)*).

The Model

The primary purpose of the proposed model is to aid in the development of the strategies for creating employment and generating income for the rural people in general and the womenfolk in particular.

The majority of population in developing countries live in the rural areas with employment provided by the agriculture sector. About two-thirds of the employment for a total of three-fourths of the rural population in the developing countries is provided by agriculture alone. The present model could form an important component of employment generating as well as small-scale industrial development programmes (SSID). More specifically, it is expected to provide the necessary prong to the Entrepreneurship Development Programme (EDP) efforts in respective countries.

As an approach, the proposed model could stand by itself, that is without being integrated as a component of an EDP or SSID programme, it could be taken up as an approach by a development agency in its efforts to identify, train and promote potential entrepreneurs. Figure-1 presents the basic structure of this model.

It is misconception that planning economic activities for women requires any special expertise and different techniques. With some training, women from the villages are able to perform almost all primary sector activities with ease and confidence and, therefore, it is wrong to assume that they can do only special types of activity. Expertise is, however, necessary for identifying characteristics of different groups of poor women in mobilizing them, in assisting them in organization building, in identifying sources or fund, training and other inputs. The model proposed for developing agro-enterprises for farm women in Asia aims to serve as an aide to the change agents. It presents a pragmatic approach to trainers, implementers, as well as planners.

Objective of the model:- The model is expected to help the users in reaching and motivating women, so that they extend a helping hand to men in their entrepreneurial venture and the women too, take to some enterprises. Although, the model focuses on entrepreneurship among women, the menfolk are not ignored in the approach; they are also to be influenced and worked with, so that the women secure the freedom and support to venture into some entrepreneurial activity with social and cultural sanctions and not hampering their familial roles. The development of entrepreneurship could be simultaneous among men and women.

The specific objectives of the model could be stated as:

1. To assess the industrial/entrepreneurial potential of the agro-products in the study area, including the availability of human and material resources and consumer demand in the local communities.
2. To provide training and resources for economically gainful activities and to create an atmosphere in which women can pursue them.

To enable women to have direct access to the resources and services they need as women and a direct voice in determining the kind and quality of these resources and services.

The two general objectives for which this model has been constructed are:

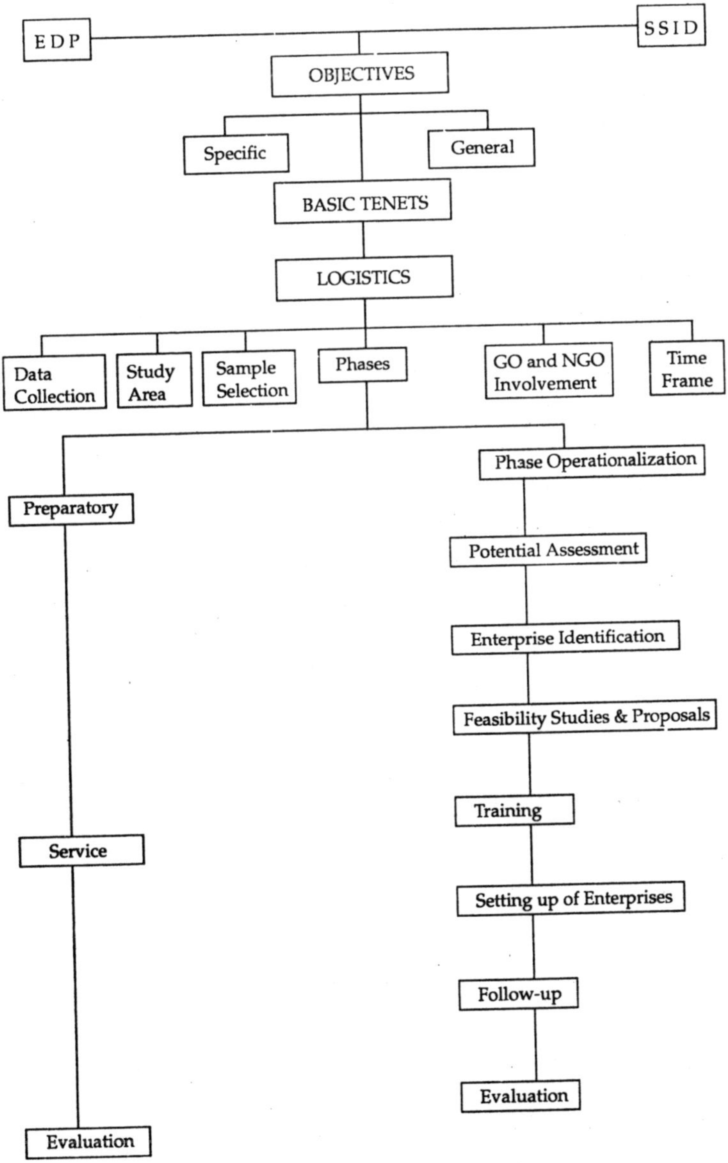

Fig. 3.1 A Model for Developing Agro-enterprises among Farm Women in Asia

1. To identify productive tasks performed by women in the farming system which are not generally ascribed a monetary value.
2. To determine the impact, both positive and negative, on women due to the introduction of new technologies in the farming systems especially in terms of employment, production and income.

Basic tenets of the model:- This model for developing agro-enterprises among farm women is based on the following assumptions:

1. Women play an important role in income-generating activities.
2. Rural women have the labour, skills and resources needed to set up agro-based enterprises which are closely associated with their farm activities.
3. Provision of adequate infrastructure and support services, including training in technical skills and management will give women the motivation and assistance necessary to develop new enterprises.
4. Women engaged in farming and related activities in the village communities can increase productivity and income if they are given required resources and services and institutional and policy support within the existing socio-cultural and economic system.
5. Demonstration of economic benefits will motivate rural women to develop entrepreneurial activities.

MODEL LOGISTICS

I. The Method Of Data Collection

Data are to be collected through an industrial potential survey. Individual and group interviews could also be held. Secondary data are to be obtained from development agencies on natural resources and the field crops, animal husbandry, forestry, and fisheries enterprises in the study area. Primary data are to be collected on the most promising resources and their potential used for developing agro-based enterprises for women should be assessed.

It is proposed that the project based on this model could be carried out in the following three phases:

1. *Preparatory Phase.* In the preparatory phase, field workers would be engaged in general information and orientation work, which would consist of sensitising the men to the importance of women having access to improved technologies and of informing the women about the types of income-generating activities available and how these can help them. The women would also be taught how to organize themselves into groups or cooperatives so that they can collectively purchase needed technologies when credit becomes available. During this phase, the technologists and field workers would also identify priority needs and collect cultural and socio-economic data for consideration while promoting income-generating activities.
2. *Service Phase.* In this phase, credit would be provided to women's groups and cooperatives to help them take up an activity. They would be taught how to operate and maintain the equipment. They would be given training (for instance, in soap making, vegetable gardening, or some other money earning activity) so that any released time can be used productively and savings are generated to pay back loans and maintain equipment properly. When necessary, credit is to be provided to enable the women to purchase any tools or equipment related to the money-earning activity. Progress should be monitored on a regular basis and advice given on how to overcome any technical, financial, marketing or social problems that arise.

3. *Evaluation Phase:-* Finally, the scheme or programme would be evaluated in terms of impact of the entrepreneurial activity on each member of the household and the community as a whole. This would clarify what, if any, further policy changes are needed.

In order to follow the phase-wise programme based on the model, the following steps are proposed:

Step 1: *Potential Assessment.* First, a study and assessment of the potential for agro-based enterprises in the target area need to be made. The questions to be raised and answered at this level are: (a) What do the rural women do in the rural economy? (b) What are the bases for cooperation and conflict among rural women? (c) To what extent are women engaged in moneymaking activities? (d) What is the balance of power between men and women? (e) Are there women leaders? Or are there any potential women leaders?

Step-2: *Enterprise Identification.* Second, identification of specific new enterprises for recommendation to rural women is to be made. At this level, attention will be focused on identifying agro-based rural industries with consideration to (i) the resource based rural industries which involve low capital and simple technologies and (ii) the rural products which enjoy a considerable demand.

Step 3: *Feasibility studies and proposals.* Third, feasibility studies based on the resources available in the target area, including market, financial and technical analyses are to be prepared. Preparation of small project proposals along with the feasibility in terms of (i) practicability and (ii) profitability should be looked into. The important questions raised would be:

On practicability. (a) Can such an activity be taken up and operated by the woman herself? (b) Is it convenient for the woman to take up? (c) Can it be easily sustained?

On profitability. (a) Does it provide more income? (b) Are there no marketing problems?

Step 4: *Training.* The fourth step comprises the identification and training of potential women entrepreneurs. From the sample mentioned below the potential women entrepreneurs are to be selected for training.

Step 5: *Follow-up.* The fifth step includes guidance and assistance given to the trained women entrepreneurs in establishing and running their small enterprises.

Step 6: *Evaluation.* Evaluation of the action programme.

II. Selection of the Sample

Women from the following two different socio-economic classes in the rural agricultural sector of the selected area could be the centre for focus in the project based on the proposed model:

(i) Women belonging to landless households or households with insufficient land to fulfill, on its basis alone, the family's subsistence needs and who, in addition to their roles as child bearers and as family domestic workers, need to hire themselves out as wage labourers to help provide an adequate income for themselves and their families.

(ii) Women belonging to small cultivator households, which have adequate land for subsistence but which have to depend essentially on family labour for cultivation and who, in addition to their reproductive roles and domestic chores, need to do some manual work on the family farm, although they do not have to hire themselves out as wage labourers.

Women of agricultural labour households constitute a major focus of concern since, economically they are amongst the worst off and in many Asian countries they constitute the largest percentage of rural woman workers.

III. Study Area

A cluster of villages could be selected from the developing countries. The project using this model could be taken up simultaneously in the selected countries involving the local Department of Small-Scale Enterprise Development (Ministry of Industry, Department of Small-Scale Industries). The local Department of Small-Scale Industries could be involved in the identification of potential woman entrepreneurs and suitable small-scale enterprises and organizing the training programmes and the follow-up support systems to help the identified potential woman entrepreneurs in establishing and running their enterprises.

IV. NGOs Involvement

Experience has it that besides the government, few NGOs are actively involved in promoting small enterprise development among rural and urban women. When it comes to urban areas, we have, what are called livelihood projects, especially promoted among the slum dwellers in metropolitan centers. Some of the NGOs operate in limited jurisdictions covering especially the underprivileged and weaker sections in the community. If partnership of such NGOs could be secured in the project as partners or, sole agencies in terms of identifying the entrepreneurs and candidate enterprises for different types of individuals and groups, it would be more effective and it would also serve as a demonstration of successful entrepreneurial development among women which may have a spread effect in the neighbouring areas. The project could also be extended, wherever it is feasible, to involve both the Government Department of Small-Scale Industries and one or two NGOs.

The project could be spread over a period of two years for one cycle of operation.

Prospective Outcome

The model is expected to yield the following results upon successful operationalization:

(1) Enable women in need, of whatever class, to work for monetary gain.

(2) Women will become able to act in meeting their own needs and that of their families and will have alternatives to dependency on males.

(3) Women who contribute income to the family will have increased authority to make decisions, and increased access to resources enabling them to act on those decisions in the aspects of life and work which are already their sphere of responsibility.

(4) The economy will benefit through an increase in needed production from shifting rural women's work from domestic to commercial production, increasing family income and savings, thus, enhancing the fungibility of the womenfolk in the household.

(5) It is likely to empower women and alleviate their poverty.

When used as an approach, the proposed model is also expected to help indirectly the development agency to:

(1) Study the development and dissemination of labour-saving technology for household activities, particularly in rural areas.

(2) Examine the role of women in the unorganized sector, for instance the contribution to family

income, measurement of productivity in various activities etc.,;

(3) Examine the appropriateness of census data for analysis of the position of women and monitoring of their position over time;

(4) Calculate cash contributions by rural women to the family income.

Conclusion

The concern for gender development is unquestionable and imperative. The only meaningful approach to enhance the economic and social status of women is through enabling and facilitating them through self-employment and income-generating activities.

One can think of several approaches to remedy the gender imbalances in development, but one substantive approach which is close to the available natural, material and human resources is the one that the present model purports. The usefulness of this approach depends on how seriously and faithfully it is translated into action. Unless there is something exclusive, answering the cause and ameliorating the economic conditions of women, any grand designs and diluted approaches in the name of women development will hardly succeed.

REFERENCES

1. Campbell, M.J., (ed.), 1990, New Technology and Rural Development – The social Impact, Routledge, Chapman and Hall Inc., New York.
2. Dixon Ruth, B., 1978, Rural Women at Work: Strategies for Development in South Asia, Johns Hopkins University Press, London.
3. Epstein, T.S., and Watts. R.A., (ed.), 1981, The Endless Day – Some Case Material on Asian Rural Women, Pergamon Press, Oxford.
4. Setty, E.D., 1980, Developing Entrepreneurship Among Women, Man and Development, Vol. II, No. 3, pp. 92-96.

5. Setty, E.D., 1991, Rural Industrialization, Small Scale and Cottage Industries in Asia, UNCRD Working Paper No. 91,-2, United Nations Centre for Regional Development, Nagoya, Japan.

Note:- Please See APPENDICES-II (A), II (B) & II (C)

"It may be noted that in Appendix-II(C), some of the items mentioned under Appendix-II(A) & II(B) are repeated. However, since the list of items is issued by the Small Scale Industries and Tiny Sector, Ministry of SSI, Govt. of India, 2000, and it may be mentioned that the list may be relevant to the prospective or ongoing entrepreneurs."

4

Empowerment and Development of the Poor Through their Participation

A Case Study From Bangladesh

Introduction

Empowerment is both a means and an end in itself. Empowerment through legislative, political, economic and social means will facilitate development among women. Similarly any development measures encouraging women creating and providing opportunities to them in the field of especially entrepreneurship development would empower them. Empowerment and development are related to each other. One serves as means and the other as the end and vis-a-vis. While we speak of empowerment and development we have a dual approach simultaneously providing opportunities effecting changes, so that we can achieve twin objectives in respect to the women folk in any society. In this context, it would be interesting to look at a case what BRAC (Bangladesh Rural Advancement Committee) has done dealing with the poor and their development. As one could see, it was a collective and sustained approach where the poor were brought together wherein they gain the strength. As Mohd. Younis, the Father of Grameen Bank, has pointed out, "When the Poor stand alone they are poor, but when they are brought together they gain strength."

While discussing the dual objective of empowerment of women and developing entrepreneurship among them, the case study in respect of what BRAC has been doing in Bangladesh is quite relevant.

If we are looking for an organization generating a genuine, authentic, systematic, meaningful, enlightened and highly motivated popular participation of the poor in their poverty alleviation and social empowerment programmes, we can cite Bangladesh Rural Advancement Committee, popularly and widely known by its acronym *BRAC*. It is a non-governmental organization, perhaps the largest in Asia. A giant private organization working for the poor. It does not simply dole out relief to the poor and the disadvantaged but it works with them at the grassroots and steadily helps them help themselves. We may call it a process of development with dignity for the poor.

BRAC is a multi-faceted organization with diverse activities all converging in terms of its philosophy and strategies on two major goals: alleviation of poverty and empowerment of the poor.[1]

Formed in 1972, BRAC began its activities with the objectives of relief and rehabilitation of thousands of displaced people during the war of liberation. The rehabilitation task was carried out successfully and the normalcy has come back to the people. But this was largely a relief measure and so BRAC moved on to multi-sectoral village development programme focusing on the poor. Over the past twenty-seven years since its birth, BRAC has emerged as a parallel agency to the national government in the field of development especially in reaching the poor.

MANAGEMENT OF BRAC

A Governing Body is vested with the management of BRAC. The Executive Director and Founder of BRAC, Mr. F.H. Abed is the Chief Executive Officer. Mr. Abed is the creative, imaginative and guiding force behind this massive programme of developing the poor. At the top, mid and field levels, BRAC is managed by development managers with years of professional experience. BRAC pursues a system of participatory and decentralized management. BRAC programmes are planned through participation of all levels of workers. Within the framework of programme plans, each level of management is encouraged to exercise appropriate authority, to embrace creative solutions and to generate innovations. BRAC provides its managers freedom to take initiatives which stimulate participation and a continuous search for excellence.

Since BRAC demands a high level of work ethics and performance standard not commonly found in Bangladesh, it decided to develop its management cadre from within the organization. Consequently, a policy of recruiting young people with high educational qualifications for placement at the lowest level of programme operation has been pursued over the past two and a half decades. This policy exposes potential managers to the dynamics of grassroots mobilization and problem solving. As a result, large numbers of qualified and experienced development practitioners stand ready to manage future expansion.

Over the years BRAC has pursued a vigorous policy of management development through training at home and abroad including post-graduate and doctoral level degree courses. It has set up its own Management development Programme to take responsibility for management training and value creation.

Bringing women at the top management is a valued policy of BRAC. This is done not only to promote gender equity but also for balanced development of the society. In pursuance of this policy BRAC has started grooming the potential woman workers for managerial positions.

Collaboration with Public Sector

BRAC considers it important to develop a system of effective collaboration with the public sector. It feels that such cooperation can enhance the capacity of people's organization and support of the process of development of the poor. Thus BRAC has established linkages with various Ministries such as Health, Relief and Rehabilitation, Fisheries and Livestock, Education etc. This cooperation has also been useful for the government to strengthen its existing programmes and increase their effectiveness. A few cases may illustrate the kinds of collaboration and their results.

BRAC assisted the Ministry of Health and Family Welfare in achieving the goals of its Expanded Programme on Immunization (EPI) in 124 up-zillas of Bangladesh. BRAC provided training to the government staff on programme management and created a demand for immunization at the community level through social mobilization. The results have been highly satisfactory both for the government and BRAC. Evaluation studies conducted by BRAC as well as by some external agencies have shown that the highest coverage of EPI in Bangladesh was in those areas where BRAC worked.

BRAC's poultry development programme is another illustration of collaboration with the public system. BRAC has trained several thousand destitute women on poultry rearing and vaccination of birds. These women, trained as vaccinators, have been linked to the government's department of livestock which supplies free vaccine. These women now provide vaccination services to the villagers for a small fee. By cutting the poultry mortality rate, the programme ensured increased production of eggs and birds.

Education, sericulture and family planning are some of the other areas of collaboration. BRAC feels that such partnership with the public system can strengthen the process of sustainable development of the rural poor.

People's participation is accomplished through the social mechanism of forming Village Organizations both for men and women and their periodic meetings to deliberate over issues that various development programmes that are carried on by BRAC.

Over the years, BRAC has grown into a multi-faceted organization with more than 8600 men and women workers and a variety of development programmes in various parts of the country. Its basic rural development activities have until now been organized over 11,842 landless groups in some 5,414 villages. A separate Rural Credit Project was initiated in 1990 to institutionalize the credit component. The wide-scale Oral Therapy Extension Programme (OTEP) teaching a home-based oral solution for the prevention of diarrhoea has reached all the households in the country expanding into a more extensive primary health care programme. The Women's Health and Development Programme, embarked in early 1991, aims to pursue a dual purpose of decreasing maternal and infant mortality. BRAC's non-formal primary education programme has so far opened more than 6,000 schools for poor rural children, especially girls.

BRAC activities include: Rural Development Programme (RDP), Rural Credit Project (RCP), Women's Health and Development Programme (WHDP), Training, Management Development Programme (MDP), Income Generation for Vulnerable Group Development (IGVGD), Rural Enterprises Project (REP), Non-Formal Primary Education Programme (NFPE), Research and Evaluation Division (RED), Craft Development and Marketing Services through Aarong and several other commercial projects.

Empowering the Poor Facilitating their Participation

Empowering is a social, psychic and to a limited extent a material (in the initial stages) process. It has to grow over a period of time in the once socially and economically poor and disadvantaged groups at the individual, family and the community levels and between both the sexes and amongst all the age groups. Empowerment in the psychic and social sense does not come about to the target population by receiving money and other material things alone.

The poor or for that matter any marginalized group can feel a sense of power when they are recognized, when their voices are heard, when they can choose and have their choice, when they are partners in decisions and deeds that concern them and the larger emphasize here that BRAC's approach to its twin objective of poverty alleviation and empowerment is through identification and organizing landless poor into viable, functional social groups. Here the dynamics or call it chemistry of development is interesting. Empowerment secures social strength, negotiating power, accessibility to resources and thus contributing to alleviation of poverty and the decrease in the poverty level is likely to increase empowerment, one supporting and strengthening the other.

BRAC has made a pragmatic approach in organizing the poor into groups with specific functions and responsibilities to be carried out by the general membership, office bearers and the small group leaders. With one strategic social stroke, it has facilitated and encouraged people's participation in their development. There is a fusion of the clientele group and BRAC as a development agency. The bridge between the development agency and the people is narrowed. This has come about what may be called as institution building that BRAC has successfully accomplished. As mentioned earlier, this organizational mechanism of institution building contributed a great deal to real people's participation. In this context we may briefly look into BRAC's objectives of development and the methodology of its organizing the clientele groups and the functions and some highlights of the Village Organizations.

Institution Building

Before we look into the institution building process in BRAC, a word on what is an institution is in order. The terms institution and organization are commonly used interchangeably and this contributes to ambiguity and confusion. Three categories are commonly recognized: (a) organizations that are not institutions (*e.g.*, a firm of lawyers); (b) institutions that are not organizations (*e.g.*, law); and (c) organizations that are institutions (*e.g.*, courts) or *vice-versa* institutions, that are organizations.[2]

To the extent that an organization has acquired special status and legitimacy for having satisfied people's needs and for having met their normative expectations over time, one can say that an organization such as BRAC, VO, has become institutionalized. In general, institutions, whether, organizations or not are complexes of norms and behaviours that persist overtime by servicing collectively valued purposes. Institutions are stable, valued, recurring patterns of behaviour. Institutions change over time, decay and some institutions are born. It is a continuous social process.

We find that BRAC has spelled out activities as underlying its approach to institution building *vis*-a-*vis* village organizations. They are[3]:

(a) Resource mobilization,
(b) Organizational discipline,
(c) Social corruption, vices, superstition,
(d) Financial discipline,
(e) Economic activities,
(f) Local body participation/influence, and
(g) Social justice.

BRAC tries to translate the above activities which may be taken as its objectives in empowering the landless poor and alleviating their poverty as follows:

(i) Remind people where they are, why they are, what they are,
(ii) Functional and consciousness raising education,

(iii) Leadership training and developing leadership,
(iv) Monthly issue-based meetings,
(v) Stimulating economic activities,
(vi) Secure for the poor the khas land, water bodies for fishing (ox bow lakes) and markets,
(vii) Secure for the poor the facilities meant for them,
(viii) Raising their political consciousness and social awareness,
(ix) Savings,
(x) Credit, and
(xi) Non-formal primary education.

BRAC's Institution Building

BRAC's institution building may be viewed as three pronged: within BRAC, in the client groups it served and with the development departments of the government. Within BRAC as an organization, the noteworthy and laudable procedures, norms, regulations, work ethics relate to personnel selection, training, job rotation, target fixing, monitoring, reporting and development communication within the staff and between the staff and the clientele system.

The whole process of setting up an Area Office, selection of villages in the service area, conducting of pre-survey, followed by detailed socio-economic surveys, identification of the landless poor, meeting them individually and in small groups and making them reflect on the deplorable conditions they live in, the scope and potential for their modest growth and development once they organize themselves into groups, forming them into what are called Village Organizations (VOs), for male and female members, followed by a series of training programmes, functional education, consciousness raising education, leadership, management and enterprise related education and training and the introduction of savings and credit system and the weekly and monthly meetings constitute the institutional building in the client system.

The functional relationship BRAC has established with the government development departments in respect to poultry development, livestock, fishery, apiary, sericulture and irrigation through Deep Tube Wells may be construed as mentioned earlier, institution building. In other words, the whole gamut of institution building revolves around new structure and functional mechanisms developed by BRAC in formulating, implementing and evaluating its programmes to empower and enrich the landless poor.

The Village Organizations (VOs)

The VOs as organized, monitored, supported, educated, motivated and developed by BRAC constitute the bedrock of its promotional operations in respect of the landless poor. The VOs provide a forum for interaction, mutual help, individual and collective initiative and social action. The secret of BRAC's success and popularity in serving the poor, owes a great deal to the VOs. One may imagine as to what would have happened to RDP and RCP and other programmes in the absence of VOs. BRAC's socio-economic programmes have filled in a vacuum which should have been filled in by the government and other agencies like Grameen Bank and NGOs. The landless poor in a helpless state with feeble hopes for a minimal meaningful life, found an anchor and hope in the VO which may become their own self-managed organization.

Structure of VOs

An Area Office covers approximately 100 village organizations (VOs)-50 for landless women and 50 for landless men, with a combined membership of 6,000 to 7,000. It is not in fixed ratio. We find that two-thirds of the VOs are female VOs. The minimum size of a VO is 45 and the maximum 55. Each VO comprises small groups of 5-7 members. BRAC has introduced an interesting principle that in the small groups of VO, there will be no close affinal or consanguineous kin. The small group is headed by a Secretary. The larger group is managed by a Management Committee (MC) consisting of 7 members, which includes a Chairman, a Secretary and a Treasurer. Members of the MC are either elected or selected for a period of one year and no member can be on MC for more than two terms, thus giving an opportunity for all members of group to serve on the MC over a period of time. The group meets once in a week on a fixed day and hour to organize their financial activities, viz., small savings and weekly loan installment payments coordinated by the *Gram Sevak* (GS) and once in a month to discuss the issues that interest the group, facilitated by a BRAC official – a programme organizer.

Growth of VOs

The VOs have been increasing in number as new areas are added under BRAC's constantly increasing volume of activity, with the same pattern of surveys, identification of the landless poor and forming them into VOs. The progress of the VOs up till the end of December, 1991 is shown in Table 4.1

Emphasis on Female VOs

In the cultural context of Bangladesh, the idea of separate organization for women is prudent and pragmatic. BRAC's policy of emphasis on women's progress is reflected in the significantly large number of female VOs as of December 1991 (7,781) as compared to male VOs (4,061) and female membership (419,213) as compared to male membership (197,923).

Elements that Strengthen and Keep Going the VOs

We may discern two sets of elements or activities that strengthen and keep going the VOs. The first set of elements constitute the whole process of contact with the group members, motivating and mobilizing them and organizing them into larger and smaller groups followed by Functional, Consciousness Raising Education for all members and training

TABLE 4.1

Village Organization Status by the End of December 1991

Programme	No. of branches	Villages covered	Village organizations (Total)	VOs Male	VOs Female	Membership (total)	Male	Female
All Total	125	5,414	11,842	4,061	7,781	617,136	197,923	419,213
Total RCP+RDP	120	5,198	11,376	3,911	7,465	598,123	192,149	405,974
RCP	30	1,682	3,687	1,284	2,403	201,118	62,714	138,404
Year 6	10	568	1,232	424	808	69,222	22,539	46,683
Year 5	20	1,114	2,455	860	1,595	131,896	40,175	91,721
RDP	90	3,516	7,689	2,627	5,062	387,005	129,435	267,570
Year 4	20	982	2,468	259	1,509	126,760	44,190	82,570
Year 3	20	889	2,108	886	1,222	144,955	47,037	67,918
Year 2	20	924	1,917	577	1,340	96,966	28,001	68,965
Year 1	30	721	1,196	205	991	58,324	10,207	48,117
HSD	4	166	363	144	249	15,760	4,85	10,907
SP	1	50	103	36	67	3,253	921	2,332

Source: BRAC Report, No.1, December, 1991.

in leadership and management for the selected members of the group. The second set of elements are the recurring, regulatory weekly and monthly meetings wherein the substantive activities of the group such as savings, loan repayment and life issues are transacted.

It is found that Functional Education is a key element in the process of institution building. An FE course is obligatory for all group members under RDP. It is also a pre-requisite for credit entitlement. FE plays a crucial role in conscientising the target population and emboldening them to confront the problems they face.

The process of preparing and educating the members of the VOs may be described as going through three phases: in the first year, it is mainly preaching the dos and don'ts. In the second phase which lasts for three years (RDP), it is preaching and regulating the members' behaviour in credit operations and other social programmes. The third phase (RCP) may be described as commercial relationship. It is a gradual movement and the whole process is institutionalization aiming at taking people to a state of self-reliance and sustainability. This is evident to a large measure in the field situation.

Effect of VOs on their Members

Based on the empirical evidence collected through interviews, meetings and discussions with the female and male members of VOs in several villages in the districts of Narsingdi, Pabna and Natore (several areas of RDP and branches of RCP) recently and corroborated by the non-members, the better off people in some of the villages, feel positive about the whole process of VO formation and its functioning.

The members of the VOs are especially, the female feel that BRAC through its VOs has kindled new hopes for them for a better life. It facilitated accessibility to credit and means to go in for self-employment in small enterprises and trade. The members expressed a sense of achievement that they have learnt to sign their names and are becoming aware of what they are, why they are, what they are, what they can do by themselves, the resources they have and what they can expect from external sources.

The members of the VOs who were interviewed were unanimous that the VOs have brought them into a forum for individual and collective growth. It brought in a new value system, group work ethics, group identity, group solidarity, group commitment, identity of a common cause, discipline, order, a habit of savings and a certain degree of social cohesiveness. The members have learnt that so long they live up to the functional norms of the VO, their interests would be served. Further, the female members of the VOs feel that they have gained some respectability at home and in the community by virtue of their supplementing their family's income through their earnings (some of them through self-employment in chicken raising, sericulture, deep tube well etc.) and by virtue of the new knowledge they have gained through education and training. The very fact of women sitting together exclusively and deliberating over polygyny, divorce, dowry, child marriage and ill-treatment meted out to them by the male members in their families is an unprecedented and an uncommon phenomenon in the local culture. In a sense, it is a revolutionary change, especially among the poorest-segments in Bangladesh society.

The members of the VOs indicated in the interviews that the credit programmes channeled through VOs foster and build discipline among them. It is a question of weekly payment of loan installment due, and a small amount of savings. This element of compulsory weekly payment and answerability to the peer group in the VO, is said to keep the members alert, sensitive and responsible in repayment. They say it is a question of individual prestige and honour, to pay on time, however poor a person is. Credit programmes through VOs not only contribute to economic betterment but also bring in a social behavioural transformation. What is to be reckoned here is the VO which serves as an organization comprising members and at the same time as an institution with a set of newly established norms, procedures, regulation, obligations, rights and duties, all of them ensuring the interests of the individual and the group.

The process of building rural organizations has already initiated considerable social changes, both individual and collective, in the rural disadvantaged people, especially women. Both men and women say that they are more aware of their rights as citizens and how they have been exploited by the rich. One-woman member of a VO (Putia, Natore Region) has put it, "To be together is strength".

In material terms, in six years time from 1981 to 1987, per capita real income of the programme households has increased by 116 per cent while the real income of the non-programme households has declined by 15.6 per cent. Zafar Ahmed reports in the same paper that in the year 1981, 89.7 per cent of the non-programme households were below the poverty line and 10.3 per cent above the poverty line. But overtime, the poverty situation amongst the non-programme households has deteriorated. In the year 1987, the percentage of below poverty line households has increased to 97.4 from 89.7, while the households above the poverty line has declined from 2.6 per cent in 1981 to 0.3 percent in 1987.

But the situation in the programme households is almost the opposite. In the year 1987, the below poverty line households has declined from 91.2 per cent in 1981 to 25.9 per cent in 1987, and above the poverty line households has increased from 8.8 per cent in 1981 to 74.1 per cent in 1987. This shows an appreciable effect of VOs and the poverty alleviation programmes carried through them on the households who have been members of the VOs.[4]

Besides the weekly savings and loan repayment meetings, the monthly so-called issue-based meetings, however unspontaneous they are, they provide a continuous education to the members. Whether the issues related to khas land (government land), women's exploitation, dowry, child marriages, health issues, wages and village touts are resolved or not, they are deliberated upon in a group sitting. The group sitting normally encourages the individual to voice his/her feelings and opinions. The discussions are not casual but deliberate and purposeful. The individual in such group sittings leans on the group and the group sometimes shares the individual's views and supports the individual's stand. Public opinion sometimes for or against an issue gets crystallized and gains momentum in such group meetings.

Despite the positive and facilitating factors in respect of the monthly meetings of the VOs, there are a few limitations pertaining to them. Sometimes, the issues discussed in the monthly meetings are not the keenly-felt-needs of the members, that they have no resources and strength to resolve them, that the issues are not spontaneous, that the issues have deep roots in the value system and the tradition of the larger society.

Maturity Level of VOs

The VOs as chief instruments and vehicles of institution building are deliberately built-groups with certain values, norms, procedures, objectives, expectations, rights and obligations, and naturally each VO is to be treated as an unique social entity. It is a growing organization. The VOs are at different levels of maturity in terms of regular attendance to weekly and monthly meetings, payment of savings and loan installments and managing their individual and collective enterprises. It is gathered that some of the VOs in the RCP areas are managing the credit operations in the absence of BRAC personnel. The maturity of the VOs is manifest in the level of awareness, self-confidence and in articulation of ideas for development among the members of VOs. The case in point is the female VO in Baichitola village in Maheshpur Area Office, Pabna District. The women interviewed at Baichitola were quite clear as to the usefulness of the VO and that they would work towards advancement, strengthening their organization. They feel that the VO as a new forum has given them a social shelter for development. It is gratifying to note that the survival rate of the VOs is extremely high. The dropout cases of members of VOs and what is called disintegration of VOs has been negligible.

It may be relevant here to briefly describe the forming or dissolving of village organization. As mentioned earlier, the minimum number of members to form a VO is 45. Sometimes, it takes a couple of months to reach this minimum number. When members in the target population, say some 20 or 30 come forward for a VO, it is tantamount on their part to mobilize the strength in order to reach the minimum required and once the minimum is reached, the VO is formed formally. Similarly, when the members leave the VO on their own accord or asked to leave, when found that they did not satisfy the conditions to be members of the VO, the VO is dissolved. The reasons for the members voluntarily leaving the organization are their not being satisfied with the VO and inconvenient timing of the weekly meetings. The weekly meetings are held in the mornings before 7.30. It is fixed. An instance was reported by the BRAC monitoring Division that a Vo of fishermen had to be dissolved because, the fishermen found it to be impracticable to attend the weekly meetings in the morning at which hour they are to do fishing. The fixed hour of the weekly meeting inconvenienced the fishermen.

Future of VOs

The VOs as deliberately built vehicles of development of the landless poor, as the media at the village level for BRAC for its development operations are slowly taking roots in the social and livelihood pursuits of their members. It may be observed that the VOs in the context of prevailing socio-economic conditions of the landless poor, are the only foothold and anchor for the poor. The VOs are to be described primarily as associations or organizations of people and are in the process of establishing themselves as institutions. The VOs have a specific function to fulfill, to serve as an institutional, social-collective force to reach the poor to the basic minimum level of life. They may continue to be useful organizations, even after BRAC withdraws from them. However, it may be pointed out, that the VOs in a sense are transitory *ad hoc* organizations, unlike other social, economic and political institutions. Their survival is a question of their function in respect of the clientele for whom they were created. Even though, the VOs may not continue with the present structure and functions, they may continue in a modified form. The form it would take and the strength it would gain and the needs it would serve largely depends on the local clientele group.

The whole process and operation associated with VOs has brought in a great degree of self-regulation and maturity on the part of the VOs. In one sense, the VOs are project related and time-bound organizations meeting the economic and social interests of the group, but at the same time, they are not as pointed out above as enduring and strong as religious and social institutions such as a mosque, church, marriage or caste. It appears as though that the VOs require the paternal support of BRAC for some more years, so that the VOs become part of the social institutional fabric of the poor.

It is reported that many VOs have been developed into well-managed democratic institutions which have been able to resolve local conflicts, undertake joint economic schemes and lobby for government services. By being strong in number and unified in purpose, many VOs, it has been reported, have been able to decrease their dependence on local elite for guidance and advice in resolving conflicts and exploitation in money lending.

Conclusion

It will not be far from truth to say that BRAC has been exceedingly successful in applied social sciences in understanding the landless poor, their socio-economic milieu, in establishing rapport with them, in motivating them, organizing them and forming them into larger and small groups, imparting them with functional knowledge and skills, infusing confidence and hope in them inducing initiative in them for social and economic movement forward.

In building and in facilitating the VOs as live and active social organizations, the secret of the approach lies in BRAC meeting the psychological, social and economic needs of the landless poor at the individual, family and community level.

The structure of small groups within the VO, the constitution of a Management Committee (MC), the system of electing or selecting small group leaders and MC members, and the periodic rotation of leadership and the functions assigned to the group leaders and MC, reflect a system of built-in checks and balances, and also contributing equal opportunity to the members to participate in the activities for their betterment.

The VOs are growing people's institutions and they are at varied states of maturity and BRAC may have to continue nurturing them for some more years. The VO concept is a significant and innovating idea in BRAC's development strategy, the nucleus ingredients being credit, weekly savings and loan installment payment meetings and the monthly meetings.

The effects and impact of VOs on their members have been impressive. They have kindled hope in the members, unity, individual and group action for social and economic betterment.

ACTIVITIES OF VILLAGE ORGANIZATION

Resource Mobilization	Organisational Discipline	Social Corruption	Financial Discipline	Economic Activities	Local Body Participation	Social Justice
Govt. Khas	Regular Meeting	Bribe Divorce	Budgeting Procedure	Income and employment generation activities	Participation in all local committees/ bodies expert pressure and influence for administration	Participation & influence on local issues
Food for work	Participation & collective development	Nepotism Dowry	Accounts	Conformity with social values appropriate to the local situation		Assurance of social fair services
General Wages	Human & Material control	Theft Polygamy	Proper recording of financial transactions			
Govt. Support Services	Intra & Inter organizational cooperation	Women status Usury rate of interest	Periodical reports/ statement			
Govt. Subsidized resources	Collective responsibility Documentation and record keeping	Unfair wages	Fund generation proper utilization of fund			

While speaking of the sustained success of BRAC, we have to give extra weightage to the factor that BRAC's clientele are the disadvantaged and distressed poor. Organizing them and working with them is a laudable achievement. The poor and their participatory planning and development is an unique lesson that others may emulate.

NOTES AND REFERENCES

1. The material in this case study is based on: (i) BRAC Report, 1990; (ii) BRAC 1992 Diary and (iii) the author's own observations in the field. The author would like to express his sincere thanks to BRAC and to the Donor Liaison-Office, Dhaka.
2. Uphoff, Norman, (1989). *Local Institutional Development*, Kumarian Press; p. 8.
3. BRAC documents (please refer to Appendix I for details).
4. Zafar Ahmad, (1991). *Group Approach to Empowering Women: An Emerging Development Paradigm from South Asia;* BRAC (1991).

5

Role of Banks in Entrepreneurship Development

In many instances whether it is men or women motivated to take to some entrepreneurial activity by themselves may not be in a position to finance their enterprises. Financial institutions especially the banks by their assistance to the neo or ongoing entrepreneurs really create a positive impetus for accelerating and successfully running the enterprises small or large. When we say banks, the concept stands for all kinds of financial institutions helping the entrepreneurs in their ventures. Here, we may briefly look into the role of banks in entrepreneurship development.

Entrepreneurship development as a socio-cultural concomitant to small-scale industrial development in the country envisages a multi-institutional approach. Of several institutions engaged in the promotion of entrepreneurship, banks constitute a significant factor. The paper attempts a brief discussion on the role of those banks could play as vital partners in the task and the approach to inducing entrepreneurial ventures on the part of a large number of people in the country.

Most of the Asian countries have of late adopted a deliberate policy of promoting and encouraging small enterprises as a strategy for the overall development of their countries. During the past five decades, India has been engaged in the task of promoting and developing entrepreneurship.

Priority has been accorded to small-scale industries and stimulating and finding entrepreneurs. The agencies promoting entrepreneurial development try to cater to the needs of two types of clientele: the spontaneously emerging entrepreneurs, and those who have been induced to take up entrepreneurial activity by the promotional agencies.

Banks as Major Partners in EDP

Though organizations such as the District-Industries Centres, Small Industry Service Institutes and other state corporations are engaged in the primary task of stimulating and supporting entrepreneurial activity, it is the banks and other financial institutions that have a major role in developing entrepreneurship. Until recently, the activity of EDP has been rather confined to the promotional agencies but today the banks are more involved not only in the financing the enterprises of the entrepreneurs, but they do associate themselves in stimulating, and motivating entrepreneurial activity.

The volume of activity on the part of the banks in entrepreneurial development is not only quantitative but also qualitative. There is a change in the orientation of the banks' role in this field. Today, the need and the emphasis is to go beyond the financing of the enterprise. It is to motivate and develop entrepreneurial climate in the community. In the context of developing entrepreneurship, we are dealing with induced entrepreneurs, and the banks have to take into account the limitations on the part of the new entrepreneurs, and appreciate their problems and their unfamiliarity with banking institutions.

The banks are not alone in the field; several agencies as mentioned earlier are engaged in the task of EDP and unless there is an inter-institutional coordination, the effectiveness of the whole activity will be lost. There is a need for teamwork in the case of agencies engaged in the task. The banker as a major promoter of EDP has to work in unison with other promotional agencies.

In the interaction between the banker and the customer, the communication on the part of the banker may be emphasized. Whether this interpersonal communication is oral or written the banker has to see that he speaks and writes to the customer in the wave length of the latter, so that the customer understands and appreciates the role of the bank, and the bank in turn, builds up confidence in the customer and contributes to the credibility of the bank. The personnel of the bank who meet and interact with the customer need a special kind of orientation especially in the case of rural-tribal entrepreneurs.

As we have mentioned earlier, the banks are to be participants in the journey of EDP right from the start of the process. Instead of indulging in mutual accusations (DICs blaming the financial institutions and the financial institutions blaming the DICs etc.), it is desirable that they join hands right from the beginning as a team and help the entrepreneur. Their association may have to start right from the point of identification of entrepreneurs and training them till the enterprise becomes viable.

It is presumed that banking institutions are facing some institutional problems. Since the banks are playing and need to play a significant role in EDP, the banking system has to attend to these problems and streamline the entire working system-internal as well as inter-institutional to help and facilitate rapid and sustained growth in the field of entrepreneurial development.

Role of Banks

With the nationalization of major commercial banks in 1969, banks have been playing a pivotal role in development financing—the small sector in particular, as also contributing to the development of backward regions of the country with the abetment of other developmental institutions.

In the context of the continuing paucity of entrepreneurial

talent and scarcity of investable resources, commercial banks in India are playing a dynamic and positive role in igniting the forces of innovation and helping to foster and broad-base new entrepreneurship.

The functions of development banking include providing loans and working capital, formulation of project ideas, identification of specific projects suitable to local conditions, location and induction of new entrepreneurs into entrepreneurial activity and offering of technical and managerial guidance.

The public sector banks have been experimenting with wide range of special schemes to finance engineers, doctors, technically qualified entrepreneurs apart from promoting several schemes for funding self-employment endeavours among the weaker sections of society and the educated unemployed. Wherever possible, banks are collaborating with other developmental institutions representing industry, trade or commerce. Various schemes have been in the preparation of area potential studies, bankable projects and collection of information useful to potential entrepreneurs. For enterprises that are export-oriented, apart from financing, banks offer a wide range of services.

Specific to entrepreneurial activity, nationalized banks are guided in their endeavour to provide the following services:

- Assisting entrepreneurs in selection of industry, preparation and evaluation of project reports and conducting market survey.
- Providing short-term and long-term finance.
- Assisting in obtaining clearance, machinery and equipment.
- Assisting in setting up production and control processes, offer management and technical guidance.

EDP in Backward Areas

In order to accelerate industrial development in backward areas, banks are now involved in identifying industrial potential and motivating entrepreneurs to take up activities to exploit it. Banks are identifying and training entrepreneurs by conducting EDPs for them. Each of these programmes is followed by a support phase which provides counselling and consultancy services on a continuing basis. Banks are nominating project leaders to assist entrepreneurs in product selection and see them through various phases of the project until the unit is established.

Equity Fund Scheme

The State Bank of India introduced an Equity Fund Scheme in 1978 to help small but credit-worthy units to expand their equity base. First of its kind to be implemented in the country, the scheme extends assistance to small units in the form of loans ranging from Rs. 5,000/- to Rs. 50,000/-. The loans are repayable in a period of seven years, after a moratorium of five to seven years.

Secondment of Bank Personnel

Another contribution that banks are making towards EDP is by deputing their officers for posting to District Industries Centres as Credit Managers. These officers facilitate entrepreneurial activity by speeding up completion of formalities relating to sanctions, approvals, quotas, etc. These personnel are also actively involved in designing and organizing training programmes and coordinating such programmes in various parts of the country by preparing training manuals.

Conflicting Situations

While the policies and priorities of the Govt. are directed towards development banking and while the focus is on weaker sections and inducing entrepreneurship or industrial activity among the people who are new to these, and who have never approached the banks for any developmental purpose, the managers of branches who are the ultimate people in assessing, appraising and advancing loans to new entrepreneurs, meet with certain dilemmas; on one hand the directives from above are to lend money to a variety of customers, who may not, in terms of security meet the requirements, but at the same time, such customers are to be helped. And in such a context, the branch manager meets with a conflicting situation; whether he should discharge his functions as per the policies and directives of the government or not and at the same time ensure security of the money he lends and save his position. Many of the branch managers of banks today may be experiencing this kind of difficulty.

As it is, it is the promotional agencies like the DICs who make promises to the entrepreneur that he could/would secure bank loan for his enterprise. Sometimes, the promotional agency might not have looked into it in detail, the technical and economic feasibility of the enterprise and also studied the background and competence on the part of the entrepreneur; and when the entrepreneur meets the banker with all expectations, he fails to meet the requirements as per the banker. Since a number of institutions are engaged in the task of EDP, the banker as a promotional agent whose stake is around 80% in the venture of the entrepreneur, there is a dire need for the banker to be a major promoter and more involved in the process of EDP.

The banks could play a significant and substantive role in all the phases of entrepreneurship development. This could be on their own initiative and more often in collaboration with the DICs and other agencies in the field of ED.

Role of Banks: A Vision

The banks and other financial institutions as instruments of economic development and welfare of people have basically two things to work with the material resources and the human resources. Wherever finance is a factor to harness and boost these two basic resources, it will be the banks that would play a prime and sustaining role. The banks as they are doing today, will extend their support and guidance technical and managerial, to the ongoing and potential entrepreneurs and establish themselves as pervasive and enduring institutions.

It may be the individual who meets the banker and who establishes an enterprise, but as the individual is placed in the social-cultural network, there is a need on the part of the bank to go beyond the individual, developing rapport with the group and the community of the individual. The banks are to motivate the individual, and to do so, they have a role to educate the community in which they operate, to make the bank a partner in the development of community resources and in raising the standards of living in the community. The banks through their activities and involvement over a period of time, should become an integral system of the individual and community development.

Statistically speaking, the banks today may be touching only a small segment of the economic community in the country. The vision that one envisages is that banks extend their supportive limbs to all potential individuals and families in developing them so that they develop the resources towards attaining a meaningful quality of life.

6

Extension Education in Aid of Agricultural Marketing

Extension which may be called as an applied social science though began with agriculture, the very concept and the methods are applicable to several fields and especially to the field of small scale industrial development. One of the major problems that governs small-scale and cottage industries is marketing of goods and services. The chapter though here deals with agricultural marketing, the principles and the methodology are equally relevant and applicable to industrial extension.

It is paradoxical that agricultural extension tries to help the farmers with a package of improved farm practices to improve and increase farm production and productivity, but unfortunately, it stops with the production function only. Negligible attention is paid by the extension agency in helping the farmer in the marketing of the produce. There is a need for a new kind of extension education especially in helping the farmers in securing remunerative prices for their hard earned produce.

Before we look into extension education in aid of agricultural marketing let us briefly look into the concept and other dimensions of extension education.

(1) The Concept

(i) Helping people by means of education to put useful

knowledge to work for them, is the essence of extension education.

(ii) The process of selling across new ideas and new techniques based on the knowledge of recent advances in science and technology to people who need to use it most is generally called "Extension" and the method is "Education".

(iii) It is working with people for their betterment.

(iv) It is a two-way communication.

(v) It is an applied education.

(vi) It aims at change in the ways of life of people through education.

(2) Activity-wise it consists of

(i) Imparting of new knowledge

(ii) Imparting of new skills

(iii) Change of outlook/attitude

(iv) Supplies

(v) Services

(3) It is based on the triple tenets of faith

(i) Faith in the individual

(ii) Faith in democracy

(iii) Faith in science and technology

(4) As an applied education it comprises

(i) Research findings

(ii) Accumulated field experiences

(iii) A judicious dose of appropriate technology

(iv) A body of philosophy, principles and methods based on behavioural sciences.

(5) Philosophy of Extension

(i) Extension has a philosophy of democracy.

(ii) Extension has a philosophy of co-operating with agencies that are interested in the common welfare of the people.

(iii) The basic philosophy of extension is centred around the welfare of the individuals and their families.

(iv) The great principles underlying the philosophy and extension are:

- The individual is supreme in democracy.
- The home is a fundamental unit in civilization.
- The family is the first training ground of the human race.

(v) Extension has a philosophy of working out problems by group action, based upon the needs of the people and developed by the people.

(vi) Extension has a philosophy of education for all.

(vii) Extension has a philosophy covering teaching.

In the words of Seaman A. Knapp "What we hear we may doubt. What we see we may possibly doubt but what we do we cannot doubt".

(viii) Extension has a philosophy of truth and seeking for truth.

(ix) Extension has a philosophy of culture, it recognizes the customs, manners, conventions, norms, habits and behavior of the people.

(x) Extension has a philosophy of leadership (working with local leaders – developing new leadership)

(xi) Extension has a philosophy of the dignity of the individual.

(xii) Extension has a philosophy of local responsibility (people's participation)

(6) Principles of Extension

(i) Extension work must be educational.

(ii) Extension must work through understanding the

traditions, customs, manners, and cultural values of the people so that it is in harmony with the culture of the people.

(iii) Extension work must be started where the people are, at their economic, educational, social, physical and cultural level. The technical knowledge, education, intelligence, capacity of understanding and group and physical standard should be considered.

(iv) Extension programmes should be based on the interests and needs of the people, which are determined by general acceptance and full support of those for whom they are chalked out. They should not have undue support from the government, except that of technical guidance and essential finances, the government acting as a catalyst.

(v) Extension should use democratic methods.

(vi) The implementation of an extension programme must be done by the people through their local leaders, the govt. agency giving proper guidance at the appropriate time.

(vii) As extension is a two-way channel, the extension worker should not hesitate to learn from the people while he helps them solve their problems.

(viii) The extension programme should be started first with those problems which appear simple yet, are very important and urgent in nature.

(ix) Extension programme must be flexible. It should permit adjustments to local needs.

(x) Extension work must always be educational. It should be persuasive and convincing but never coercive.

(xi) Extension must be a continuous and an on-going process.

(xii) It should evaluate and re-adjust or modify according to need.

(xiii) Extension programme must suit young and old, men and women. Extension work should be challenging and satisfying.

(xiv) Extension should work with all classes of people irrespective of race, creed, caste or community.

(xv) Extension work must not be combined with regulatory functions.

(xvi) Extension work must develop programmes gradually.

(xvii) Extension must promote the fuller utilization of local resources, both physical and human.

(xviii) Extension must keep in view the national policies and programmes.

(xix) Extension must use the community approach.

(xx) Extension work should be supported by technical expertise, services and supplies.

The proper recognition of the philosophy underlying extension work and applying the principles are bound to bring in the desirable changes among people to reach the ultimate objective of:

- Developing finer families
- Living in better homes
- On more productive farms
- In more progressive communities

(7) Main Components of Extension

(a) programme planning

(b) programme implementation

(c) Programme evaluation

- The entire process of planning for agricultural

marketing development implies a need for change.

- The question then arises; change from what, to what, by whom, where, by what methods?

"If we could but know where we are now, and where ought to go, we could better judge what to do, and how to do it" – Abraham Lincoln.

(a) Programme Planning focuses on:

- Needs
- Resources
- Obstacles
- Processes - Steps
- Methods
- Evaluation

(b) Programme Implementation implies:

(i) Organizing wide publicity to the programme
(ii) Drawing up a plan of action
(iii) Evaluating the programme during and after its execution
(iv) Four pillars of implementation
  - Research
  - Service
  - Supplies
  - Credit

(c) Programme Evaluation:

Evaluation is an integral part of extension cycle. The following steps illustrate the place and importance of extension evaluation in the entire extension cycle.

1. Analyse situation
2. Identify objectives
3. Determine objectives
4. Plan programme

5. Decide on subject – matter or methods
6. Make changes as needed
7. Plan evaluation
8. Collect information
9. Summarize and report findings
10. Interpret and use findings

(8) Extension Methods in Aid of Agricultural Marketing:

(i) Farm and home visits
(ii) General meetings
(iii) Group contacts
(iv) Campaigns
(v) Working with voluntary and local leaders
(vi) Exhibits and models
(vii) Tours and excursions
(viii) Literature-leaflets, folders, circular letters and newspapers on prices and prospects of remunerative marketing agri-products.
(ix) Farmers' calls.
(x) Radio/TV programmes

Prior to helping the farmer in marketing his produce there is a greater need to help him produce more at an economical cost. This leads us to a closer view of the farmers' culture and psychology.

Farmers share a village agricultural point of view. It is characterized by:

- *A holistic outlook*: Agriculture is a central activity, but it is only part of a whole, a connected way of life. For example, things which can be contributed to farm work like money and labour are constantly required to meet other family needs as well. The village family allocates these resources by looking at the whole.
- *Environmental Sensitivity*: All farmers have to be extremely sensitive to their environments in order

to survive. They sense from collective and individual observation what elements of the environment are critical to their success as farmers. They are particularly sensitive to cyclical things like rainfall and storm patterns. More than any one else, they know the mini-environments of their individual farms intimately.

- *Local Focus*: Small-scale farmers especially know a lot about local things and much less about regional, national or global things. Most of these farmers' *interests* are local as well.
- *Self Interest*: Each small-scale farmer has a list of priorities that helps him make decisions. This list defines a farmer's self-interest, which is a central part of his worldview.
- *Farmer's bias*: A farmer's view of things is coloured by the physical and economic realities of farm work. These practical preoccupations are uppermost in a farmer's mind.
- *Tradition, fatalism and adaptability to change:* Carrying out the tradition of farming is a normal and reliable habit of mind. This unchanging habit of mind is negatively reinforced by adverse outside opinions about village people like small-scale farmers. It has also been reinforced by the inability of tradition to contend with the new problems brought on by accelerated change. As a result, one of the extremes of a small-scale farmers' point of view is a kind of fatalism and feeling of impotence amid rapid change. The other end of the spectrum is a real, though often talent openness and adaptability to change, for farming is a constant process of successful adaptation. Like other people, small-scale farmers are ambivalent towards change.

For small-scale farmers with all the above characteristics, change is not worthwhile unless it is:

- Culturally appropriate
- In agreement with self-interest
- Respectful of tradition
- Clearly beneficial
- Not economically risky

Elaborating on economic risk, John Guy Smith offered this description in 1970:

> "Farming is subject to numerous risks from weather, pests, diseases, price fluctuations and other uncertainties. For the small-scale farmer, these risks are accentuated by his precarious economic condition. Much of a small-scale farmer's supposed conservatism is really a very shrewd attempt to avoid or minimize risk".

For example, Yigi Kamara grows rice in Sierra Leone. Every year, he grows his crop during May to September, the rainy season. In August and September, while waiting for the harvest, the stores from the previous year dwindle, and there is a "hungry season". Yigi plants millet and cassava on a hillside in March and April to deal with this. In order to grow rice year round and perhaps even grow a surplus, Yigi is thinking of building gravity-fed ditches and dikes in a swamp near his hill farm. The work will take four months, from January to May. Is it worth the effort? If he doesn't plant millet or cassava, will there be enough food this "hungry season"? Can he afford a shovel? Will his family be able to harvest, thresh, store and grind all the expected new rice? Can he sell some to make it worthwhile? What will his neighbours say? What about the old stores about the dangers of working in the swamp?

Small-scale farmers like Yigi change as individual cultural beings, as practical farmers, and as economic producers. They have considerable resources which they bring to bear on the problems of agricultural production and livelihood in developing countries:

- Expertise in local technologies and a variety of practical skills (e.g. – masonry, carpentry, etc.)
- Expertise regarding local conditions affecting farming
- Status as independent economic unit
- Experience as farmers (traditions)
- A practical, critical viewpoint
- Adaptability
- Openness to producing a usable surplus
- Their limitations include:
  - Lack of capital beyond family supply
  - Habit of not investing in or using credit or outside inputs
  - Interests and roles which compete with agriculture
  - Little access to outside agricultural support services
  - Reluctance to take risks

Along with these, however, there are factors from beyond the village which also limit the small-scale farmer's ability to deal with change. Most directed technological change, like the promoting of new practices, is based on the priorities and interests of development planners and leaders. This may exclude small-scale farmers or be irrelevant to their needs. Governments, development agencies and private business promote change this way. Example may be mechanization or mono-cropping which benefit large-scale farmers and foreign markets more than small-scale farmers.

Understanding People

Self-interest is the basis for all that a farmer does. The source of a farmer's motivation, whatever it may be in a given case, can be quite obscure to the extension worker. A farmer who seems to be strong, intelligent, financially secure, and aware enough to be successful, may still cling to his timeworn practices rather than opt for something new that he perceives to be against his interest. Neither repeated contact with an extension agent nor weighty scientific evidence will change his mind. The farmer's personal concerns – his religion, his desire for material possessions that he feels can be more quickly had by other means – are foremost in his mind. As such they are of primary concern to extension workers.

An extension agent needs to learn what the people he lives with value and consider important. This understanding is at the heart of the two-way communication process. Without it, the extensionist can gain no perspective on the appropriateness of the change he promotes. Nor can he determine what training methods are most suitable to local people's needs. Finally, and perhaps most importantly, the agent will be unable to emphasize or even communicate effectively with his friends and neighbours.

To learn anything about a person's self-interest requires time and shared experience. It takes hours sweating over blow blades, eating from the same bowl and walking together in sadness in a funeral procession. The "methods" used are informal, but the information gleaned is of crucial importance. The farming aspect of a villager's life, is connected with all other aspects. Labour resources for farm work are also labour resources required by virtue of kinship and money for improved livestock strains can just as easily become money for a niece's school fees. As an extension worker enters a community, and begins to make initial social contacts, he should take note of the various special interests people display in order to better understand how to go about his work.

Administering Credit

Farmers can exercise certain options only when they have the financial resources to do so. Accumulating these resources (*sometimes called "capital"*) is a necessary first step toward innovation and change. Farmers can accumulate resource by saving surplus income or borrowing resources from other sources. To the small-scale farmer saving presents a major problem because even the diligent application of customary farm practices does not often yield much surplus beyond home needs. One of the major catalysts of potential farmer innovation in developing countries is therefore the provision of credit.

There are many kinds of credit: informal sharing of a plough and family communal labour, village-level borrowing at the money lender's bank loans or input-credit schemes. Beyond the village level, credit is both a powerful tool and a potential cause of dependence. Cooperative ventures and capital-sharing are better ways to help small scale-farmers gain access to the resources for change.

Farmers themselves have various motives for using credit:

Consumer Credit

- *Survival* – when a crop failure or family illness causes the normal balance of home needs and harvest to go out of balance
- *Family and Social Obligations* – when a wedding, funeral or other family obligation requires money or resources not at hand
- *Consumption* – when something the farm family wants is beyond normal means
- *Investment in the Home or Cottage Industry* – when the farm family wants to buy a labour-saving device *(corn grinder)*, set up cottage industry *(sewing machine and cloth)* or repair/expand a house.

Agricultural Credit

- *Survival of Farm Enterprise – (e.g. securing seed or using a cultivator)* securing resources necessary to keep the farm going
- *Paying for Seasonal Labour* – Extra labour beyond

the family may be needed to plant, weed or harvest when there is no surplus to provide wages

- *Acquiring inputs* – purchasing new tools, fertilizer or equipment to carry out a new package of practices
- *Increasing Efficiency* – sometimes farmers wish to substitute animal or machine power for human power for land preparation, for example, but need to borrow to employ it before realizing profits.
- *Marketing* – while waiting for a good price for their produce farmers may need to borrow to survive
- *Expanding the Scale of Farm Business* – to acquire additional land, to finance farm improvements *(clearing land, building storage facilities, constructing irrigation works, etc.)* to increase herd size.

It is important for the extension worker and farmers to understand why and how credit is extended to farmers. Credit being a form of dependence on resources beyond the farmer's control, it should be carefully and cautiously used. When the motivation of the lender is different than the farmer's motivation, there is much less opportunity for informality, for leeway with regard to the repayment of loan, and generally for sympathy for the farmer's precarious position. It is of prime importance that the extension worker and farmer seeking credit be aware of the motives of lenders.

Locally, credit can be extended as a social obligation or an aspect of friendship or family responsibility. However, credit is most often proffered in order to earn interest on the loan. This is the basis of commercial lending in and out of the village. Beyond earning interest, credit is loaned to facilitate sales, to assure the delivery of farm products or as public service through development projects. These motives are important to consider in seeking credit with farmers.

Most of the cost of a commercial loan is interest. Interest

is calculated in a variety of ways, each resulting in a different amount of credit and a different costs. A common form of interest for small-scale farmers is the advance sale of crops, in which the lender is promised crops at current prices even though the price will be higher at harvest time. The different in price constitutes a loss to the farmer which is a form of interest, or credit cost.

Credit "terms" are all the conditions, including credit costs, that are part of an agreement between lender and borrower. The usefulness of credit is a measure of the costs and terms versus the returns or results or credit use. Cost/benefit is calculated in monetary terms for most commercial credit, although timeliness, social appropriateness and other considerations also must be weighed. Most especially, the extension worker must help a farmer weigh the value of credit against the danger of dependency on factors beyond the farmer's control. This must always be part of the calculation of credit cost/benefit.

Because most commercial credit is extended for profit, it is rarely extended to the small-scale farmer. What with the uncertainties of weather, pests and diseases, the limited money-making ability of the small-scale farm, and the inconvenience of the administering credit to a far-flung clientele in rural areas, the small-scale farmer is often not considered a good "risk".

Other forms of institutional credit (through development project or agro product distributors), where these exist, are more readily available to small-scale farmers, but do not allow freedom to use the loan for any purpose. The loan must go to producing a certain crop or buying certain inputs. Thus, it is not easy to help small-scale farmers gain access to credit.

The process of acquiring credit involves, first, surveying a farmers' needs and clarifying with him the specific need to borrow capital. Secondly, the farmer and extensionist must inventory local credit sources. Next, extensionist and farmer must calculate the costs of credit and estimate the returns to the credit to determine the cost/benefit of employing the credit opportunities identified. This would include clarifying the terms of credit. Finally, the extensionist must help the farmer honour the terms of the loan and re-pay it when due.

One facilitating means for the farmer to secure credit is the village cooperative society. It can not only serve his credit needs but it can also be used effectively in marketing his farm produce at a reasonably better price at the appropriate time to the benefit of the farmer.

Providing Storage

Storage facilities constitute a significant factor in agricultural marketing.

Approximately thirty per cent of grain in storage all over the world is lost because of insects, rodents and moulds. For the small-scale farmers with whom extensionists work, this is a major problem of every day life. In villages, protection from such pests and moulds is lacking. Since this is a vital area in which to help the farmer, attention may be focused on the following topics:

- The Grain Storage Problems
- Grain Is a Living Thing
- Grain, Moisture and Air
- Preparing Grain for Storage
- Grain Dryer Models
- Enemies of Grain
- Storage Methods

Extension workers must focus some of their attention on issues beyond the production of agricultural products. By helping a farmer double his grain or vegetable yield, an extensionist may cause a major storage problem. Where does the new grain go? How does the farmer protect it from pests, moisture, thieves? The technical information necessary to solve storage problems is to be provided to the farmers. An extensionist can help by encouraging farmers to plan their storage strategies. Also, farmers can determine the most appropriate storage facilities and strategies with the extension worker's help. Finally, adequate storage is the most practical marketing tool a farmer has. He or she can hold onto a crop until prices become favourable if storage is adequate. The importance of storage facilities cannot be over emphasized.

Besides storage, pooling of grain by the farmers at the village level and also of grading of grain or agri-products are conducive to fetching better prices. These could be done through the local cooperative or Farmers' Association.

Marketing Agricultural Products

The extensionist is often in a good position to help farmers understand and participate more successfully in the marketing system. One of the largest and most uninviting areas the small-scale farmer enters by virtue of change is the market place. In it, he is subject to the forces of supply, demand, big business and government policies and regulations. Here, if anywhere, the farmer needs the direct assistance an extensionist can provide.

There are two main ways in which extensionists can help small-scale farmers successfully approach the market system: by organizing large-scale cooperative groups aimed at gaining local or regional price advantages, or by securing favourable prices through timely marketing, and or through cooperative marketing.

The process of helping farmers secure price advantages through timely marketing involves four steps:

I. Establish who controls the crop/animals at harvest and under what conditions:

(a) Advance sales: farmers may receive payment in advance for a crop thereby obligating it to a buyer.

(b) Contracted sales: farmers may contact to sell a crop to buyer at a certain price for certain quality and quantity.

(c) Loan or credit restrictions on sale: farmers may have to sell a harvest when a loan payment is due.

(d) Tenancy or rent restrictions on sale: farmers may have to sell or give part of a harvest to a landowner or local leader due to tenancy terms, rent due or local customs.

II. Estimate the costs of holding products off the market.

(a) Estimate the average length of the "holding period" between the middle of the period of average high price and average low prices.

(b) Estimate roughly the cost of holding each product *(rice or any product)* off the market. *(eg.–storage facility cost or depreciation; storage losses; handling costs, etc.).*

(c) Estimate the profit or loss to the farmer by holding a crop out of the market. (This depends on the difference between the cost of holding out and the anticipated seasonal price rise).

Net Benefit:-

Estimate Price rise – Estimated holding cost
= Net Benefit (per unit of crop)

III. Decide to hold crop or sell.

Before a farmer can contemplate marketing strategies, his crop must be free at harvest of any restricting arrangements. If the crop is free at harvest, and if the net benefit of holding the crop out of the market place is significant (more than 25 per cent), then the extensionist can advise the farmer to hold his crop out until the price rises to the seasonal average high price.

There are other strategies for successfully participating in the market system. They are listed as one of the *TOOLS*, "interventions by Farmers in the Market System". This tool also serves to illustrate the points raised in this section.

ILLUSTRATION

The Farmer has a vested Interest in	*Because it Determines*	*And He Probably know it's related to*	*But He Probably does not know it is related to*
Market	Which commodities the can produce	Transport facilities, quotas, 'monopoly' control	Effect of government policies
Marketing Standards (Weights, Grades)	How he prepares his crop for market	Local customs. Buyers' preferences	Legislation Processors' preferences.
The Availability and quality of direct Marketing services (weighting, timeliness or payment credit, others	His choice of buyers for his crop	His personal relationship with buyers. The buyers' honesty. The buyer's resources.	Buyer's management ability How much it costs the buyer to perform marketing functions.
Overall marketing Efficiency	Marketing margins and the price he receives.	How efficiency the transport and assembly functions are performed.	Management and technical skills. Productivity of labour. Many and varied costs. The less visible market functions.
Competitiveness of the system	Marketing margins and the price he receives. His choice buyers.	Number of potential buyers, and alternative markets. The buyers' financial and political power.	Control of financing. National policies. The subtler forms of influence.
The market equating supply and demand (price determination)	More than any other factor determines the prices he receives for his products, planting and harvesting schedules, and his farm enterprise mix.	Orderly marketing. Seasonal factors. The size of the total crop. Distant demand factors beyond his control.	National policies. How much of the consumer price is absorbed by the market process. Internal supply and demand. Costs of holding the crop.

TOOL

Checklist for Collecting price Data

SOURCE OF DATA (Current)

- Actual sales
  - reported by farmers
  - reported by local people
  - reported by handlers of products
- Reports by ministries, market publications, etc. (Historical)
- Recent memory
  - as above
- Official reports and studies as above.

ANALYZING DATA:

- Collect data from sources
- Convert all data to common units of value.
- Check prices to eliminate abnormally high or low prices.
- Make sure information on prices is relevant to the community in which farmers/clients live.
- Establish average prices by observing them over a regular period of time (2 or 3 weeks).

TOOL

Interventions Farmers Can Make in the Market System

Farmers can influence four factors which affect the prices of their products over a short period of time:

- Time of sale
- Choice of buyer
- Collective or individual marketing
- Condition of the product

Farmers can learn about their options concerning these

four factors with extension workers. Often the price of a product is lower near normal harvest time, so holding the product in storage is often a way to gain a higher price. Storage depends on perishability, facilities, farmer's ability to wait for income, etc. The choice of buyers is often limited for small-scale farmers, due to transportation costs. Collective marketing is advantageous when costly transportation is a means to a higher price. Collective marketing involves thorough planning of harvest, handling and storage as well as price and profit-sharing agreements. The extension worker can help point out the need for these considerations and can facilitate the process of dealing with them.

It may not be out of place here to briefly look into the marketing of rural industries products. In a larger sense they are allied to agri-products.

Marketing Rural Industries Products

Rural Industries Products

The problem of marketing rural industries products stems from the poor socio-economic background of the artisans, competition from the better-equipped factory sector, lack of sufficient infrastructural facilities in producing raw materials, products not changing rapidly enough with consumer tastes and preferences, labour-intensive technology, inadequate storage facilities and the non-availability of distribution channels.

S. Vanaja Rao (Economic Times, Jan. 10, 1984) observes that few organizations serve as a link between village industry producers and the market and makes out a case for a district-level organization for procuring raw material and finding markets for the finished products.

To assist the marketing of rural industries products she suggests:

- The KVIC *(Khadi & Village Industries Commission)*

open more bhandars and bhavans (emporia) at the block and district level.

- The KVIC renovate existing bhandars and bhavans and set up a big emporium at each state headquarters, supported by a number of bhandars.
- A separate marketing organization to be set up for each village industry for raw material supply and procuring finished products for sale to bhandars and bhavans.
- Action should be taken against government departments which do not purchase reserved items from the KVIC/Small Scale Sector.
- The KVIC and other organizations engaged in marketing V&CI products should take the assistance of the public distribution systems and the marketing outlets of corporate public sector organizations.
- Sale of some products can be made on a contractual basis while for others, intensive sales drives can be encouraged.
- Commercial banks should come in a big way to provide assistance to entrepreneurs who take up marketing and distribution of these products.
- The government-controlled media should publicize these products on a preferential basis.
- The quality of products be improved.
- The KVIC should supply suitable machinery and spares that will enable production of improved products.
- The staff or managers of the KVIC and retail organizations should be better compensated to attract suitable persons to man sales depots *(incentives)*.

Mass Media

Vehicles of information normally classed under the heading of "mass media" – television, radio, newspapers, magazines, and newsletters – can be used by extension agents. Usually, extensionists involved in mass communication efforts adopt other training methods to a larger audience size. Role-plays and dramas are shifted from verandah and village clearings to stages where a hundred or more people can view them simultaneously. Poster designs originally intended only for local use can prove successful enough at calling attention to some new aspect of agriculture to warrant mass production and distribution through Ministry channels over a much wider area.

Media within the realm of possibility for extension work include periodicals, fairs, and radio. Periodicals can be used as discussion starters in farmer meetings where at least a portion of those present are literate. Agricultural fairs are conducted in many developing countries to encourage agriculture development. Volunteers can make use of these fairs by encouraging some of the farmers in certain areas to compete for prizes in farm produce competitions. Such prizes can be valuable form of reward and recognition for a farmer's achievements. Radio provides the most exciting opportunity of any of the standard mass communication devices. This medium can be put to use as a simple information vehicle – to relay announcements of upcoming farmer meetings in an area, for example, or it can be employed in more creative ways. Extensionists with experience in radio broadcasting and production may be able to work within Ministry channels to produce simple and yet highly effective advertisements on the radio for new techniques. Serialized skits, songs and humorous stories are very popular in countries where national radio stations, receive widespread attention.

Radio and TV in local languages would be an effective media for disseminating marketing information.

Conclusion

At the field level there is a greater need to carry out marketing extension education by the village level extension functionaries, village panchayats, youth clubs, farmers' forums, mahila mandals. Though some of the above mentioned people's organizations have their own unique functions as people's institutions, they can be used as an effective means and media to disseminate market information to the farmers. There is a greater need to have a synergetic effect of personal field extension and mass media such as, Radio, TV and newspapers. The extension functionaries to be effective as agri-marketing specialists may have to acquaint themselves with the ongoing agri-marketing practices and the problems and bottlenecks in respect to transportation, communication, storage facility, staying capacity and credit requirements on the part of the farmers. The agricultural marketing extension agents are to be aware of the existing system of agri-marketing and the better prospects available outside the system and also create better prospects in respect to profitable marketing of agricultural produce.

There is a need for continuous concerted efforts on the part of the farmers themselves, farm leaders, local institutions, extension agents to really help the farmers not only produce more but also to have better price for their products.

7

Small-Scale Industrial Development in the Asian Context

Introduction

In the context of the majority of the population in the developing countries in Asia being ruralite, engaged predominantly in agricultural and allied activities with low income levels and in a relative sense with a poor quality of life – against a background of considerable to abundant natural and human resources and potentialities for economic development leading to fuller employment, increased incomes and better quality of life – the obvious and only alternative is to go in for a gradual, well-supported, and sustained rural industrialization, promoting small-scale and cottage industries in the rural areas. All countries in Asia, in principle, recognize the importance of small-scale industries and the role they should play in the socioeconomic development of the people, but in terms of political commitment, industrial policies, organizational structure and institutional support and incentives provided, there is considerable variation from country to country. Some countries (e.g., India, Indonesia, the Philippines), have accorded small-scale and cottage industries a primary position in their planned economic development. Some are concerned simply with industrial development and export markets and devote little attention to balanced regional development or even distribution of small-scale enterprises in the rural areas among various segments of the population. The programmes of rural industrialization are not supported by realistic and coordinated action at the field level, especially entrepreneurship development. It may be stated here that there is no shortage of potential entrepreneurial talent in the rural areas. What is required is the creation of conducive climate for entrepreneurial development which in turn would generate and foster small employment for both the sexes to lead a qualitative life.

With the exception of Brunei, Hong Kong, Singapore, and to some extent South Korea and Taiwan Province of China, the economies of other Asian countries from Afghanistan to Vietnam are basically rural and agricultural with a population ranging from 60 to 90 percent living in rural areas and pursuing predominantly agricultural activities. Consequently, a major part of the labour force in these countries is engaged in activities falling under primary sector with comparatively low per capita income and low standard of living. This is the state of affairs in respect to over fifty per cent of the world's population which lives in South and Southeast Asia. Improving the quality of life of millions of people in Asia is an enormous and a challenging problem and solutions or answers to this problem are to be found within these countries. In essence, it boils down to generating employment, increasing income, basically harnessing and utilizing the primary and secondary resources that the countries are endowed with.

During the past few years many Asian countries realized the importance of promoting and developing small industrial enterprises as a part of their overall strategy of national economic development. In many instances, this was based on evidence of the failure of the strategy of developing large-scale industries to solve problems of unemployment, poverty, regional imbalances and economic inequality. In spite of this realization on the part of the policy-makers, administrators, planners and industrial extension agents, the progress made in this direction has been far from satisfactory and at any rate, varied from country to country. Since many of the Asian countries have common economic, social, cultural and to a large measure political characteristics and face similar socio-economic problems, the approach and methods discussed in the following pages would, it is believed, ensure a meaningful, realistic and sustained growth and development of small-scale and cottage industries in rural areas and thus, realize the triple objective of generating local self-employment, increasing income and making use of local primary and secondary resources, both material and human.

It is in order here to briefly look into the sub-categories within rural industries that are in vogue in different countries in Asia.

Rural Small Industries

The term 'industry' covers any productive activity involving collection, processing, manufacturing, repairing, addition or alteration, servicing etc. Small industries as a category are distinguished from medium, large or heavy industries. Though the primary criterion for 'small' is the size of the unit, definitions of small industries vary a great deal. Across the countries in Asia, there is no uniformity of definition of small industries. Agencies involved in the development of small-scale industries provide different criteria in defining this category of enterprises. At times, the criteria chosen vary from agency to agency such as the Ministry of Industry in charge of small industry development and finance institutions within the same country. The usual bases used in 'defining the small-scale industries are the number of employees, the capital invested on plant and machinery and the volume or the value of the output. Even with these criteria, diversity in definition is in vogue in different countries.

Rural industries, for all practical purposes imply rural small-scale and cottage industries inclusive of handicrafts and artisan enterprises. It is, however, necessary to indicate clearly the distinction between 'handicrafts' and 'village industries'. The handicraft industry is cottage or small-scale industry, the products of which are artistic in nature and require individual skill and craftsmanship in their manufacture. The handicrafts are both rural and urban in nature. Although, it is a labour intensive industry, it produces higher value-added items or articles whereas, the village industries produce articles of daily use for the people.

Cottage industry is usually defined as one which is carried out wholly or primarily with the help of members of family either as a full-time or part-time occupation. These industries are traditional in character, i.e., son inheriting the skill from the father. It is an industrial enterprise carried out by individual households mainly with the household workers and sometimes or occasionally employing outside labour. The fundamental characteristic of this category of industries is that the work is or, can be done as and when the household members find it convenient and not on the basis of any regular working hours or working days. Crafts or handicrafts requiring personal skill of producers and having individualistic rather than mass character fall in this group. Sometimes, the terms 'cottage and village' as prefixes to category of industries are used interchangeably.

The criteria such as, number of employees, the amount of capital investment on plant and machinery, and use of electricity or otherwise, and sometimes the kind of products manufactured and the service rendered by in regard to small industries relate to policy measures and institutional support such as fiscal support, credit policy, labour legislation, research and development, state support in the form of reservation, purchase preference, allocation of scarce raw material, freight structure, electricity rates, price subsidies, import of machinery and equipment, excise duty, income tax and free or subsidized preparation of a bankable project. Further, the sub-categorization within small industry as traditional cottage or village industries, modern small-scale industries, handicrafts and artisan enterprises is for the purpose of institutional jurisdiction, promotion and development. India provides an interesting example of this kind of organizational, and development administrative set-up. In India the village and small industries sector is divided into eight sub-sectors namely, Khadi (hand spun and hand woven cloth), village industries, Handlooms, Sericulture, Handicrafts, Coir, Small-Scale Industries, and powerlooms. The Khadi and Village Industries are under the jurisdiction of the Khadi and Village Industries Commission, modern small-scale industries under Small-Scale Industry Board and Development Commissioner for Small-Scale Industries and the other sub-sectors, mentioned above, each come under a national board.

Small industry, by definition, may be considered to include all forms of small-scale enterprises with fewer than one hundred employees. Further, within the major sub-category of small-scale industries, we have what are called traditional sector and modern sector. The traditional sector by import implies the age-old ones which have been there as part of rural economy and the modern ones are of an organized nature dealing in manufacturing, engineering, processing and servicing, more usually with modern, sophisticated technology.

Traditional small industries are engaged in the type of manufacturing that is common and caters to the needs of a traditional economy, whether rural or urban. These types of small industries are characterized by products, techniques, markets and organizations and are in a position to change to modern small-scale industries, although they are not free from the problems of such industries that are commonly found in the developing countries. The traditional small industries still can cater to the needs of the emerging economy and use the advantages of modern science and technology.

Small industries, as mentioned earlier, can be rural or

urban, located in the village, in a small market town, or a large city. Here, energy may or may not be used. The type of products produced, the value of the product, the physical resources available for production, the number of workers, the organization, the total capital investment, the type of business, the market arrangements and the efficiency of production are the features that distinguish one industry from another. It may be noted that the traditional small industries do not disappear as developing countries become industrialized.

Developing countries as of now are at various stages of transition from traditional modes of manufacturing to modern ones. In some Asian countries, traditional systems of manufacturing are still important particularly where cottage industries still predominate in rural and urban areas. In the developing countries the traditional artisan and cottage industrial workers coexist with the factory sector that utilizes highly developed production techniques and organizational methods. The spread of education, planned socio-economic development, a gradual increase in income levels, increase in purchasing power and change in taste and life-styles have a profound influence on change towards modern small-scale industries.

Even though, industries in general as secondary sector activities are spread both in rural and urban areas, their concentration predominantly has been in urban centers, while primary sector activities comprising agriculture and allied economic pursuits have been the main stay in rural areas. In view of the inherent limitations in respect to agriculture in sustaining the growing population, the time has come to gradually promote and develop small-scale enterprises in rural areas along with improvements in agricultural practices towards higher productivity. This process of generating industrial activities in rural areas may be called "Rural Industrialization".

The theme "Rural Industrialization" has recently emerged in the context of improving living conditions of the rural people in developing countries. These countries in their attempts to develop rural areas have placed greater emphasis on agricultural development. Most of the developing countries are characterized by high rates of population growth and predominantly depend on agriculture as means of livelihood. Agriculture as a means has limitations in terms of inadequacy of arable land, irrigation facilities and natural calamities as flood, drought and the system of land tenure. Even where agriculture can be developed, it is clear that it cannot absorb the additional labour force caused by rapid population growth without decreasing labour productivity. Although the agricultural sector is of prime importance in the improvement of the living conditions of the rural people, sustainable rural development cannot be achieved by developing the agricultural sector alone and unquestionably the other sectors must be included in a meaningful integrated approach.

Manufacturing activities in rural areas are usually on a small-scale. In view of this, small-scale industries in rural areas may help to diversify the rural economy and stimulate income-generating opportunities for rural people. There are a number of positive factors that facilitate promotion and development of small enterprises in the rural areas. Large-scale industries usually absorb a large share of the investment but generate only a small number of employment opportunities, whereas, the small-scale industries employ a large proportion of the labourers employed in manufacturing in developing countries. Moreover, in the rural areas there are people who are able to accumulate small amounts of capital and are willing to venture into some entrepreneurial activity. Small-scale industry then provides a good starting point for the mobilization and utilization of both their talents and their capital. Employment opportunities available in urban centers in the developing countries are not sufficient to absorb the influx of rural labour in search of employment, and the problems that this creates are well known. A possible and in a way, the only solution would be for rural industries to create employment opportunities for local labour and thus reduce rural-urban migration. Large-scale industries very often depend on technology from industrialized countries and therefore show a high degree of dependence. Most small-scale industries in the rural areas, on the other hand, can be developed with indigenous technology that is familiar to the people. It does not mean the modern technology could not be introduced to rural areas. In course of time, any useful, efficacious, cost effective and high productive technology will spread all over urban and rural areas.

Despite low productivity, lack of quality control and inefficient management of resources in many instances, the rural industries may have to stay and some of them will adapt to changing demands and technology and some may disappear. Even if they are less efficient in comparison with the large and medium industries, they serve a purpose and the question is not to ignore and overlook them, but to revive and revamp them.

National policies can in certain circumstances affect industries located in rural areas and their survival may be at stake. Most of the small-scale industries sell their products in their own locality and competition arising due to national policy decisions can sometimes disrupt them. They can be particularly vulnerable to competition arising from foreign products and domestic products from large-scale industries mostly located in metropolitan centres. If a country wants to pursue a free market policy, the types of industries which can survive in rural areas may be limited because in many respects the entrepreneurs from rural areas are at a disadvantage compared with their counterparts in urban areas. Manufactures in urban areas usually have added advantage of economies of scale, access to credit, modern technology, information, management skills and marketing strategies. Efforts centred around promoting small-scale industries in rural areas may have to recognize the above constraints and take adequate measures.

Financing of small-scale industries appears to be an important problem. One of the first things that Japan did at its early stages of industrial development was to build an extensive network of financial institutions. In most of the Asian countries such a network, especially in the case of small enterprises in rural areas, is lacking. This lacuna should be filled through institutional credit reaching the very small-to-small enterprise in the rural areas.

Changes in formal financing institutions for the promotion of small-scale industries are desirable, but liberalizing credit facilities alone would not suffice. Changes have to be combined with other institutional support. Production is rather straightforward but selling the product is a challenging task for the small-scale entrepreneur. In some rural industrial development programmes, the state has assumed the responsibility of marketing. Although such a help in the initial stage is desirable, taking the entire responsibility of marketing by the state leaves the entrepreneurs unaware of the difficulty of marketing and they may assume that it is the duty of the state to market whatever they produce. In other words, if the marketing responsibility is carried on by the state for a prolonged period, it is likely to deprive the entrepreneurs, the opportunity of developing their marketing skills. It may be for sometime, but not all through. If small-scale industries in the rural areas are to be successful, the rural entrepreneurs should share the responsibility of marketing. Then the producers will be more responsive to the conditions prevailing in the marketplace. This is one of the areas where small-scale entrepreneurs do not have sufficient knowledge and where industrial marketing extension services can play a helpful role.

Against the preceding brief discussion of rural industrialization as a theme, we may at length look at the prevailing economic situation in most of the countries in Asia and how industrialization could be the answer.

Prevailing Economic Situation

The economic situation as of today in most of the developing countries may be summarized as under:

- Heavy population
- Unemployment
- Under-employment
- Majority of the population living in rural areas
- Predominance of agriculture
- Low levels of production
- Low productivity
- Low per capita income
- Low economic growth rate
- High population growth rate
- Agriculture having reached a saturation point in some developing countries.

Industrialization: The Answer

Under the conditions summarized above, against abundant human resources and under-utilized material resources that the developing countries are endowed with, the answer is industrialization. There seems to be no other way out. As the late Sir M. Visvesaraya, an eminent Indian engineer and administrator has put it, 'Industrialize or perish'.

Rural Industrialization in Asia

The rural areas in Asian countries like their counterparts in other developing countries have tremendous difficulties to overcome. Often there is only subsistence farming which has a very low productivity yield. There is very little capital available and, in some cases, a great lack of skills. An additional obstacle is the low population density which makes it more difficult to use human labour as an effective national resources.

The main problems are acquisition of knowledge and capital accumulation. These are the real obstacles to progress. Very little capital can be brought in from outside and because practically the whole nation has the same needs, it is quite inadequate. Capital accumulation is a central problem in village development in all the countries of the region and the income of the villagers is so low that they cannot enlarge production. They simply cannot afford machines, fertilizer etc., neither can they pay for experts.

Indeed, the most important element for the development of industry is knowledge. Although some traditional industries in Asian countries have been highly developed in the past, some of them are on the decline today. The development of skills, rather than the provision of physical facilities, is the bottleneck.

The most attractive method to develop these skills is indeed education. The gradual training process is then a productive period, instead of a too costly investment because there are only limited resources to draw from. The existing elementary subsistence farming creates little surplus available for investment.

One of the major problems facing many of the Third World countries today is how to create a strategy which will lead towards rapid economic development and industrialization. It is to be realized that the industrialization of the rural areas plays a vital role; mechanization of agricultural production and rural industry will have to develop together. This line of argument appears self-evident given the conditions of many Asian countries. Yet, in reality what is actually happening is with minor exceptions, quite the opposite: industrial growth has tended to hug the city areas and the industries have tended to be capital intensive, large-scale monopolies. The villages and towns in the rural areas are rarely increasing in wealth and in some places there is an actual decline.

All the countries of Asia are committed to rural development although different strategies are followed. Rural reform community programmes and rural industry schemes have received increasing priority in all the countries. Although the rapid social and economic changes in most Asian villages certainly offer escape routes for a small number of enterprising individuals, it should be borne in mind that the objective of rural development is the social development of the community rather than the individual[1].

The level of poverty and technical knowledge in many rural areas of the region remains extremely low by any measurable standard. While no self-respecting nation will emphasize this point, it remains an indisputable fact which has failed to disappear. Moreover, with rapid population growth of the last five decades, the overall level of poverty has increased too. The future capital of the Third World can only come from the labour of the people in the community itself. This is the only form of political strategy which can conceivably bring the people out of their poverty.

With these conditions in mind, it is argued that the future prosperity of agricultural countries in the Asian region lies in the working hands of the villagers, who are a hidden resource which needs to be mobilized. Investment in rural areas does not, in this view, require foreign capital for finance, it requires the release and nurturing of the technical skills of the people to face and overcome the problem of production and development for themselves. The rural industries have been growing steadily over the past few decades in the Asian countries, playing a vital role in the economic structure of these countries, contributing significantly to the GNP and also generating employment for a large number of people.

Unfortunately however, in most of the countries in Asia reliable statistics on rural industries are not available. The variations in the criteria for definition employed in different countries, together with the non-availability of adequate and accurate statistics make international comparison difficult, if not impossible, while one endeavours to trace the growth of rural industries.

The kind of Industrialization

There are as they are organized and operated today, large-scale, medium and small-scale industries besides cottage industries and the new type that has been recently conceptualized and added to the categories, the tiny sector. The large and medium industries have their place depending on the nature of the product, raw materials, locational advantages, national requirements, priorities, transportation and the interests of the general public. But the large and medium industries are only a partial answer to the socio-economic needs and problems of the developing countries. The promotion of small industries and supporting and sustaining the traditional cottage and village industries in rural areas plays a much-needed complementary role in balanced development.

Disadvantages of Large-Scale Industrialization

Industrialization in any country is to be viewed with reference to the local context, the economic, demographic and social conditions. There cannot be a blind imitation of small or large industry. Ideas, programmes and technology are to be adopted suited to the indigenous conditions. While the large industries have a place and play a vital role in the national economy, they suffer from certain disadvantages in the context of developing countries. These disadvantages are relative in nature. They are in a way associated with the political and economic systems, nature of the population, and the resources with which the country is endowed. Briefly some of the disadvantages of large-scale industrialization are:

- It requires large capital resources beyond the capacity of developing countries to raise on their own.

- It involves substantial foreign exchange which is not available in adequate amounts from the export earnings of these countries.
- The large-scale units take longer gestation period resulting in immediate inflationary trends in the economy.
- Because of the sophisticated nature of technology and techniques adopted, it has to depend for quite some time on technical know-how from abroad.
- Employment potential per unit of capital investment in large-scale industries is too small to afford much relief to the growing unemployment problem.
- Centralized large-scale industrialization creates various social problems associated with overcrowded industrial urban centers.
- Most often, large-scale industrialization has resulted in concentration of economic power in fewer hands, it failed to provide solutions to regional economic imbalances and generated monopolistic tendencies.

Under the foregoing disadvantages of large-scale industrialization, the prudent policy and approach could be dispersal and decentralization of industries which has, in large measure, the following advantages:

- Developing countries generally lack know-how and workers skilled in technology, small-scale and cottage industries, normally, do not require a high level of technology.
- Small-scale and cottage industries are labour-intensive and do not require large amounts of capital. The energy of the unemployed and underemployed should be used for reproductive purposes in an economy in which capital is scarce.
- Small-scale industrial projects can be undertaken in a short-span of time and hence can increase

production with direct implications both in the short and long run.

- Most of the developing countries are rich in certain agricultural, forest, extractive, mineral and marine resources, hence small-scale and cottage industries can be based on the processing of locally available and produced raw materials.
- It is possible to save and earn foreign exchange by producing and exporting goods processed from local resources employing local unutilized and under-utilized labour.
- Small-scale industrial enterprises, whether traditional or modern, provide a training ground for local entrepreneurs for upward movement. The knowledge and managerial skills gained through small-scale industrial enterprises can be transferred to other sophisticated enterprises.
- By creating opportunities for the small businessmen, small industrial enterprises can bring about a more equitable distribution of income.
- The growth of small-scale and cottage industries in the developing countries will help to create economic stability in society by diffusing prosperity and by checking the expansion of monopolies and concentration of wealth in a few hands.
- The development of small-scale and cottage industries will create employment opportunities in the rural areas of the developing countries where unemployment and underemployment are relatively high. This will tend to reduce the exodus of workers from the rural to the urban areas in search of jobs.
- The development of small-scale and cottage industries will make possible a transfer of manufacturing activities from the congested urban centers to rural areas. This dispersal and de-

concentration of manufacturing away from the urban areas is a policy pursued by most of the developing countries.

- Apart from the linkages between agricultural or rural development and small-scale industrial enterprises, there is an essential linkage between large and medium-scale industries and small-scale industries in the sense that the former create opportunities or facilities for the growth of the latter. Certain large-scale industries create work subcontracted to ancillaries and even to very small units as in the case of Japan.
- The development of small-scale and cottage industries in rural areas will contribute to balanced regional development and a relative local self-sufficiency and social justice. It also contributes to rehabilitation of displaced persons.
- Small-scale enterprises have their own place in a country's economy. Imperfect competition which characterizes most of the economies of the developing countries protects the small firm's markets and enables them to exist even where they are not efficient in terms of cost. The imperfection may be due to rational factors like transport cost, which can hardly be eliminated. It may be due to differentiations in taste, that is, there may be an individuality of product to which the consumers really attach significance and to irrational factors which are also important in determining demand.

And so, industry alone with a wider spread embracing all rural communities can draw the hidden unemployed off the land into production and so long as they are left on the land, agriculture cannot increase its efficiency. Industrialization must jolt the agrarian sector out of its deep sleep. This transformation is to be brought about in a phased manner with systematic and realistic planning schemes carried on by a rightly orientated and trained administrative and developmental personnel.

The Role of Industry in Integrated Rural Development

Integrated rural development (IRD) though connotationally sounds comprehensive, operationally it aims at redressing and alleviating the problems of the poorer segments of the rural population[2]. In the series of approaches, strategies and methods towards rural development during the past five decades, the IRD is the latest, and purportedly, the most effective approach in bettering the lot of the rural poor and yet its operationalization suffers from shortcomings at the community level. The concept of integrating and mobilizing the material and human resources at the community level is wanting.

Some rural development efforts in terms of political overtones, economic objectives, organizational process, plan formulation and programme implementation are a new kind of experience for the people and the development agencies. We are in the process of finding, learning, new and better ways of doing things. There is always a need to look back and take stock of things, so that we can have a clearer perspective of the situation, avoid the pitfalls, overcome the barriers and discover effective approaches and alternatives towards substantial and sustained development in rural areas.

In the meaningful and substantive development of rural areas, along with other sectors of economic and social development, industry must be accepted as an important component of any integrated rural development programme[3]. The nature and pattern of rural industrialization, both small-scale and cottage or handicraft industries will, however, depend on the material and human resources of the area concerned. In the formulation and execution of an integrated rural development programme, the role of rural industrialization has not been adequately recognized, in spite of its importance, nor is it always reflected adequately in the rural development programme of the developing countries.

Industrialization, in general, is also of great significance to rural development. Industry helps develop the skills and disciplines necessary for modern economic society. It is looked upon as the principal means of breaking the traditional barriers to growth.

Though it is rather obvious, we may briefly look into how industry supports rural development even at the cost of repeating some aspects mentioned earlier in support of rural industrialization.

Industry Supports Rural Development

Industry supports integrated rural development in several ways. First, in almost all countries there are cottage or handicraft industries producing a variety of articles for rural and urban consumption and for export. The traditional and socially inherited skills on which these industries are based can be further developed and upgraded. Secondly, there are manufacturing industries that are closely linked with agricultural development, industries producing fertilizers, pesticides, agricultural machinery, equipment and tools (mechanical, hand-operated and animal-drawn) and industries in respect to the maintenance of machinery and transport equipment. Some of these industries are operated on large and medium-scales and although they may be located outside the rural areas, they contribute substantially to increasing agricultural productivity by supplying inputs for rural development which largely means agricultural development. Thirdly, there are industries based on the processing of local raw material from agriculture and fisheries – food processing, leather and textiles; and from forestry construction and furniture. There is enough scope to develop many small-scale enterprises in the rural areas. Lastly, other industries not included in the types mentioned above, but satisfying some of the basic needs of the rural population or linked with infrastructural development may be developed in the rural areas as part of the policy of decentralization of industrial development.

Industrial Development Programmes as a Component of Integrated Rural Development

A certain geographical area is usually taken as the unit for integrated rural development, selected on the basis of criteria formulated in the light of the objectives of government policy on rural development. The criteria may vary from area to area in a country, depending on the needs and resources of the area, both material and human. An industrial potential techno-economic survey is essential to obtain information on the size of the area, the composition of the population by sex and age; employment and unemployment and the main occupations; actual and potential resources for economic and social development; and infrastructural facilities. As the purpose for collecting all this information is to prepare an industrial development programme for the area, one has to look for the kind of viable non-agricultural and other industrial enterprises in the light of the available resources of the area such as raw materials, the supply of labour, technical know-how, entrepreneurship, the availability of finance and the internal and external demand for the products that maybe produced in the area. National machinery at different levels is necessary to prepare, coordinate and implement rural development programmes. Several countries in the Asian region have such machinery for providing institutional support.

Elements of a Rural Industrialization Programme

In view of the interrelated nature of development a broad, integrated approach should be adopted for rural industrialization. Mere credit facilities for small-scale industrial promotion are not enough though necessary. Development of small-scale enterprises in rural areas is limited by such factors as lack of technical knowledge, inefficient marketing, poor design of products and lack of skill in planning and managing industrial enterprises. A programme for developing industries in the rural areas should consist of measures to deal with the numerous limiting factors simultaneously.

A rural industrialization programme as a part of integrated rural development may, therefore, encompass the following elements:

- The selection of an area on the basis of the desired criteria;
- A survey to assess the human and natural resources of the area;
- Identification of potential enterprises for incorporation in the industrial development programme for the area;
- Project preparation and evaluation;
- Financial or credit support;
- Industrial research and advisory services;
- Procurement of raw materials and equipment;
- The establishment of industrial estates or centers with basic facilities;
- Industrial training;
- Marketing support in the initial stages.

Almost every developing country in Asia has a programme for developing small-scale and cottage industries, but these programmes seldom constitute a significant part of integrated rural development.

Broader Implication of Rural Industrialization

While the role of small-scale and cottage industries is important in rural industrialization, it is not sufficient by itself to lead to the desirable scale of industrialization to deal with the problems of the disadvantaged and weaker segments of the population in the rural areas. Rural industrialization traditionally associated with small-scale and cottage industrial enterprise, should really imply a mix of industrial enterprises which may be large-, medium-, small-scale or handicraft in character, depending on the availability of or access to requisite infrastructural facilities and the cost of providing such decentralized infrastructure, raw material and markets.

Though the emphasis in rural industrialization is on small-scale and cottage industries, since they meet the situation which exists in rural areas, there is nothing preventing the rural population benefiting entrepreneurially and industrially through the location of large- or medium- scale industries in the rural areas. Whether industrial location is rural or urban, the core question is to what extent and in what ways, would it enable the rural people to benefit in terms of increased employment and income and a better quality of life? The answer is, clearly, that it would lead to improved rural development.

REFERENCES

1. Rizwanul Islam, ed., "Rural Industrialization and Employment in Asia", *Asian Employment Programme* (New Delhi: ARTEP, 1987).
2. E. Desingu Setty, "Field Approach to Integrated Rural Development", *Journal of Rural Development*, Vol. 7(6) (Hyderabad: National Institute of Rural Development, 1988), pp. 675-688.
3. United Nations Economic and Social Commission for Asia and the Pacific (UN/ESCAP), "Administration of Rural Development in ASEAN Countries", *Proceedings of the Colloquium* (Jakarta, 1983), pp. 189-240.

8

Rural Industrialization in India

India provides an example of consistent and progressive industrial policy measures beginning 1948 and upto the present. In gradual succession these policy measures were aimed at rural industrialization, promotion and development of overall socio-economic development of rural as well as urban population. These measures encompass organizational and institutional support in terms of identification of viable small-scale enterprises, potential entrepreneurs, and institutional credit, a variety of incentives, infrastructure, training, common facilities, supply of raw material, machinery and equipment and support for marketing of products. The small-scale industries have been accorded a priority status in terms of reservation of certain products to be exclusively produced by the SSI units and preferential bulk and higher quantum of purchase of SSI products by the governmental and quasi-governmental organizations. The Government of India through the Ministry of Industry, the State Governments and a plethora of national and state level organizations with diverse functions coordinate the promotion and development of small-scale and cottage enterprises in the country. In the pages that follow a brief profile on the development of small-scale and cottage industries in India is attempted.

Industrial Development Policies

Industrial Development Policies as a significant and set of progressive measures for industrial development, the Government of India has successively formulated industrial development policies right from 1948 down to 1991 as shown below:-

The nucleus for the industrial policy measures in India is enshrined in the 'Directive Principles of State Policy' of constitution of India. In view of the imperative need to promote and develop village and small industries, the Government of India, soon after attaining independence, came up with its first industrial policy resolution in 1948 which had the following emphasis:

'Cottage and small industries have a very important role in the national economy. These industries are particularly suited for better utilization of local resources and for the achievement of local self-sufficiency in respect of certain types of essential consumer goods. The hearty expansion of cottage and small-scale industries depends upon a number of factors like the provision of raw materials, cheap power, technical advice, organized marketing of their produce and where necessary safeguards against intensive competition from large-scale manufacture. Most of those fall under the provincial sphere and are receiving the attention of the government of the province and the states.'

In pursuance of this policy measure, a significant place for promotion of cottage and village industries was accorded in the First Five Year Plan (1951-56). During the period of First Five Year Plan the government had launched industrial pilot projects in selected community development blocks and had set up all India level Boards for Handlooms, Handicrafts, Sericulture, Coir and Khadi and Village Industries to advise and assist in the formulation of development strategies for them. Certain degree of protection to the small-scale sector in terms of reservation of certain spheres of production, exclusively for the village and small industries sector, non-expansion of capacity of and imposition of cess on large-scale sector and also arrangements for preferential supply of raw material to the decentralized industries was accorded.

The Industrial Policy Resolution of 1956, reflects the experience gained in the First Five Year Plan and had a slight shift. It stated that while some basic and heavy industries would be set up, simultaneously Government of India would stress the role of cottage and village and small industries in the development of the national economy. It aimed at dispersal of small enterprises all over the country to make use of the local resources, to develop and upgrade local skills, to meet the local consumer demands and to avoid unplanned concentration of population in urban areas, migrating from rural areas.

In 1970, prior to the announcement of the third Industrial Policy Resolution of February 1973, the Government of India formulated special schemes of incentives in favour of small industries such as subsidy on investment, subsidy on transport of raw materials and finished products and schemes of concessional finance from banks and also certain fiscal concessions to industries that are started in the backward areas selected for this purpose. These concessions are operative up till now.

In 1977, there was change of government at the centre and the new government announced its own industrial policy. Besides several policy measures, one highly significant outcome of the new policy was the creation of District Industries Centre, one for each district in the country. It was envisaged that the DIC would function as a 'single roof' providing the entrepreneurs of small-scale and village industries with all the services and support required by them for starting and successfully running their enterprises. The DIC is headed by a General Manager assisted by a team of technical staff covering economic, credit, raw material and machinery and equipment, extension and marketing and other special activities wherever they existed.

The policy in general, envisaged that the thrust of the new industrial policy would be an effective promotion of cottage and small industries widely dispersed in rural areas and small towns and whatever can be produced by small and cottage industries must only be so produced. It paid attention to the tiny sector within the small sector with an investment of Rs. 100,000 on plant and machinery, located in towns with a population less than 40,000 and villages. It further said that the government would consider introducing special legislation for protecting the interest of cottage and household industries with a view to ensuring that those activities which provide self-employment in large numbers get due recognition in industrial development. It also indicated that the focal point of development for small-scale and cottage industries will be shifted from big cities and state capitals to the district headquarters. This last component of the policy resulted in the creation of District Industries Centres all over the country. The policy also has laid emphasis on the promotion of ancillaries as linkages to nucleus plants and large industries.

The announcement of the industrial policy of July 1980, coincided with the formulation of the Sixth Five Year Plan (1980-85). The policy statement sought to harmonize growth in the small-scale sector with the large and medium sectors. The emphasis was on fostering complementarity between the large and small sectors so that the dichotomy between the two sectors does not impair the economic pattern. An important element in the new policy was the raising of investment limits in respect of tiny and small-scale industry.

Establishment of nucleus plants in backward districts was another salient feature of the policy statement. It was envisaged that this would foster ancillarization and functional linkages between large and small industries and bring about economic federalism. Other measures proposed in the policy included the strengthening of the existing arrangements for the provision of credit facilities, establishing of buffer stocks of essential and critical raw materials for the use of small units, providing the benefits of research and development in order to facilitate easy flow of technology, modernization and establishment of an early warning system to prevent sickness and to take appropriate and timely remedial measures.[1]

The same tenor of emphasis on village and small-scale industries continues in the Seventh Five-year Plan document (1985-90). It says that provision of village and small-scale industries will continue to be an important element in the national development strategy particularly because of its very favourable capital output ratio and high employment intensity and this sector would: (a) assist in the growth and widespread dispersal of industries; (b) increase the levels of earnings of artisans; (c) sustain and create avenues of self-employment; (d) ensure regular supply of goods and services through use of local skills and resources; (e) develop entrepreneurship in combination with improved methods of production through appropriate training and package of incentives; (f) preserve craftsmanship and art heritage of the country. The plan document adds that the strategy for achieving the above objectives would consist of upgradation of technology and modernization, supply of adequate inputs promoting specialization in production and export oriented industries, strengthening and enlarging skill profile and entrepreneurial base and management practices to increase opportunities for self-employment and strengthening the programmes of ancillarization to establish and improve linkages between large and small industries leading to harmonious growth of the total industrial sector.[2]

In the Industrial Policy of 1990, the Government have been considering the need to take measures for promotion of small-scale and agro-based industries and to change procedures for grant of industrial approvals.

- The policy focuses on re-orienting industrial growth to serve the objective of employment generation, dispersal of industry in the rural areas, and to enhance the contribution of small-scale industries to exports it has been decided to take the measures enumerated below.

- The investment ceiling in plant & machinery for small-scale industries (fixed in 1985) would be raised from the present Rs. 35 lakhs to Rs. 60 lakhs and correspondingly, for ancillary units from Rs. 45 lakhs to Rs. 75 lakhs. In order to enable small-scale industries to play an important role in the total export effort, such of the small-scale units which undertake to export at least 30 per cent of the annual production by the third year will be permitted to step up their investment in plant & machinery to Rs. 75 lakhs.
- Investment ceiling in respect of tiny units would also be increased from the present Rs. 2 lakhs to Rs. 5 lakhs. However, with regard to their location, the population limit of 50,000 as per the 1981 census would continue to apply. Steps will be taken to ensure better inflow of credit and other vital inputs and to improve the infrastructure support to the constituents of the Tiny Sector.
- Presently, 836 items have been reserved for exclusive manufacture in the small-scale sector. Efforts would be made to identify more items amenable to similar reservation. Encroachment and violation by large-scale units into areas reserved for small-scale sector will be effectively dealt with.
- A new scheme of Central Investment Subsidy exclusively for the small-scale sector in rural and backward areas capable of generating higher level of employment at lower capital cost would be implemented.
- With a view to improving the competitiveness of the products manufactured in the small-scale sector, programmes for modernization and upgradation

of technology would be implemented. A number of technology centres, tool rooms, Process and Product Development Centres, testing centres, etc. will be set up under the umbrella of an apex Technology Development Centre in Small Industries Development Organization.

- To ensure adequate and timely flow of credit of the small-scale industries, a new apex bank known as SIDBI has already been established. One of the major tasks of SIDBI and other commercial banks/ financial institutions would be to channelise need-based, higher flow of credit, both by way of term loan and working capital, to the tiny and rural industries. A targeted approach will be adopted to ensure implementation and to facilitate monitoring this objective.
- The existing regime of fiscal concessions will be reviewed both to provide sustained support to the units in the small-scale sector and to remove the disincentives for their graduation and further growth.
- All new units upto an investment of Rs. 25 crores in fixed assets in non-backward areas and Rs. 75 crores in Centrally notified backward areas will be exempt from requirement of obtaining licence/ registration.
- For the import of Capital Goods, the entrepreneur would have entitlement to import upto a landed value of 30% of the total value of plant and machinery required for the unit.
- For imports of raw materials and components, imports will be permissible upto a landed value of 30% of the ex-factory value of annual production. The ex-factory value of production will exclude the excise duty on the item of production. Raw materials and components on OGL will not be

included within this 30 percent limit. For all licensable items of raw materials and components, import-licensing procedures will continue to operate.

- 100% export oriented units (UOUs) and units to be set up in export processing zones (EPZs) are also being delicensed under the scheme upto an investment limit of Rs. 75 crores.
- The above proposals will be applicable to all manufacturing items in a specified list. The list shall follow the nomenclature of the Indian Trade Classification based on the Harmonised System. In such section of the classification, apart from positive mention of approved items, those not permissible shall be specifically excluded from the benefit of the proposals listed above. Approval for excluded items will be as per the existing industrial policy regime and procedures.

The latest industrial policy of 1991 which briefly refers to the earlier industrial policies as mentioned below:

The Industrial Policy Resolution of 1948 was followed by the Industrial Policy Resolution of 1956 which had as its objective the acceleration of the rate of economic growth and the speeding up of industrialization as a means of achieving a socialist pattern of society. In 1956, capital was scarce and the base of entrepreneurship not strong enough. Hence, the 1956 Industrial policy Resolution gave primacy to the role of the State to assume a predominant and direct responsibility for industrial development.

The Industrial Policy Statement of 1973, inter alia, identified high priority industries where investment from large industrial houses and foreign companies would be permitted.

The Industrial Policy Statement of 1977 laid emphasis on

decentralization and on the role of small scale, tiny and cottage industries.

The Industrial Policy Statement of 1980 focused attention on the need for promoting competition in the domestic market, technological upgradation and modernization. The policy laid the foundation for an increasingly competitive export base and for encouraging foreign investment in high technology areas. This found expression in the Sixth Five-Year Plan which bore the distinct stamp of Smt. Indira Gandhi. It was Smt. Indira Gandhi who emphasized the need for productivity to be the central concern in all economic and production activities.

These policies created a climate for rapid industrial growth in the country. Thus on the eve of the Seventh Five Year Plan, a broad-based infrastructure had been built up. Basic industries had been established. A high degree of self-reliance in a large number of items-raw materials, intermediates, finished goods had been achieved. New growth centres of industrial activity had emerged and had a new generation of entrepreneurs. A large number of engineers, technicians and skilled workers had also been trained.

The Seventh Plan recognized the need to consolidate on these strengths and to take initiatives to prepare Indian industry to respond effectively to the emerging challenges. A number of policy and procedural changes were introduced in 1985 and 1986 under the leadership of Shri Rajiv Gandhi aimed at increasing productivity, reducing costs and improving quality. The accent was on opening the domestic market to increased competition and readying our industry to stand on its own in the face of international competition. The public sector was freed from a number of constraints and given a larger measure of autonomy. The technological and managerial modernization of industry was pursued as the key instrument for increasing productivity and improving our competitiveness in the world. The net result of all these changes was that

Indian industry grew by an impressive average annual growth rate of 8.5% in the Seventh Plan Period.

Government is pledged to launching a reinvigorated struggle for social and economic justice, to end poverty and unemployment and to build a modern, democratic, socialist, prosperous and forward-looking India. Such a society can be built if India grows as part of the world economy and not in isolation.

While Government will continue to follow the policy of self-reliance, there would be greater emphasis placed on building up our ability to pay for imports through our own foreign exchange earnings. Government is also committed to development and utilization of indigenous capabilities in technology and manufacturing as well as its upgradation to world standards.

Government will continue to pursue a sound policy framework encompassing encouragement of entrepreneurship, development of indigenous technology through investment in research and development, bringing in new technology dismantling of the regulatory system, development of the capital markets and increasing competitiveness for the benefit of the common man. The spread of industrialization to backward areas of the country will be actively promoted through appropriate incentives, institutions and infrastructure investments.

- Government will provide enhanced support to the small-scale sector so that it flourishes in an environment of economic efficiency and continuous technological upgradation. (For further details of Industrial Policies, please see Appendix-III(A) & III(B)).

Basic Approach And Measures Initiated

The basic approach towards development of small-scale

industries as outlined in various policy resolutions and national plans can be summed up as to create employment opportunities with relatively low investment, to meet a substantial part of the increased demand for consumer goods and simple producer goods, to facilitate mobilization of resources of capital and skill which may otherwise remain unutilised, to help in raising the levels of earnings and standards of living of a large number of artisans, craftsmen and entrepreneurs, to promote entrepreneurship widely with focus on villages and small towns, to make small industries export-oriented and to help upgrade quality of products, and to remove regional disparities through a deliberate policy to encourage growth of non-farm occupations in villages and small towns. The development strategy, all through, comprises of: (a) protective discrimination; (b) integration between small and large-scale industries; (c) elaborate schemes of assistance and incentives administered through a large number of government departments, agencies and institutes; (d) modernization of technology without displacing labour; and (e) adoption of an area approach in development planning.[3]

In order to translate the above strategies into action, programmes on some aspects of small-scale industries are being implemented. They comprise the following:

1. Reservation of items for manufacture in the small-scale sector: The policy of reserving certain lines of manufacture for exclusive production in the small-scale sector has been pursued since 1967 to provide protection to the small-scale sector against competition from medium and large industries. A standing committee of the Ministry of Industry reviews the list periodically to ensure that production in the small-scale sector is economical and of acceptable quality. As new products and new processes capable of being manufactured in the small-scale sector are identified, they are added

to the reserved list. Beginning with 46 items in 1967-68, it rose to 869 items by March 1988. Reservation of items for production in the small-scale sector is covered under section 29B of the Industries (Development and Regulation) Act of 1951 with an amendment passed in 1984.

2. Reservation of items manufactured in the SSI sector for Central Government Purchases: The policy of reserving certain products for exclusive purchases from the small-scale sector under the central government purchase programme, was introduced in 1956 by identifying 16 items. It was only in 1976-77, that the number was increased to 241. As of March 1988, it stood at 409. In addition, four categories of handicraft products (14 items) and 14 items from handlooms were also listed for exclusive purchase from the village industries category. Two other categories introduced sometime back for purchases from the small-scale sector are: purchase to the extent of 74 per cent (14 items) and purchase to the extent of 50 per cent (28 items). The list is periodically reviewed.
3. Referred items and items of mass consumption selected for intensive growth during he Sixth Plan period (1980-85): One hundred and fourteen products were identified for this purpose. They include products reserved for manufacture in the small-scale industry as well as others. These products have growth potential and offer greater scope for employment generation.
4. Items banned for manufacture in the small-scale industry sector: Items banned for manufacture in the small-scale sector announced periodically by the Small Industries Development Organization (SIDO) refer to products where capacity is saturated and further expansion is not considered advisable.

The number of such banned items as of January 1987 was 11.

EDP though primarily it depends on the individual interest and initiative in view of the need and complexity of several enterprises individuals alone cannot meet the requirements for promotion and sustaining their enterprises. In this context, the State comes forward with comprehensive industrial development policies from time to time. Wherein it focuses the kind of role that is to be played by the state by the financial institutions and the kind of reservation, enterprises need these small scale sectors and also detailing the kind of incentive in terms of that the state should provide to the entrepreneurs, the industrial policy stands as a guideline, a support system, encouragement and helping the neo-entrepreneurs, thus contributing to industrial activity generating employment, income and thus taking the state economically and socially forward to higher levels of living. The issuing of industrial policies by Govt. of India began in 1948 and periodically upto 1991. Each industrial policy spell-out in detail the role of the state and other institutions in the state.

Plan Oultlays and Progress of Village and Small-Scale Industries

The emphasis on the promotion and development of small-scale and village industries is reflected in the outlays earmarked under public sector in the Five Year Plans. Though in terms of percentage the outlays appear small, in financial terms, the allocation appears to be substantial.

Though the progress of small-scale and village industries is not attempted here either fiscal year-wise or the Five Year Plan-wise, it may be mentioned here that the increase in the number of SSI units has been significant. At the end of March 1988 there were a little over 1.06 million registered small-scale units and 0.52 million unregistered small-scale units. Ninety per cent of establishments registered under the Factories Act were small-scale units with investment on plant and machinery not exceeding Rs. 2 million (Annual Survey of Industries, 1984-85). This figure and the following facts are based on the earlier definition of small-scale industry with an investment on plant and machinery not exceeding Rs. 2 million over 5,000 products are being manufactured by small-scale industrial units (SIDO industries). Village and small-scale industries (unregistered manufacturing sector) account for about 39 per cent of the total value of production of the manufacturing sector (national income computation for 1986-87 at 1980-81 prices). Small-scale factory establishments, with 90 per cent of units account for 5.3 per cent of the total fixed capital of all factories, provide employment to 33.7 per cent of the total, have share of 20.4 per cent of the total output and contribute to 16.6 per cent of the value added by manufacture.

Employment generated in small-scale factory is nine times that of large establishments for an investment of Rs. 100,000 in fixed assets. Small-scale industrial units provide employment to about 11 million persons.[4]

Institutional Framework

Prior to looking into the institutional framework across several levels in the country to carry on multiple tasks of a complex and stupendous programme of small industry development, we may briefly look into the concept and definition of the subcategories within what is called small industry. The concept and definition of small-scale industry have changed over years with the changing circumstances and pressing problems of the Indian economy. Currently, a small industry is defined as an industrial unit with investment on plant and machinery not exceeding Rs. 3.5 million and not exceeding Rs. 4.5 million if it were to be an ancillary unit. Within this sub-sector, there is a separate category of tiny units. A tiny unit is defined as a unit with an investment on plant and machinery not exceeding Rs. 200,000 and located in villages and small towns. These definitions have been formulated for implementing the composite loan schemes for providing loans which include fixed and working capital and for implementing specific development programmes. Table 8.1 shows actual plan outlay for village and small-scale industries.

TABLE 8.1

Plan period	*Public sector outlay for village and small-scale industries (Rs. Million)*	*Total public Sector outlay (Rs. Million)*	*Share of village and small-scale industries in the total outlay (%)*
First Plan: 1951-52 to 1955-56	430	19,600	2.0
Second Plan: 1956-57 to 1960-61	1,750	46,000	4.0
Third Plan: 1961-62 to 1965-66	2,410	85,770	2.8
Annual Plans:			
1966-67	430	21,650	2.0
1967-68	420	20,850	2.0
1968-69	410	23,760	1.7
Fourth Plan: 1969-70 to 1973-74	2,430	157,790	1.5
Fifth Plan: 1974-75 to 1978-79	5,925	394.262	1.5
Annual Plan: 1979-80	2,557	121,765	2.1
Sixth Plan 1980-81 to 1984-85	19,451	1,092,917	1.8
Seventh Plan: 1985-86 to 1989-90	27,527	1,800,000	1.5

Source: Small Industry Bulletin for Asia and the Pacific, No. 23, p. 95

We may just have a glance at plan outlay of States and Union Territories under Village and Small Industries. The following Table 8.2 provides figures from 6th Plan to 9th Plan.

TABLE 8.2

(Rs. in Crores)

States	*Sixth Plan Outlay*	*Seventh Plan Actuals*	*Eighth Plan Agreed Outlay*	*Ninth Plan Agreed Outlay*
Andhra Pradesh	30.00	107.15	141.60	394.48
Arunachal Pradesh	2.75	7.73	13.00	34.32
Assam	30.00	55.00	109.68	174.77
Bihar	47.00	87.86	120.32	197.65
Goa	*	5.21	16.80	28.55
Gujarat	61.50	208.18	435.00	369.65
Haryana	19.46	48.95	135.19	111.83
Himachal Pradesh	9.05	12.78	47.50	80.00
Jammu & Kashmir	34.70	46.77	101.50	**
Karnataka	74.00	163.95	756.31	565.00
Kerala	49.80	69.29	304.00	509.00
Madhya Pradesh	33.40	76.38	105.87	314.82
Maharashtra	60.26	88.53	225.78	362.30
Manipur	12.50	14.62	22.00	42.84
Meghalaya	4.00	6.78	11.11	32.00
Mizoram	4.00	16.37	37.50	59.73
Nagaland	5.00	8.83	18.00	85.28
Orissa	27.00	68.39	114.00	68.70
Punjab	20.61	17.79	119.92	24.16
Rajasthan	19.50	25.69	170.94	300.63
Sikkim	3.60	3.32	8.80	25.00
Tamil Nadu	80.00	276.62	269.00	600.00
Tripura	8.50	13.42	34.50	37.99
Uttar Pradesh	125.23	162.41	261.20	204.47
West Bengal	60.00	69.04	223.52	213.06
Total States	821.07	1,661.06	3,803.05	4,836.23
Union Territories				
Andaman & Nicobar Islands	1.00	2.64	6.90	38.00
Chandigarh	0.60	1.56	2.64	3.09

States	Sixth Plan Outlay	Seventh Plan Actuals	Eighth Plan Agreed Outlay	Ninth Plan Agreed Outlay
Dadra & Nagar Haveli	0.55	0.90	3.25	5.74
Daman & Diu	2.50	0.24	2.76	1.28
Delhi	25.64	45.15	27.00	59.90
Lakshadweep	0.30	1.21	3.40	9.16
Pondicherry	4.60	13.20	27.20	78.00
Total UTs	35.19	64.91	73.15	195.17
Total (States & UTs)	857.05	1,725.97	3,876.20	5,031.40

Note:- 1). *: Included in Daman & Diu.
2). **: Not yet finalized.

Further, Table 8.3 provides details plan-wise right from 6th Plan to 9th Plan outlay for other than Village and Small Industries.

TABLE 8.3

(Rs. in Crores)

(Other Than Village & Small Industries)

States	Sixth Plan (1980-85) Outlay	Seventh Plan (1985-90) Outlay	Eighth Plan (1992-97) Outlay	Ninth Plan (1997-2000) Outlay
Andhra Pradesh	75.66	219.30	130.90	567.65
Arunachal Pradesh	7.51	2.75	13.94	11.78
Assam	24.75	53.10	214.25	205.27
Bihar	51.65	146.60	339.00	140.97
Goa	@	@	19.70	6.00
Gujarat	99.60	129.44	233.50	835.35
Haryana	11.40	20.55	85.33	32.85
Himachal Pradesh	9.00	16.27	28.70	70.00
Jammu & Kashmir	38.07	38.75	93.20	131.90

contd...

States	*Sixth Plan (1980-85) Outlay*	*Seventh Plan (1985-90) Outlay*	*Eighth Plan (1992-97) Outlay*	*Ninth Plan (1997-2000) Outlay*
Karnataka	88.68	95.00	228.44	461.00
Kerala	109.70	131.00	506.52	616.86
Madhya Pradesh	35.55	56.35	360.27	798.15
Maharashtra	131.90	302.00	588.68	540.30
Manipur	7.50	10.30	18.00	83.67
Meghalaya	5.50	13.10	32.06	70.00
Mizoram	0.58	2.35	7.25	9.19
Nagaland	7.00	20.20	32.00	35.74
Orissa	38.00	100.35	671.94	54.79
Punjab	61.07	88.71	43.00	257.14
Rajasthan	64.09	144.64	365.07	1,452.75
Sikkim	2.94	5.42	12.00	45.00
Tamil Nadu	91.77	155.00	281.00	802.91
Tripura	5.46	6.25	30.50	41.35
Uttar Pradesh	198.12	429.03	308.35	322.18
West Bengal	213.34	226.00	853.96	1,113.23
Total States	1,378.84	2,412.46	5,497.56	8,706.03
Union Territories				
Andaman & Nicobar Islands	0.00	0.00	0.00	0.00
Chandigarh	0.49	0.19	0.20	0.00
Dadra & Nagar Haveli	0.00	0.00	0.00	0.00
Daman & Diu	6.00	11.85	0.02	2.32
Delhi	1.98	12.00	3.50	50.10
Lakshadweep	0.00	0.12	0.46	0.00
Pondicherry	1.74	3.34	21.69	107.00
Total UTs	10.21	27.50	25.87	159.42
Total (States & UTs)	1,389.05	2,439.96	5,523.43	8,865.45

Note:- 1) @: included in Daman & Diu.

Source:- http://planningcommission.nic.in/plans/planrel/fiveyr/10th/volume2/v2_ch7_1.pdf

In the Indian context, it is relevant to look at the small-scale sector as distinct from the village industry sector. The village and small-scale industry (VSI) sector has been divided into different sub-sectors for administering assistance programmes and specialized institutions have been set up to look after each of the sub-sectors at the national level These cover sub-sectors of Khadi (Handspun and hand-woven cloth) and village industries, handlooms, handicrafts, power looms, sericulture, coir and other small-scale industries. Categorization of the VSI sector based on the national level organizations implementing the promotional and assistance programmes is given below:

CATEGORIZATION OF THE VSI SECTORS

S.No.	*Commission/Board*	*Implementing Agency*
1.	Khadi and Village Industries Commission (KVIC)	KVIC at the Centre and KVI Boards in the states
2.	All India Handlooms and Handicrafts Board	Development Commissioner (Handlooms)
3.	All India Power loom Board	Textile Commissioner
4.	Central Silk Board	Central Silk Board
5.	Coir Board	Coir Board
6.	All India Small-Scale Industries Board	Small Industries Development Organization (SIDO) with Development Commissioner (Small Scale Industries – DC (SSI) – as the headquarters organization.

Power looms and small-scale industries are referred to as the modern sector and all the others as village/rural traditional industries are the decentralized sector. The tiny units can also be included under the decentralized sector. The concept of rural industrialization thus encourages village and tiny units located primarily in rural areas. As stated above, village industries cover those industrial units falling under the purview of the organizations listed at 1,2,4,5. Modern small industry sector coming under the purview of the All India Small-Scale Industries Board is thus given a residuary status, by having jurisdiction over all industries falling outside the purview of the other all India boards and at the same time falling within the stipulated investment ceiling on plant and machinery.

Khadi & Village Industries Commission

A brief special mention may be made of the All India Khadi & Village Industries Commission (KVIC). The apex organization located in Mumbai and its constituents in the states carry on very significant promotional programmes in the field of Khadi and other traditional 26 village industries. The KVIC network comprises 26 State Khadi and Village Industries Boards, 1114 Registered Institutions and about 30,008 Industrial Cooperatives of Artisans covering about 150 thousand villages.[5] (Please see Appendix-III (B) for a brief profile of KVIC)

Under textiles, the KVIC covers cotton, silk and woollen handspun and hand-woven fabrics. The village industries under its purview comprise:

1. Bee-keeping (Apiary)
2. Cottage match, manufacture of fireworks and incense sticks
3. Pottery
4. Soap
5. Flaying, curing and tanning of hides and skins and ancillary industries connected with the same and cottage leather industry
6. Ghani oil industry
7. Handmade paper
8. Manufacture of canegur and khandasari
9. Palmsugar and palm products industry
10. Processing of cereals and pulses

11. Manufacture and use of manure and methane gas from cow dung and other waste products (such as flesh of dead animals, night soil, etc.,)
12. Limestone, lime-shell and other lime products
13. Manufacture of shellack
14. Collection of forest plants and fruits for medicinal purposes
15. Fruit processing and fruit preservation
16. Bamboo and cane work
17. Blacksmithy
18. Carpentry
19. Fibre,other than coir
20. Manufacture of Household utensils in aluminium
21. Manufacture of gum resins

Most of the above village / cottage industries are located in the villages. The value of the products under KVIC during Sixth Five Year Plan was Rs.9290 million and it provided employment to 3.7 million persons. During the Seventh Plan, the value of output of this sub-sector is targeted to increase from Rs.9,290 million in 1984-85 to about Rs. 20,000 million by the terminal year 1989-90. The employment coverage in this period is likely to increase from 3.7 million persons to 5 million persons. The targets set for Khadi and for village industries would account for growth rate of 7.1 per cent for Khadi Production and 17.5 per cent for village industries output.

India has developed a most comprehensive network of institutions in the public sector for the promotion of small and to some extent, medium industries. These institutions cater to the different needs of these industries, and taken together, they have schemes and programmes to attend to virtually all types of problems. As mentioned earlier, the components of this institutional framework are at national, state and district levels. This is necessitated by: (a) India being a large and diverse country; (b) industry being a concurrent subject between the union and state governments; and (c) small industry being geographically widely scattered and dispersed.[6]

The comprehensive institutional network involved for the promotion of small-scale industries in the country is presented in the following tables:

INSTITUTIONAL SETUP FOR SMALL-SCALE INDUSTRY DEVELOPMENT IN INDIA

1. National Level – Ministry of Industry, Department of Industrial Development

(a)Small Industries Development Organization (SIDO)

- Policy formulating, coordinating and monitoring agency;
- Maintains close liaison with the central ministries, Planning Commission, state governments and other organizations concerned with small-scale industry development and serves as the secretariat for the All India Small-Scale Industries Board;
- Provides a comprehensive range of industrial extension services including technical, managerial, economic and marketing assistance through its network of 26 small industries services institutes, 32 branch SSSIs, 41 extension centres, 4 regional testing centres, 1 product and process development centre, 2 footwear training centres and 4 production centres. In addition, 20 field-testing stations are being established in areas of concentration of specific industries for providing testing facilities to small-scale industries.

(b)National Small Industries Corporation (NSIC) with four regional offices

- Supply of machinery on hire purchase basis;

- Registration of units for participation in the purchase programmes of the Central and state governments, and other central institutions;
- Marketing assistance – internal and export;
- Development of prototypes of machinery and equipment, and other facilities
- Basic and advanced training in selected trades and technologies through its four-prototype development and training centres.

(c) Commissioner for Industrial Cooperatives

- Coordination of policies for industrial cooperatives.

(d) Specialized Institutions

(i) National Institute of Small Industry Extension Training (NISIET), Hyderabad

- Interdisciplinary approach in the areas of training; research and consultancy relating to development and management of small-scale and village industries (earlier known as Small Industry Extension Training Institute – SIET)

(ii) National Institute for Entrepreneurship and Small Business Development (NIESBUD), New Delhi

- Coordinates research and training in entrepreneurship development and devises specific training programmes suited to various categories of entrepreneurs specially from the weaker section of the society.

(iii) Central Institute of Tool Design (CITD), Hyderabad

- Training in the design and manufacture of tools, jigs, fixtures, dyes and moulds;
- Advisory and consultancy services including assistance in the design and development of tools;
- Recommend measures to standardize tools, tooling elements, components etc.

(iv) Central Tool Room and Training Centres (at Ludhiana, Delhi, Calcutta and Bangalore)

- Provision of tool room services and facilities in designs, manufacture and training. Tool rooms at Delhi and Bangalore are owned by the respective state governments.

(v) Central Institute of Head Tools (CIHT), Jalandhar.

- Provision of improved technology, raw materials, designs and testing for hand tools industry.

(vi) Institute of Design of Electrical Measuring Instruments (IDEMI), Bombay

- Provision of technical consultancy in the design and development of electrical and electronic instruments, calibration and testing, tool design, tool fabrication, prototype fabrication and training.

(vii) Central Machine Tool Institute, Bangalore.

(viii) Central Institute for Plastics Engineering and Tools, Madras (Ministry of Petroleum and Chemicals)

(ix) National Institute of Foundry and Forge Technology, Ranchi.

2. State Level

(a) Directorate of Industries: With a network of District Industries Centres at the district level, industries officers at the sub-division level and extension officers at the block level.

- Registration of small-scale units and recommending cases of large/medium industries to appropriate authorities
- Raw material quota
- Import quota
- Financial assistance under the State Aid to Industries Act

- Industrial estates
- Technical consultancy
- Training of entrepreneurs
- Industrial cooperatives
- Compilation of statistics
- Overall administration of the village and small-scale industry sector and maintaining close liaison with the central and state level organizations concerned with industrial development.

(b) Small Industry Development Corporation

- Supply of scarce raw materials through raw material depots
- Machinery on hire purchase
- Marketing assistance
- Joint ventures in the small-scale sector
- Entrepreneurship development
- Trade centres
- Industrial estates

(c) Industrial Infrastructure Corporation; Industrial Area Development Board/ Authority

- Plans and develops industrial estates and industrial areas

(d) Industrial Development Corporation

- Promotion of industrial units in the medium and large-scale including joint and public sector ventures
- Planning and development of industrial estates and industrial areas (in some states)

(e) Industrial Investment Corporation

- Finances medium and large units up to a certain investment ceiling with direct participation in share capital and underwrites new issues

(f) Agro Industries Corporation
   - Supply of agricultural machinery / equipment on hire
   - Development of agro-based industries
   - Sale of agro-inputs like fertilizers and pesticides

(g) Electronics Development Corporation
   - Promotion of industries in the field of electronics including joint sector and public sector projects.

(h) Leather Industry Development Corporation and other similar commodity corporations
   - Development of specific types of village and tiny sector units relating to a particular trade

(i) Rural Industries Marketing Corporation
   - Marketing of village industry products and provision of a variety of services needed by village and tiny units (Gujarat State has setup this corporation)

(j) Industrial and Technical Consultancy Organization (Sponsored by IDBI/IFCI/ICICI)
   - Technical consultancy services to small and medium-scale projects)

3. Financial Institutions

(a) Reserve Bank of India (RBI)

The country's central bank, responsible for currency and monetary regulation and other central banking functions besides being banker to the government. Also responsible for supervision of all banking institutions, provision of rural credit exchange control.

Entrusted with the administration of the credit Guarantee Scheme, under which government guarantee is provided for advances granted by banks and other credit institutions to small industrial units. The administration has since been transferred to the Deposit Insurance & Credit Guarantee Corporation.

(b) All India Term Lending Institutions

(i) Industrial Development Bank of India

Coordinates in conformity with national priorities the activities of institutions engaged in financing, promoting/developing industry; operates with schemes such as:

- Direct assistance
- Soft loan scheme
- Technical development fund
- Refinance of industrial loans
- Automatic refinance
- Special refinancing facility
- Rediscounting of bills
- Seed capital assistance
- Subscriptions to shares and bonds of financial institutions
- Development assistance fund

(ii) Industrial Finance Corporation of India (IFCI)

- Long term loans to new industrial units and also for expansion, diversification, renovation or modernization of existing units both in rupees and foreign currencies, underwriting of equity, preference and debenture capital
- Risk capital foundation provides soft loans as part of equity capital to new entrepreneurs, particularly technologists and professionals
- Benevolent reserve fund provides assistance for development purposes

(iii) Industrial Credit and Investment Corporation of India (ICICI)

- Currency loans to small enterprises under its Rupee Assistance Programme and foreign currency loan

(iv) Industrial Reconstruction Bank of India (IRBI)

- Provides financial and other types of assistance to sick or closed industrial concerns, and operates, in the case of small units, through state level agencies by way of sanctioning 'Line of Credit'
- Provides managerial assistance
- Guidance for renovation and modernization

(v) Export Import Bank of India (EXIM Bank)

- Finances, facilitates and promotes foreign trade of India
- Coordinates the working of institutions engaged in financing export and import
- Finances export of consultancy and related services, assists Indian joint ventures in third countries, conducts export market studies, finances export oriented industries and provides international merchant banking services.

(vi) National Bank for Agriculture and Rural Development (NABARD)

- Refinancing the farm and non-farm operations in rural areas
- In the non-farm sector, village and tiny sector industries located in rural areas are supported through refinancing

(viii) National Cooperative Development Corporation (NCDC)

- Promotes and finances cooperative enterprises in processing, marketing, storage and export relating to agro-based industries
- Agro-service centres
- Promotion of units for production of fertilizers, pesticides and insecticides

- Workshop for fabrication of agricultural machinery/implements
- Margin money for processing units
- Technical training

(c) Other Financial Institutions

(i) Export Credit Guarantee Corporation (ECGC)

- Supports and strengthens export promotion drive (a) by providing a range of risk insurance covers to exporters against loss in export of goods and services, (b) by offering guarantees to banks and financial institutions to enable exporters to obtain better facilities from them.

(ii) Deposit Insurance and Credit Guarantee Corporation (DICGO)

- Operates four guarantee schemes:(a) small loans guarantee scheme, (b) small loans (small-scale industries) guarantee Scheme, (c) small loans (financial corporations) guarantee scheme, and (d) service cooperative society guarantee scheme

(iii) State Financial Corporation (SFC)

- Provides long and medium term loans for acquisition of fixed assets of small and medium-scale industries
- Guarantees payment for purchase of machinery from suppliers within India
- Guarantees loans raised by industries from commercial banks, cooperative banks etc.
- Foreign exchange loans under World Bank line of credit
- Special capital assistance upto Rs.200,000

(iv) Commercial Banks

- Provide term finance and working capital advances classified under cash credit, overdrafts, demand loans, purchased/discounted/advanced against inland bills, purchased/discounted/advanced against import bills and clean advance.

(v) Regional Rural Banks (RRBs)

- Provide banking facilities in remote and unbanked areas among other places of the selected districts and provide credit to agriculturists, artisans and other self-employed persons belonging to weaker sections. The loans are given in kind.

(vi) Cooperative Banks

- Provide credit to farm and non-farm cooperative societies.

(d) Research Laboratories

- National laboratories coming under the purview of the Council of Scientific and Industrial Research (CSIR) and of other organizations and ministries of the Central Government
- Research laboratories established by state governments for research and development of new products / processes.

The National Research Development Corporation (NRDC), New Delhi releases the patents of new processes / products developed by national laboratories for commercial exploitation.

(e) Association of Small-Scale Industry Entrepreneurs

- Federation of Association of Small Industries of India (FASII)
- Indian Council of Small Industries (ICSI)
- National Alliance of Young Entrepreneurs (NAYE)
- State Small Industry Associations
- District small industry associations

- Associations at state and national levels for specific groups of industries
- Chambers of commerce & industry and their federations.

The All India Small-Scale Industries Board with the Union Minister for Industry as the Chairman is the apex contemplative and advisory forum for the small-scale sector. As the Board meets only once or twice a year, it operates through a number of standing committees for detailed deliberations on various aspects. The standing committees operating at present are on policies and programmes; development of industries in the North Eastern region; ancillary development, quality improvement and marketing assistance including exports; credit facilities, taxation and modernization; and industrial sickness. The secretariat for the Board is the office of the Development Commissioner (Small-Scale Industries), headquarters of the Small Industries Development Organization (SIDO).

Central Organizations

The principal central institutions assisting the small-scale sector are the Small Industries Development Organization (SIDO) and the National Small Industries Corporation (NSIC) under the Ministry of Industry. The SIDO was established in 1954. It acts as a policy formulating, coordinating and monitoring agency for developing of small-scale industries. It coordinates the work relating to the development of small industries on an all-India basis by evolving an all-India policy and programme for the development of small-scale industries; coordinating the policies and programmes of various state governments, programmes and development of large and small-scale industries and programmes for the district industries centres, and development of industrial estates and ancillaries all over the country. It also acts as a liaison between different states and between the states and central ministries, planning commissions, the Reserve Bank of India and financial institutions.

The SIDO renders such technical assistance as may be required by the state governments for preparing schemes within the overall plan allocations. It assists the Ministry in regulating central assistance to the states for the development of small-scale industries.

An important function of the SIDO is to suggest a pattern of small-scale industries development for the country as a whole. This involves responsibilities for indicating the lines of manufacture which are suitable for the small-scale sector, and giving it all assistance in the form of promotion, procurement of raw materials and machinery, and other technical advice from time to time.

The SIDO provides a wide range of extension services through its network of small-scale industries service institutes, branch institutes, extension centres, regional testing centres and other institutions at the field level.

The National Small Industries Corporation was set up in 1955. Its primary function is to help small entrepreneurs in setting up small industries by providing both indigenous and imported machinery and equipment on hire purchase basis, assisting small units in marketing their products through participation in the Central Government Stores Purchase Programme. Through its prototype development and training centres, the Corporation develops prototypes of machinery for transfer of technology and know-how for commercial production and imparts training to skilled workers and entrepreneurs in various technical fields.

State Level Institutions

Prominent among the sate level institutions assisting the small-scale sector are the Directorate of Industries, Small Industry Development Corporation and State Financial Corporation. The Directorate of Industries is the executive agency for the village and small-scale industry sector. It acts under the overall guidance of SIDO and the concerned central institutions associated with various programmes of assistance. Its functions include regulatory and development activities. In the recent years, its emphasis is on utilizing the regulatory functions for more effective performance of developmental functions. It implements certain programmes of assistance and oversees the implementation of other schemes with the help of specialized agencies operating at the state level for village and small-scale industries. Its main asset is the extensive network of field offices in every district of the state, at the district, sub-division and block levels.

The main functions of the Small Industry Development Corporation are: supply of scarce raw materials to units in the small-scale sector, supply of machinery on hire purchase, provision of marketing assistance and promotion of entrepreneurship through various schemes. The State Financial Corporation provides long and medium term loans for acquisition of fixed assets of small and medium-scale industries.

Through various schemes of financing for small and medium-scale units, it is actively involved in attracting entrepreneurs to backward and rural areas.

District Industries Centres

An important institution set up at the district level for industrial promotion is the District Industries Centre (DIC). It is a major structural innovation introduced in May 1978 to serve as a unified agency for industries under a single roof. Compared to the earlier pattern of district industries officer/ assistant director of industries, the institution has been upgraded and headed by a senior person designated as general manager. He is of the rank of joint director of industries and in certain cases deputy director of industries. There are in all 422 DICs in the country covering 428 districts. With a senior officer posted at the district level, powers have been delegated to him in a number of areas and many organizational innovations are either introduced or contemplated in various states to provide a wide range of services and support to entrepreneurs and artisans.

The general manager has four functional managers concerned with the functional areas of economic investigation, village industries, credit, marketing, infrastructure and raw materials. It is planned to augment the strength of functional managers with three project managers specialized in different product groups, based on the needs of a particular district. It is hoped that the team will be able to give area orientation and project orientation to its activities simultaneously for helping entrepreneurs in various ways. In many states, sub-divisional set up has come into being with an assistant director of industries and an industrial promotion officer posted at the sub-divisional headquarters. In addition, at the block level, an extension officer (industries) is in position. In the recent past there have been some changes in some states especially in Andhra Pradesh, the block as a unit changed to Mandal. In some states, he looks after two to three blocks. It is hoped that an extension officer will be given the jurisdiction of not more than one block in the near future, to cope with a number of developmental schemes for which he is held responsible as a field level functionary. Strong district and lower level teams are an important aspect of industrial administration in the country.

Economic Information Service

In the package of services needed by entrepreneurs at the pre-investment,. investment and post-investment stages, economic information service and technical and management consultancy are quite prominent. Some of the important consultancy needs of entrepreneurs at various stages are detailed below:

- To identify industrial potential of a region and suggest project ideas;

- To prepare project profiles, feasibility reports and other pre-investment studies;
- To prepare detailed project reports and when called upon, render turn-key services in project implementation;
- To identify potential entrepreneurs, provide them with technical and management assistance and train them to shoulder the entrepreneurial responsibility;
- To undertake the techno-economic appraisal of feasibility/project reports;
- To undertake market research and surveys for specific products;
- To undertake project supervision and follow-up and where necessary, render technical, management and administrative assistance;
- To undertake studies for expansion/ modernization/ diversification;
- To undertake diagnostic studies of sick units and monitoring of the rehabilitation programmes;
- To provide industrial and management consultancy services.

Economic information services are made available through a number of studies carried out by promotional and consultancy organizations. These are techno-economic surveys at the district/regional level, industry surveys, product profiles, feasibility studies, market surveys and surveys dealing with impact of specific programmes. These were initially undertaken by the SIDO on an extensive scale and gradually, at the state/district levels, by small industries corporations, technical consultancy organizations and district industries centres have pursued them. Training and research organizations like the National Institute of Small Industry Extension Training (NISIET) have prepared select studies on these themes and evolved guidelines for incorporating the foci considered relevant at various periods in the studies carried out by them from time to time.

Information service provided to entrepreneurs at the SISIs and at other institutions at state and district levels is based on the findings of studies of the type referred to above carried out by a number of agencies. This service helps prospective entrepreneurs in selecting suitable product lines. An existing industrialist is assisted to know about the competitive position of his industry and market, and guided in the expansion/ diversification of his product lines.

The Small Enterprises National Documentation Centre (SENDOC) established at the NISIET is a storehouse of information on all aspects of relevance to the small-scale industry sector. The Centre has close links with all national laboratories, specialized research institutions and development agencies in the country, and prominent international organizations concerned with industrial development. It captures technological management and economic information from a variety of sources and disseminates the same to entrepreneurs and development functionaries. Dissemination of information attempted through various journals and ad-hoc publications as an anticipatory information service relates to specific products processes and regions.

Similar documentation centres have been established in a number of national level research laboratories to provide information on specific product groups to entrepreneurs and development agencies.

Entreprenership Development

Entrepreneur being the kingpin of industrialization, emphasis was given to development of entrepreneurship of various categories as part of the small-scale industry promotional efforts. With the special programmes launched in 1971 to provide large-scale self-employment opportunities for the educated, unemployed, technically qualified, skilled and experienced persons, development of entrepreneurship became an important element in the strategy for stimulating industrialization. Entrepreneurs are trailblazers or innovators. They can be identified through certain demographic, social, economic and psychological tests and such characteristics can be developed through educational and training programmes. Thus entrepreneurship can be stimulated, increased, regulated and controlled.

The need for achievement, affiliation and power have been regarded as the most significant characteristics of successful entrepreneurs in the pioneering studies carried out by David C. McClelland and his team at the National Institute of Small Industry Extension Training (NISIET) in the mid sixties. Through these and subsequent studies, and experiments carried out by NISIET and a number of other institutions in the country, more insight was gained into the nature of entrepreneurship, and the ways and means of promoting and developing qualities of entrepreneurship relevant for small scale industries and small business.

Among institutions specialized in this field mention may be made, besides NISIET, Hyderabad, Entrepreneurship Development Institute of India, Ahmedbad; National Institute for Entrepreneurship and Small Business Development (NIESBUD), New Delhi; and Management Development Institute, New Delhi. Recently, the National Board for Entrepreneurial Development was established with the Union Minister for Industry as the chairman. At the operational level, Small Industries Development Organization through its network of SISIs have organized a large number of programmes all over the country. Financial institutions, particularly the State Bank of India and technical consultancy organizations promoted by the all-India financial institutions have organized a number of programmes on entrepreneurship development at the district level, taking clues from the patterns advocated by specialized institutions. The Indian Investment

Centre, New Delhi, is another institution which has made a significant contribution in this field.

Intensive campaigns are organized extensively for attracting entrepreneurship. In the initial years, they were conducted at the state level and in recent years focus is on district and taluk level campaigns. All organizations concerned with small industry promotion come together in a particular location, publicize the opportunities available and facilities offered for starting small-scale units, and enthuse entrepreneurs through counseling. On the strength of the preparatory work done earlier, the campaigns enable a large number of entrepreneurs make up their mind on the product lines they intend to pursue. Clearances are given on the spot by the concerned agencies to entrepreneurs who are in an advanced stage.

As entrepreneurial development programmes gathered momentum in the seventies, more streamlined procedures were adopted for identification and selection of entrepreneurs, and to provide them techno-managerial training. Selection procedure evolved consists of administering psychological tests like TAT, risk taking, personal efficacy; finding out the socio-economic views. Among the states, mention may be made of Gujarat where systematic efforts were made to develop entrepreneurial qualities among employees, workers, merchants and all those who evinced interest in pursuing self-employment avenues in various vocations – industry service and business. The programme was not limited to small-scale industry alone nor to people with relatively high level of education, including technical education. People with smaller means and with low level of education were helped to become self-employed.

The integrated model for entrepreneurship development evolved by NISIET in the early seventies is the result of its experience and realization that entrepreneurship development is a multi-disciplinary and long-range plan executed through well orchestrated institutional support. The main components of this model are: (a) local agency to initiate and support potential entrepreneurs till the break-even stage; (b) inter-disciplinary approach; (c) strong information support; (d) training as an important input for entrepreneurial development, monitoring and evaluation; (e) institutional financing and counseling services. These steps may also be categorized as stimulatory, support and sustenance activities needed for development of entrepreneurship. The inter-disciplinary training programme of twelve-weeks duration include economic aspects of self-employment including industrial opportunities and acquaintance with the environment for establishing a venture; feasibility studies for selected product lines; management of new enterprises.

Programmes were organized for training the trainers who could in turn put across programmes at the district level. In this effort NISIET was instrumental in the establishment of the entrepreneurial motivation training centres in Assam.

The type of entrepreneurs selected by various agencies for the programmes organized by them included educated unemployed, science and technology graduates, technically qualified, skilled or experienced persons, women entrepreneurs, retired defence personnel, entrepreneurs from tribals and other economically weaker sections, entrepreneurs interested in ancillary units, those interested in industry, service and business (small enterprise and not necessarily small industry) and artisans. The nature of the programme was modified to suit the needs of specific categories.

One important direction in which programmes are being pursued is to look for entrepreneurship in smaller towns and rural areas. This needs to be intensified further through a cluster approach. Grouping entrepreneurial activities in different clusters and planning interrelated activities and services would be useful in the context of small towns and rural areas. Manufacture of products needing simple technology, and goods and services required in the neighbouring areas could be the focus for reaching smaller towns and rural areas through this programme.

In the context of rural areas, 'Training of Rural Youth for Self Employment (TRYSEM)' is a scheme started in 1978 to cater to the age group of 18-35. Another scheme known as 'Providing Self-employment to Educated Unemployed' (SEEU) was started in 1983 with focus on educated unemployed persons with low level of education in the age group of 18-35 interested in self-employment ventures requiring total investment not exceeding Rs.25,000/-. Developing entrepreneurs through self-employment ventures has thus been one of the major goals of smalls-scale industry programmes for quite some time.

Training

Training was visualized in its totality for the benefit of the small-scale sector right from the early years. Based on the needs identified, programmes of training and institutional framework were evolved at various levels. Technical and managerial training is an integral part of the extension services rendered by SIDO. Basic consideration in organizing these programmes is the scope for developing new enterprises and improving the productivity of existing ones. Over the years, small-scale industries have developed a greater degree of sophistication. Skills, managerial talents, technical know-how and entrepreneurship required for these industries are of a high order. New institutions have been established to provide specialized series including training to certain categories of industries.

SIDO conducts technical and managerial training programmes for small industries through SISIs, extension centres, and training and production centres. Short courses are organized on various aspects of management and technical areas. These include trade-oriented, process-oriented, and product-oriented courses. Mobile workshops are attached to SISIs visit areas of concentration of artisans for demonstration and training purposes. Training through mobile vans is imparted to interested artisans in areas such as blacksmithy, carpentry, leatherwork, general engineering, woodwork, etc.,

NISIET provides composite non-technological training in almost all aspects connected with small industry development, emphasis being on development, management and behavioural science programmes at national and international levels. It trains development and extension personnel of organizations associated with small industry development in the country and from a large number of developing countries, and existing and prospective personnel from various organizations are also organized periodically. It thus serves as an apex training, research and consultancy organization in the small-scale sector.

The National Institute for Entrepreneurship and Small Business Development (NIESBUD) coordinates the training and research activities for entrepreneurship development in the small enterprise sector. It also undertakes specific programmes to cater to the needs of various target groups. Its programmes are mainly for motivators, trainers and entrepreneurs.

Some of the central institutions which provide specialsied training for technical personnel concerned with specific industry groups are Prototype Development and Training Centres of the National Small Industries Corporation, Central Institute of Tool Design (CITD), Hyderabad, Institute for Design of Electrical Measuring Instruments (IDEMI), Mumbai, Central Tool Room and Training Centres, Central Institute of Hand Tools, Jalandhar, National Institute of Foundry and Forge Technology, Ranchi and the Central Institute for Plastics Engineering and Tools (CIPET), Chennai.

To supplement these, the state governments have also

developed training centres, tool room and testing facilities in certain line of manufacture. At the grass root level for development of skills needed for various industries, polytechnics and industrial training institutes are operating in each district. Training programmes are being closely monitored to ensure that they cope with the requirements of the industry from time to time.

Technical and Management Consultancy and Technology Support

As part of the comprehensive extension service, technical and management consultancy services are quite important. Project consultancy is an integral part of this package deal. This indicates the need at various stages to conduct specific studies in the plant to improve productivity, efficiency and profitability with the help of effective consultancy services. Consultancy in this sense should have process orientation, i.e., a continuous consultant-client relationship where both are jointly involved in identifying and analyzing problems, finding solutions to problems and implementing them, with the major role being played by the client himself while the consultant would function more as resource person.

Key organizations providing consultancy services to small enterprises are as follows:

1. SIDO Network (SISIs, and its branch institutes, and extension centres) providing virtually free consultancy services and acting as promotional organizations;
2. Technical consultancy organizations (TCOs) promoted by all-India financial institutions (Industrial Development Bank of India, Industrial Finance Corporation of India and industrial Credit and Investment Corporation of India) providing consultancy services at subsidized rates;
3. Consultancy bureaus of banks established recently

providing services free of charge to enterprises assisted by the respective banks;

4. Private consultants and management institutions mostly serving medium and large enterprises who can pay for the services rendered. To enable small enterprises avail of private consultants, financial support from governmental institutions becomes necessary.

SISIs and TCOs have a complementary role to play in providing consultancy services. They can pool their expertise and provide consultancy services in the respective states. A roster of private consultants is maintained by SISIs, TCOs and financial institutions. They solicit the services of consultants as and when they find it necessary. The cost of such services is subsidized by the government: SISI for the work entrusted by SISI and the concerned all-India financial institution for the work taken up or entrusted by a TCO.

Management consultancy involves study of specific aspects of the unit and in some cases study of a number of technical and managerial aspects simultaneously. The integrated plant studies encompass areas such as production, inventories, layout, designs, quality control, plant maintenance, marketing, finance, costing, industrial relations, inter-personnel conflicts, training etc. Packaging consultancy services bring out practical suggestions which can be pursued by the unit for implementation.

Technical Consultancy

Small industries service institutes and industrial extension centres are equipped with workshops where small units can utilize engineering services such as machine shop, tool room, heat treatment facilities and furnaces. Laboratories are set up to provide testing facilities. Product and process development centre for glass and ceramics at Ranchi develops viable processes and products and introduces quality control measures. Prototype development and training centres of

NSIC development prototype of such equipment and tools as are relevant to the small-scale sector and provide common facility services such as testing, machining, castings, electroplating, etc., and intensive job-oriented technical training. They also design, develop and produce improved tools for use by rural artisans. Footwear training centres offer training in improved methods of footwear technology.

Technical consultancy rendered by SIDO consultants can be grouped into the following areas:

- Advice on improvement of processes, use of modern machines, production planning, layout of the factory, and material handling.
- Assistance in better product design, preparation of drawings of machines and machine parts, equipment, tools, jigs and fixtures;
- Demonstration of use of modern technical processes through workshops;
- Research on proper use of equipment, improved designs of machinery;
- Training in various technical trades for the benefit of small industrialists and artisans;
- Preparation of product profiles, feasibility studies and projects reports;
- Guidance on proper selection of machinery and equipment, make or buy policy, sources of supply of machines, erection and commission of machinery, proper maintenance, etc.

Specialized institutions such as central tool room and training centres, Central Institute of Tool Design, Institute for Design of Electrical Measuring Instruments, Central Hand Tools Institute and National Institute of Foundry and Forge Technology, provide a variety of advisory, consultancy and common service facilities for existing and prospective entrepreneurs and for developing manpower in specialized areas through training to take to employment in small scale units.

Role of TCOs

Technical Consultancy Organizations (TCOs) promoted by all-India financial institutions provide a wide spectrum of reasonably priced consultancy services to small and medium scale units and to prospective entrepreneurs. They also provide consultancy services to government departments, commercial banks and other state level developmental and financial institutions concerned with industrial development. Sixteen TCOs (including the one promoted by the Government of Karnataka) started with major focus on technical consultancy. Preparation of product profiles, feasibility studies and project reports constitutes a sizeable part of the work. Gradually they are diversifying their activities into managerial consultancy, specialized studies needed at the district and regional levels and selection, motivation and training of entrepreneurs as part of entrepreneurship development programmes. They are also entering areas such as design engineering services, turn-key assignments, retainer consultancy services, putting up functional industrial complexes, adopting sick units and training barefoot consultants who can act as a link between the consultancy organization and entrepreneurs.

One of the technical consultancy organizations covering Gujarat state (GITCO) has introduced a number of innovative experiments in developing management consultancy services for small-scale industries which are:

1) Novel approaches for reviving sick units through the adoption or retainer systems.
2) Marketing consultancy clinics organized at various locations for benefiting clusters of small enterprises.
3) Marketing assistance either by undertaking direct sale or through counseling. In case of the latter, the effort involved is in developing the product concept, identification of market segments, determination of marketing strategy in terms of

price, promotion and distribution, and procurement of orders.

Modernization and Technology Support

The scheme for modernization of selected small-scale industries was introduced in 1975 with a view to identify the problems of productivity-efficiency and obsolescence, and keeping industrial units abreast of the latest trends in production processes, product design, technical and technological development and training facilities through an effective consultancy service and other forms of assistance. Salient features of the programme include motivational and educational activities like seminars, industrial workshops, industrial clinics etc., inplant studies for suggesting modernization methods, preparation of modernization guides and industrial study reports and conducting of modernization courses. All India industry study reports are prepared for specific industries for identifying the problems of industries relating to product design, technology, machinery and equipment, managerial aspects, etc., and for taking action to overcome the problems. Under this programme, 20 industries have been selected on an all-India basis and 38 industries based on state wise concentration of units. Selection of these industries was done on the basis of present status of technological obsolescence, potential for export and possibilities of import substitution.

Intensive inplant study of small-scale units registered under this programme is conducted free of cost by consultants/ SIDO officers. For studies conducted by consultancy organizations, SIDO bears the cost upto a maximum of Rs.2000 per study. For problem-oriented consultancy, 75 per cent of the expenditure upto Rs.500 per unit will be borne by SIDO. For units from backward areas, the service is free. For organizing study visits of entrepreneurs from one area to another to study advanced technologies, better design and testing facilities in the same industry, 50 per cent of the transport cost is borne by SIDO.

Interest subsidy scheme for modernization has been recently introduced to quicken the pace of modernization for implementing the recommendations of inplant study reports prepared by SISIs. For undertaking modernization, loan is made available at 7 per cent rate of interest per annum, the difference between this figure and the normal rate of interest charged by financial institutions for loans advanced by them being subsidized by SIDO, subject to a maximum of Rs.20,000 per unit per annum. The subsidy will be available for five years for a unit located in backward areas and for three years in other areas. In respect of all the above-mentioned schemes, SISI is the implementing agency at the state level.

As part of the programme of technology upgradation and testing, a number of institutions are operating in the field. Four regional testing centres of SIDO provide testing facilities and assistance to small-scale units in improving the quality of their products and enabling them to produce goods conforming to Indian Standards Institution specifications.

A chain of twenty field-testing stations is being established in areas of concentration of specific type of industries as part of the network of regional testing centres. Specialized tool rooms and training institutes including prototype development and training centres of the NSIC provide a variety of services to small-scale units in technology upgradation. Science and technology parks are planned to be established in a number of centres in the country to provide a window to the industry for new technologies developed in various fields which could be adapted by existing and prospective entrepreneurs. Establishment of pilot plants for enabling entrepreneurs to try out processes developed in research laboratories to test their commercial viability, is also planned in these parks.

Industrial Estates

Availability of factory accommodation with a package of facilities and services has been an important attraction for small-scale units. This is provided through industrial estates and industrial areas in locations identified for intensive promotion and those where prospects for industrialization are bright. Provision of such facilities in anticipation of demand obviates the need for the entrepreneur to get clearances from a number of agencies for establishing his enterprise, which is often a cumbersome and time consuming process, and conserve his capital for production purposes rather than utilizing it for land and buildings.

The industrial estates programme of India which was started in 1955, expanded rapidly in certain periods of planned development. The main purpose of the programme was two-fold: promotion of small-scale industries and entrepreneurship on an extensive scale; dispersal of industries to less developed or backward regions, smaller towns and rural areas.

The programme also serves other purposes such as promotion of specific category of industries, relieving congestion in cities, promotion of export-oriented units, attracting foreign investment through promotion of industries, and integrating industry with urban and regional planning.

Types of Estates

Industrial estates can be categorized from three angles: (a) sponsorship; (b) nature of industrial activity; and (c) location.

Industrial estates in most cases have been sponsored by state governments. Either the Department of Industries or government corporation have developed them.

Another pattern of estates promoted is on cooperative lines. In the states of Maharashtra and Gujarat in the western part of the country, cooperative pattern is preferred as it involves the entrepreneurs to a considerable extent by pooling their own resources right from the conception of the estate proposal. The idea is to enable entrepreneurs develop the estate, construct factory buildings and make them available to its members. Land is acquired and given by the government on lease to the society. The financing pattern followed in a cooperative estate is 20:20:60. In the total project cost of the estate including building construction, members' share capital contribution is 20 per cent, and equal amount is contributed by the state government and treated as a long term interest free loan, and 60 per cent is obtained as long tern loan from a financial institution. Life Insurance Corporation of India provides finance to cooperative estates.

In many locations, industrial estates are of general-purpose type judged by the nature of industrial activity. All types of industries are permitted in them except noxious and hazardous ones. In such estates, provision is made for custom built factories where manufacturing operations demand special type of facilities. Ancillary estates are promoted for attracting ancillary units either for one parent large-scale unit or for a few parent units located nearby. Clusters of ancillary units thus promoted help parent units to provide the required services such as supply of raw material, technical guidance, quality control, etc. Single trade estates are designed to attract units of the same trade or a cluster of units belonging to a homogenous group. A functional estate is one in which the functions of one industry are sub-divided among a number of small-scale units located at one place, each functioning according to a coordinated manufacturing programme. Both single trade and functional estates offer opportunities for planning the technical and common service facilities to a greater degree and facilitate arrangements for joint purchase of raw materials/sale of finished goods. These two patterns are very often used as synonyms and referred to as functional complexes. Many states are promoting functioning complexes for leather goods, ceramic products, light engineering goods, hosiery, agro-industries, etc.

Another categorization attempted is by location:

metropolitan, urban, semi-urban estates refer to places from 50,000 to one million population; semi-urban estates refer to urban settlements upto 50,000 population; rural estates are situated in rural settlements, of generally below 5,000 population.

By March 1981, there were 799 industrial estates sponsored in the country out of which 659 were functioning and 140 were at various stages of development. At the aggregate level, more detailed picture is available as at the end of March 1979. The data relate to industrial estates and do not include industrial areas. The accent on development of industrial estates in small towns, rural areas and less developed regions is conspicuous by the large number of estates sponsored during the Third Plan period (1961-66) which could start functioning only during the Fourth Plan period. Hence, rightly, the emphasis from the fourth Plan period has been on consolidation and making the existing estates function effectively. By March 1979, the number of functioning estates was 633 as against 796 sponsored. Sheds constructed were 19,368 of which 17,451 were occupied, resulting in the occupancy rate of 90 per cent (72 to 84 per cent from 1961 to 1975). On the other hand, the occupancy position of developed plots was only 70 per cent in 1979 (75 per cent in 1975). In the 18,241 units functioning in allotted sheds and plots, production was Rs.8,030 million and employment of 286,000 was generated. Out of the completed estates of 705, there were 316 in urban locations, 179 in semi-urban and 210 in rural settlements. Occupancy rate of semi-urban and rural estates was less than that of urban estates, indicating the slow response from entrepreneurs in these locations.

Lessons of Experiences

With wide diversity in the levels of industrialization and development, the degree of effectiveness and success of industrial estates in various locations has varied.

Development and management of estates in various centres should be related to the potential and pattern suited to the locations. In centres where industrialization is of a high order, industrial areas could be the answer. Ancillary estates, functional complexes and estates needed for specific categories of entrepreneurs may be planned. Wherever possible estates may be sponsored by cooperative societies or associations of entrepreneurs.

In semi-urban and rural areas, assessing entrepreneurial response is necessary to decide on the size and type of estates. Building construction is to be attempted in consultation with the entrepreneurs to ensure that it meets their needs. In smaller towns, linking the units of estates with the resource and demand picture of the region and developmental plans envisaged promotes inter-sectoral linkages. In bigger centres objectives such as catering to institutional purchases, demand of a larger region, meeting inter-firm demand can certainly be kept in view while selecting product lines. In each of these locations entrepreneurship development of a pattern that is considered advisable for a region has to be pursued. Attracting outside entrepreneurs and technical talents from elsewhere to a less developed region is necessary to trigger off industrialization of that region. Guided entrepreneurship needs to be pursued in less developed regions.

In the units functioning in existing industrial estates, monitoring of performance is necessary for identifying the reasons for some of them not working up to optimum capacity and devise strategies to improve their performance.

REFERENCES

1. D. Nagaiya, "Small-Scale Industry Development in India: Policy, Programmes and Institutional Support" in Victor Sit Fung-Shuen, ed., Strategies for Small-Scale Industries Promotion in Asia (Hong Kong: Longman:1984), pp.8-42.

2. Planning Commission, Government of India, Seventh Five Year Plan 1985-90: A Summary (New Delhi, 1985), p.25.
3. Manas Bhattacharya, "Planning and Development of Small-Scale Industries in India" in Small Industry Bulletin for Asia and the Pacific, No.23,(New York: United Nations, 1988), p.89.
4. D. Nagaiya, Small-Scale Industries in India: Handbook of Statistics (Hyderabad: National Institute of Small Industry Extension Training, 1989), pp.10-11.
5. Planning Commission, Government of India, Seventh Five Year Plan, Vol.2, p.101.

9

Field Approach to Development of Entreprenuership

When we speak of developing entrepreneurship among women, we cannot think of this effort and programme in isolation. One can think of developing entrepreneurship among women only through creating an environment which would motivate and facilitate women coming forward to take to certain enterprises. This necessitates developing entrepreneurship in rural areas. The present chapter focuses on developing entrepreneurship towards rural industrialization. Such a measure will pave the way and create conditions which will help the women folk from different ethnic segments and economic background to gradually move and shoulder up industrial activity by themselves or with their family members.

As we have pointed out earlier, promoting and developing small-scale and cottage industries inclusive of handicrafts and artisan enterprises in rural areas is not for their own sake, nor is it simply a political strategy to appease the low-income groups in the community, but it is an indispensable measure, whatever be the approaches and methods employed towards the use of the material and human resources at the disposal of the rural communities. So long you have the choice to ignore rural industrialization and that you have better alternatives to it, you are free to pursue such a course of development. But such alternatives are few in view of the enormity of population in some countries, literacy and technological levels out-weighed by material and human resources that could be gradually harnessed and utilized to meet the minimum needs of the people.

We can safely say, irrespective of certain limitation in respect of the whole class of small-scale and cottage industries in terms of productivity, quality of products, profits and poor management of these enterprises, that there is no argument against rural industrialization and development of small-scale and cottage industries.

Promotion and development of small industries will involve, both directly and indirectly, the development of entrepreneurship. The approach and strategies for achieving industrial development may vary from those for entrepreneurship development. Perhaps, the strategies vary accordingly as emphasis is placed on either of the two. Needless to say that industrial development cannot be achieved without entrepreneurship development. Depending upon the emphasis, one becomes the by-product of the other. They are indeed two facets of the same activity.

The inadequacy of entrepreneurship is an inhibiting factor to accelerate the process of industrialization in the newly developing communities. Although there is no such thing as a zero level of entrepreneurship, the absence of an appropriate industrial and entrepreneurial climate and an industrial base, coupled with lack of access to relevant technology, has acted as a handicap for such communities, to achieve rapid industrial development. The inadequate availability of entrepreneurial talent particularly affects the development of modern small manufacturing and processing enterprises for, while large industries can be set up with expatriate capital and entrepreneurship, small industries need to have a domestic entrepreneurial base. The development of indigenous entrepreneurship especially among the rural-tribal populations is, therefore, a key issue and an imperative need on the part of the countries embarking on small industry development programmes.

Our focus in this discussion is on entrepreneurial development in rural communities. Development here means a basic, partial or total transformation, a socio-cultural change in the client community. Entrepreneur in this context is defined as one who would start an industry or take to a new enterprise which is a deviation from his traditional family occupation or profession. Further, entrepreneurship may be defined as a creative activity, the entrepreneur being an innovator who introduces something new into the economy: a method of production not yet tested by experience in the branch of manufacture concerned, a product with which the consumers are not familiar, a new source of raw material, or of a new market hitherto unexploited and other similar innovations.

The approach suggested here is field approach which may be defined s a holistic approach to development comprising the study of the social structure and socio-cultural processes that operate in a given client community. It envisages a thorough understanding of the target community in all its aspects and attempts entrepreneurial development in it, manipulating simultaneously all the key elements in the total system such as physical and human resources, institutions, infrastructure and the entrepreneur himself.

Prior to the advent of entrepreneurial development agencies, entrepreneurship grew as a spontaneous economic activity among certain traditionally entrepreneurial communities wherein this activity was institutionalized. Besides, there has been sporadic emergence of entrepreneurship among other groups based on needs and wants of people, natural resources, innovativeness, managerial and risk-taking abilities on the part of individual entrepreneurs. The rate and volume of spontaneous emergence of entrepreneurship is far behind the desired national, social and economic objectives of entrepreneurial development. Attempts during the past few years have been towards induced entrepreneurship. This was restricted to selective, sporadic and isolated approaches and the results have not been commensurate with the time and money spent on these programmes. It is relevant here to look into some sociological aspects of entrepreneurship citing India as an example.

Sociological Aspects

Entrepreneurship as an economic activity emerges and functions in a sociological and cultural setting. It could be conceived of as an individual's free choice activity or a social group's occupation or profession. In the Indian context, the supply of entrepreneurship in the past was mostly from some functionally designated communities or individual families. The ancient Hindu Varna order and its later ramifications called the caste system were partly based on the division of functions in the Hindu society. Thus we had and have the Brahmin, Kshatriya, Vysya and Sudra with innumerable sub-castes and sects in the first three and hundreds of castes or endogamous groups among the Sudra. Of the four Varnas traditionally, it was the Vysya community that was assigned the entrepreneurial activity comprising farming, trade, commerce and industry. Over the years, trade and commerce became characteristic of them. Further, the caste system, which was the later complex social stratification of the Varna order, was predominantly associated with diverse occupations and professions in a given territorial community. This stratification of Hindu society resulted in the birth of a new institution called the Hindu Jajmani system. It is a service relationship between the service or goods receiver (Jajmani) and the service and goods supplier (Kamin). The rendering of service or supply of goods on the part of a caste has become over centuries hereditary and closely associated with the caste system. The Jajmani system is a complex network of socio-economic relationship and still prevails all over rural India. Thus we had the functional groups such as priests, carpenters, blacksmiths, goldsmiths, potters, dairymen, washer-men, gardeners, water bearers, cobblers, barbers, sweepers, scavengers, oil-mongers, vegetable growers, weavers, traders and scores of others with distinct functions. An occupational or servicing group rendered service or supplied goods as the case may be and received remuneration mostly in kind annually or periodically.

In the jajmani system the farmer was the central figure and other groups served him and served each other. This kind of barter economy and socio-economic relationship streamlined and institutionalized the castes and their distinct functions, as a contrast to the Japanese society where in there has been negligible division of labour or functions. Since it became institutionalized over a period of time, it tended to be rigid, each caste pursuing its traditionally designated or customary function. Thus, as a sequence of the jajmani system, activities relating to industry, trade and commerce and small enterprises such as handicrafts made by artisans and their counterparts elsewhere in the country (Agarwal, Marwari etc.), the smith and artisan groups are examples of those who are predominantly engaged in trade, commerce and small enterprises, manufacturing, processing, the supply of entrepreneurs was sociologically and culturally limited to the traditional entrepreneurial groups. That is, only certain caste groups forced by the value system and tradition entered the field of entrepreneurship. Alongside the traditional entrepreneurial caste groups, in a sporadic way, a few individual pioneers and innovators drawn from the non-traditional entrepreneurial groups have taken to entrepreneurship.

During the past two-three decades in the context of India and other developing countries in Asia, as a consequence of a combination of factors such as increase in education, forces working against the institution of caste (in India), democracy as an ideal and value, territorial mobility, urbanization, increase in population, new impetus in science and technology, the state's intervention and emphasis on industrialization, new economic policy and diversification of occupations, a climate is being created inducing and encouraging development of entrepreneurship both among traditional and non-traditional groups.

Assumptions

In our approach to the problem of developing entrepreneurship in rural communities, a basic question needs to be answered. Does promotion and development entrepreneurship depend on inherent entrepreneurial ability or quality of individuals in a given community? If the answer is 'yes', and since the inherent factor is a constant in all societies, it ceases to be a significant change-inducing factor. We may grant that entrepreneurial ability as a consequence of social and environmental background is distributed in a given population to a smaller degree. Assuming that, how do we explain and account for the transformation of agrarian societies into industrial societies. Almost the whole western society and Japan are examples of this transformation. In the case of Japan, which lacks most of the natural material resources, it was the human resource, the quality of man and the entrepreneurial climate it has built up, that put it on the map of highly industrialized countries in the world. The kind of transformation that has taken place in once-agrarian countries leads us to make the following assumptions:

1. We assume that agrarian societies could be transformed into industrial societies. The chief element in this change process is 'time', provided that factors such as finance, technology, marketing of the product and organizational machinery – necessary concomitants of industrialization are taken care of.
2. We assume that physical and institutional infrastructure could be provided with comparative ease in developing entrepreneurship.
3. We assume that conditions could be created and

talented persons could be trained to become successful entrepreneurs.

We realize that the real problem we encounter in promoting entrepreneurship in the client community is the 'human factor', the individual in society, his network of relationships, his aspirational level, his attitudes and his group norms. This leads us to the study and understanding of the target community wherein we have to locate and develop entrepreneurship. We may call this a field approach or a total systems approach to the development of entrepreneurship.

This approach does not ignore the individual or selective approach by the use of projective tests and other psychological tools. Field approach is employed to see that the potential entrepreneur secures encouragement and support from the local institutions and environment of which he is a constituent. This modus operandi requires an understanding of the clientele community.

Aspects of the Client Community to be Studied

In the field approach, we take the entire community, be it a village, a cluster of villages, a mandal, a block, an occupational or a professional group as a unit of action. We study all aspects of the client system, physical, economic, human resources, cultural patterns, social, political and ecclesiastical structure, local institutions and institutional leadership. The study of the client system precedes the programmes related to entrepreneurial development. The data that are already available in respect to a unit of action (industrial potential surveys, lead bank surveys, techno-economic surveys, monographs, census reports etc.) will be made use of. The gaps in the aspects of the clientele group will have to be studied afresh. The major aspects to be studied of a client group may be described briefly.

Physical Conditions

It includes the physical resources that the area is endowed with, such as rainfall, terrain, quality of soil, the kind of farm activities that are in practice and enterprises that can be undertaken in the locality. This part of the study subsumes the industrial potential survey, as to how the people in the area have interacted with the given resources such as agricultural, horticultural, mineral, forest, marine etc., in the past and the resultant economic and industrial activities of the people and the related skills the people are proficient in. It will give us an idea of the ongoing activities, skills, attitudes, preferences on the part of the people and the kind of entrepreneurial activities that need modernization and innovative enterprises that could be introduced in the area.

Economic Structure of the Community

In the economic field, we study the types of production within the community, the organization of producing units, capital and labour resources, the ratio in which labour and capital resources are used, occupational structure, the functioning of the local marketing system, farm organization and land tenure. In this area, we also study the network of economic relationships the community has with the outside world.

Human Resources

Usually, the industrial potential surveys or techno-economic surveys that are undertaken by different agencies connected with industrial development pay a meagre attention to human resources. The requisite emphasis on human resources has not been there. The focus has been on economic resources and the potential thereof and not on the man and the group behind him. In the field approach, man or the human resource is at the centre. He is the starting point. Under the human resources, we go in for a census enumeration of literate population, skilled workers, technically qualified people, educated unemployed and various native skills available in the community. Another human resource is the leadership in the client group which is to be studied, promoted and utilized for introducing changes in the community. We will further deal with the resources aspect in the following pages.

Women constitute a potential human resource, untapped and underutilized and there is a need to make special efforts to promote entrepreneurship among women.

Cultural Patterns

A Community or a social group has history, a value system and tradition in terms of its occupation and or profession and choices or preference for economic activities. Individuals in the group when intend or motivated to take to some entrepreneurial activity look in for sanction and support from within the group. And so, in the field approach we make a historical analysis of the community and the patterns of diffusion and change. We look in for the direction and trend of change taking place in the community. The understanding of the cultural patterns of the group lends us some insight into the group's ethos and it will serve as a lead for further action in the filed of entrepreneurial development.

A study of the cultural patterns of the community takes us to the other intimately associated aspect of it – its social structure. In a general sense, entrepreneurship may be taken as an individual's free choice affair, but when the development of entrepreneurship comes to a rural-tribal community, it ceases to be purely an individual's affair. Here it is the group's choice. And hence the need for understanding the social structure of the group, the network of relationship between various sub-groups and institutions, and the dynamics of the group's influence over the individual and vice-versa.

In social structure of the community, we study the various constituents and the institutions in it. We may begin with the basic constituent of the society – the family, its structure, the decision-making process in the family, functional aspects of the family, and the typology of the families based on occupation and division of functions. Around the family is the kin-group with a set of consanguineous and affinal kin shaping, and influencing the individuals' decision making and behaviour. We study the kin-group in the client community, its structure and functions; intraclan, inter-clan, inter-tribal relationships and the role of certain kin in kinship circles.

Ethnic or tribal councils are significant and viable social institutions. We may say that tribal councils are almost universal among the tribes in the world. Despite the influence of Christianity, western styles of life and new politico-administrative institutions among certain tribal groups at the village-community level, the tribal councils still continue to be significant and functional in the life of a tribe. For instance in India, we find a high incidence of caste councils among the so-called lower castes. These are village or settlement-based and community-based in a region. Though caste councils are sporadic among middle-ranking and higher castes, we come across among some of them formal caste associations at town, district and regional levels. These caste associations (Sangham) are a kind of foundations to promote the education of the children and other welfare activities of the group: Wherever the caste-tribal councils obtain, whatever may be their strength and influence over the individual and group today, they are to be reckoned with as factors of influence. Positive and negative. Further, ethnic groups in a multi-ethnic community maintain or enjoy certain social balance, a particular group being predominant over the other, a particular group subservient to the other, a group dependent on another for leadership and guidance or a group blocking changes or progress in the other. In the Indian context, in the rural-tribal settings, inter-caste and caste-tribe relationships matter while attempting planned changes among them. This takes us to the study of caste-tribal council, its constitution and functions, the role and influence of the chief of the council, the council's influence over its members, and the degree of their dependence on the council in the matters economic and social. Further, we study the nexus of relationship between tribals and non-tribals.

The traditional village council (non-statutory) is another ancient social institution still in vogue in most of the villages. It chiefly deals with village affairs, celebration of local deities, sundry civil and criminal issues and divorce cases. The office of the chief of the traditional village council is either hereditary or elected. In some cases, the caste/tribal council itself functions as the traditional village council. Despite the advent of statutory village council in some communities, the traditional one, still enjoys status and influence over the local community. It is also to be studied and its relationship utilized for entrepreneurial development.

Besides the traditional institutions referred to above there are the modern associate or feeder organizations viz. Farmers' Forum, Youth Club, Women's Club, and recently organized users committees in the rural areas in Andhra Pradesh etc. which do matter as sources of influence, guidance and leadership in the entrepreneurial development programmes.

While studying the social structure of the client community we may also take into account the sacred institutions in the community, the temple, church, mosque and the sacred specialists or the religious leaders associated with the sacred institutions. Though their domain is religious/spiritual, they are significant people in the community. The entrepreneurship developer may work through them to clear the way and secure sanction and support for the potential entrepreneur to go about his enterprises.

Further, the schoolteacher also considered a friend, guide and philosopher to the local folk is a force to be reckoned with and he plays the role of a catalyst and his services may be utilized in the programme. Mention may be made of the local medical practitioner and he sometimes as a source of influence for the programmes.

The Political Structure of the Community

Entrepreneurial development or introducing of any change in the client group depends on the political leadership, power structure and the politico-administrative institutions at the village, and district levels. In other words, it has a bearing on the initiative, lead and encouragement given by the local leaders. Under the political structure we study the leadership patterns in the community. At the village level we can think of five different kinds of leaders:

(1) Hereditary leaders such as village level officials (in some cases), Chiefs of Caste-tribal councils and traditional village councils;
(2) Functional leaders who matter in specific areas;
(3) Sectional leaders who represent a class, tribe, a neighbourhood or a locality;
(4) Elected leaders of the statutory council and cooperative; and
(5) Professional leaders who are from outside the community, officials of different developmental agencies operating at the village level.

In the field approach we identify the different kinds of leaders in the community and work through them towards entrepreneurial development. Wherever the existing leadership is inadequate for entrepreneurial promotion, new organizations are to be developed. It may be noted here that a potential entrepreneur in the community may tend to look for some nodding approval and encouragement from the people whom he considers significant in the group. If the potential entrepreneur is convinced of his project or enterprise and if he can venture into action on his own, we need not bother about his environment and referent groups. But the situation in the rural and tribal areas is not so. Even if he is sure of his project and ready to take the risk and thinks that he could managc his enterprise, he has sometimes an obligation to seek the opinion and secure the approval from the significant members in the group. And so, the entrepreneurial developer enters the client system through the local leaders, expose to them the idea and prospects of some entrepreneurial activity, try to convince them so that either they encourage the potential entrepreneurs to go ahead with their ventures or do not stand in their way of movement. There is every likelihood of the local leaders sometimes playing a negative role.

On the institutional side in this field, the elected council at the village level, and village cooperative may be used as sources of information and as levers to influence potential entrepreneurs in the community.

In sum, it may be observed here, that institutions and organizations in the community may or may not have a direct bearing on or a functional relationship to entrepreneurship or economic activity. The tribal council, the caste council, the religious institutions for example, deal mostly with social aspects of the community, but as traditional and deeply rooted institutions, they influence and control the behaviour of people. The change agent tries to make use of these existing institutions and customs to communicate to the people. The leadership in all spheres of communal activity will be utilized to bring about desirable changes in the client community.

Barriers and Stimulants to Change

We may pose here a basic question. What is the supply position of entrepreneurship in developing countries today? The field experience and the rate of growth of entrepreneurship in the area of small-scale industries in most of the developing communities show that the supply of entrepreneurship (the number of entrepreneurs that take up some enterprise) in a given period of time is short of what the Industrial Development Agencies demand or in a position to support and promote. When there is spontaneous emergence or adequate supply of entrepreneurship, then the problem is to meet the new entrepreneurs' needs and providing them with physical and economic infrastructure to help them start and run their enterprises successfully. But unfortunately, the State as the chief promoter of entrepreneurship wants to, within the constraints of scarce resources, promote entrepreneurship. In this process of inducing entrepreneurship among the rural-tribal people we meet with shyness and resistance on the part of individuals and groups to go in for some enterprises. Entrepreneurial development is a basic complex change. It is met with different kinds of resistance and so it leads us to identify the barriers (areas of resistance) and stimulants (promotional factors) to change.

Foster (1973, 82-146) discusses at length the different kinds of barriers and stimulants to change. All societies are constantly in a state of relative tension. Each society can be thought of as a host to two kinds of forces – those that seek to promote change, and those that strive to maintain the status quo. These forces are locked in perpetual combat, the former trying to throw the latter off balance in order to gain ascendancy and the latter trying to prevent this from happening[1].

It is necessary on the part of the entrepreneurial development agency to identify the areas of resistance and the factors that contribute to change, here the entrepreneurial development.

We can think of three kinds of barriers – cultural, social and psychological. These are interrelated in any community. Here, basically we go in for an understanding of the value system of the client community, the factors that inhibit or promote change. On identifying the barriers, we work toward loosening their grip over the potential changees, simultaneously using the positive factors available from within the client group.

Despite barriers changes do take place in all spheres of life-religious, political, ideological, economic and social. When a group is faced with the prospect of change, there exists a balance of forces. On one side are those forces which are against change, viz., conservatism, apathy, fear and the like; on the other side are the forces for change such as dissatisfaction with the existing conditions, pride of new occupation, profession, new status or economic and social benefits that are anticipated in the new activity. Successful entrepreneurial development consists largely of choosing those enterprises where the balance is almost even and then trying to lighten the forces against change or to increase the factors that promote change.

Some of the positive factors that could be used for inducing change are motivating people to change through education and demonstration of the usefulness of the new activity, working on the desire of clients for economic gain and prestige, making use of a competitive situation obtaining in the client group, using the positive forces of authority and timing and sequencing the programmes in such a way that the total effort and process results in entrepreneurial development.

One crucial factor in working with tribal groups is their value system. The change agent needs to have a knowledge of the dominant values in the culture of the group, and working through these values, gradually bring about desirable changes in the group. The two constants to community wide changes are the tribe's identity and the tribe's moral beliefs. It is important for them to know that they can maintain their identity while making changes in their value system. It may be noted here that an important value of a tribal group is: "what they want to be".

Another important factor that is to be taken into account in our approach to bring about entrepreneurial development among tribal groups is to know what agencies have worked so far with them, what programmes have been attempted, and with what results. This leads us to an understanding of the tribe's perception, attitude and experience of the agencies and developmental programmes. For instance, community development agencies, Christian missionaries and several voluntary organizations have been working with tribal groups for their development for sometime now. An understanding of the tribals' reactions and experiences vis-à-vis the development or change agencies, whatever may be their sphere of activity, will give us an insight into their problem, and help us in avoiding the pit-falls. This will help us formulate our strategy in a manner that will make the process of change smooth and gradual.

Social change relating to entrepreneurial development is a complex phenomenon. It requires an integrated approach, a sustained effort on the part of the organizations that promote industrial development.

Problems

In developing entrepreneurship, we are confronted with several problems. The barriers we referred to earlier relate to the client community which are of general nature, but we may also look into some specific kind of problems in promoting entrepreneurship in rural communities.

The problems of entrepreneurial development are of individual, group and of institutional nature. Ultimately, it is the individual who has to take the initiative to decide on, start and manage his enterprise. He also needs the approval and support of his kin-group or community. The individual and the group constitute the client system. The institutions are to stimulate the client system towards entrepreneurial activity. The institutions are the various governmental and autonomous agencies that are concerned with entrepreneurial development. They are the source of several commissions and omissions that impede and slow down the process of entrepreneurial development. We may briefly look into some of the problems that centre around the individual, group and the institutions.

Individual

1. Lack of motivation.
2. Shyness and inhibition.
3. Ignorant of opportunities that he can avail himself of.
4. Lack of requisite managerial skills to start and manage his enterprise.
5. Lack of finance for initial investment.
6. Lack of familial and community support for his enterprise.
7. Is scared of the cumbersome and time-consuming process in establishing the enterprise.
8. Even if he starts the enterprise, he is not sure of sustained support from the promotional agencies in terms of timely and adequate credit and marketing of his products.

Group

1. Lack of awareness.
2. Preference for traditional occupations and professions.
3. Don't think of alternative avocations.
4. Apathy, sense of fear and insecurity towards government initiated and sponsored programmes.
5. Ignorant of their own potential: material and human.
6. Economically and politically weak.
7. Lack the freedom to choose and pursue their choices as a consequence to the power-sway of the local elite or the dominant caste.
8. They are more tradition-bound, and their values are, to continue with their institutionalized familial occupations.
9. They prefer to be what they want to be.

Institutional

1. Vague and unrealistic policies, and policies not supported by action.
2. Lack of teamwork and internal coordination in the agencies.
3. Lack of inter-agency coordination.
4. Bureaucratic style of working.
5. The functions of the personnel are not vested with the requisite power and authority.
6. Overlapping and duplication of functions both at the apex and operational levels.
7. A multiplicity of agencies performing a more or less similar task.
8. The field-level personnel are not supported in their promises and performance by the higher-ups in the organizations.
9. Lack of work motivation and commitment to their task.
10. Lack of relevant training on the part of the EDP personnel.
11. Lack of appreciation of the importance of human factors in development.
12. Lack of knowledge of technical know-how on the part of the personnel.

Other problems of entrepreneurial development are in respect of provision of infrastructural facilities, including finance and marketing.

The problems mentioned above though are stupendous and complex, are not insurmountable, an inter-disciplinary and multi-pronged approach is required to find solutions to these problems.

The problems listed above are not inherent or unchangeable. Through gradual entrepreneurial education, organizational and institutional support provided to the people in terms of motivation, incentives, infrastructural facilities, supply of certain inputs, credit and market support, the neo-entrepreneurs will gain confidence through their experience and success and they would be the factors creating congenial entrepreneurial climate. These problems are interrelated and they are to be looked at by the industrial development agencies and the community leaders. As mentioned above, entrepreneurial education through entrepreneurial activity and training provided to the development personnel and potential entrepreneurs would gradually create conditions favouring a positive change in the problems listed above.

Contributing Factors

In the foregoing discussion of field approach to entrepreneurial development, the focus and emphasis has been on the understanding of the client group and using the physical, economic and social resources. But when we look at the entire gamut of entrepreneurial development in terms of an action programme, we find four factors significantly contributing to entrepreneurial development. They are (1) Resources, (2) Organizations concerned with entrepreneurial development, (3) Infrastructure and (4) The entrepreneur. We may briefly examine them[2].

Resources

The resources of a client community are of two kinds: material and human. The material side consists of the natural resources, primary (nature given) and secondary (man-made) that the community is endowed with viz., climatic, geographic, agricultural, horticultural, mineral, marine, forest, animal, textile, etc. Here we examine how a given community living in a region has interacted with the resources it is endowed with. What kind of economic and industrial activities and associated skills have been generated as a result of people's interaction with the resources. This will give us an idea of the enterprises that the people in the area carry on with, and which have become a part of their culture. Based on the ongoing economic activities, we can demarcate the enterprises that need modernization and the areas in which innovation can be introduced based on the available resources. Here we move from the familiar (to the people) to the unfamiliar but associated entrepreneurial activities. What is envisaged here is that the entrepreneurship development agency should examine the potentialities of the material resources, in what manner they could be developed making use of the human material available in the target community.

A word here about analyzing resources. A resource is truly a resource in the economic sense only if it can help to produce something which somebody wants at a cost that he is willing to pay. In analyzing the resources of an area from the point of view of the area's suitability for various kinds of enterprises we cannot count among today's resources like timber located in the middle of the jungle or minerals so far underground or so far from transportation that the labour of getting them out-costs more than the materials are worth. The cost factor is all-important in appraising the industrial usefulness of an area's resources. The resources need not always be available in the immediate local community and they can be obtained from elsewhere so long the enterprise would be profitable. In fact, successful manufacturing areas rarely have a complete supply of the resources they use.

The existence of certain very evident resources, especially raw materials, within an area does not necessarily mean that enterprises based on these resources will be economical and beneficial in the area. Other resources not quite as evident may even more important than this raw material in determining the total cost of resources that go into the manufactured product, for example, technical labour, supervision and capital equipment. The total cost of all the input items is the important thing on the resource side. Also factors on the marketing side may pull enterprises to a location quite far from the origin of the most conspicuous material.

In the analysis of an area's industrial potential it is necessary to make a systematic inventory of al types of resources in the area that might be usable in some enterprises. The purpose is to determine the presence or absence of specific kinds of resources required in different kinds of enterprises and to ascertain their location, quality, abundance and probable cost. This information, when fitted together with information about the resource requirements of different industries and the market demand for the products of these industries, will enable an intelligent preliminary choice to be made of enterprises most suitable for promotion and development in the area.

The analysis of the resources can be conducted with almost any desired degree of comprehensiveness in detail. It can be merely a quick survey for general orientation based on information available in published materials or readily obtainable through quick surveys. Otherwise, it could be a comprehensive and detailed assessment of potential and usable resources based on industrial potential surveys.

Speaking of natural resources, we may think of a particular natural resource, how it is being utilized in a given area, in how many ways and how the same resource is utilized or processed in another area, or what kind of industries are based on a particular natural resource. Le us take for example, the coconut. It is cultivated in abundance in Assam (India), but it is chiefly used as a food article as it is and for ritual and ceremonial purposes, but whereas the same coconut is used in over a hundred different ways in Kerala. Coconut constitutes a base in Kerala's economy. Similarly bamboo is used in multiple ways for handicrafts in Tripura but its economic or industrial use elsewhere in India is limited to a couple of utilities. Another example is the abundant cultivation of ginger in Mizoram (India) but a total absence of any industry based on this resource in the state.

As we have pointed out earlier, industrial resources are not solely material. In the ultimate analysis it is the area's human and social resources – labour, management and organization are the key to successful industrial development. Japan and Switzerland are the most striking examples wherein the human resources have been the dominant factor in their tremendous advancement in industrial development[3].

It is the human resources that shape and control the material resources in industrial development. Ways can be found to overcome many material deficiencies if the human talents are highly developed and if environment of social, political and economic institutions is favourable. But if the human skills and institutions which make for effective industrial production are not available in an area, then no amount of material resources will bring a successful industrialization. It is the reason all the more to lay emphasis on entrepreneurship development which is the human side of industrial development.

In sum, it is the responsibility of the industrial development agencies to assess the resources available in the area, the possible industrial uses they could be exploited for and the kind of technology and infrastructure required for the newer uses of a resource and thus guide the potential entrepreneur and his group.

Organization

In a basic sense, entrepreneurial/small enterprise development is based on the individual initiative and when it is either lacking or meager, it is to be induced and promoted by the state. The situation in many of the Asian countries demand an induced entrepreneurial development and consequently we find several organizations figuring in the realm of entrepreneurial development. These are governmental, quasi-governmental and some are voluntary organizations. The nomenclatures, structure, functions, area of operation, size and number of such organizations vary from country to country. For instance, in a medium-sized state in India there are about twenty-five organizations or departments that are in a way connected with industrial development. The kind of their functional responsibilities and the degree of their involvement in industrial promotion vary. Again, India may be taken as an example which largely represents the role responsibilities of development organizations in other Asian countries. Based on the way the organizations are related to entrepreneurial/industrial development, they may be categorized into three groups.

The first group of organizations have a primary function and a direct responsibility in entrepreneurial development. They are chiefly organizations such as: (i) Directorate of Industries, (at the State level), (ii) District Industries Centres, and (iii) Small Industry Service Institutes (SISIs). These primary small industry development agencies are supposed to carry on both stimulatory and supportive kind of activities in respect to entrepreneurial development. It is the Directorate of Industries and more especially the District Industries Centres (DICs) which are charged with the task of identifying technically feasible and economically viable enterprises and identifying, motivating, selecting and training the small-scale entrepreneurs. They are to do the primary job of bringing in the entrepreneurs to the threshold of entrepreneurship. But in many of the cases, we find that the stimulatory part of their job is lacking and they are more at ease and successful in supportive kind of activities such as financial, infrastructural and technical. Concerted and persevering efforts are necessary in the filed of stimulatory activity in generating an entrepreneurial climate to bring in new entrepreneurs.

The second group of organizations which may be called secondary consisting of different corporations of finance, infrastructure, raw materials and machinery, banking and marketing mostly carry on supportive and sustaining kind of activities. These organizations are partly or distantly related to the primary function of development of entrepreneurship in the small-scale sector.

The basic task of finding an entrepreneur or responding to a potential entrepreneur lies largely on the first category of organizations.

We may call the third group of organizations as tertiary which are mostly governmental development departments or line agencies which are indirectly or remotely connected with industrial-entrepreneurial development. Departments of agriculture, horticulture, sericulture, sylviculture, pisciculture, animal husbandry, mineral, power, irrigation, highways, transport, communications, education, both basic and technical, textile and so on, fall under this category. Though these departments or agencies are not directly connected with industrial-entrepreneurial development, any improvement or expansion in them contributes to industrial development. They are the sources, feeder and support agencies which generate the potential for industrial development and ultimately contribute to its promotion.

The purpose of this brief preceding discussion is not just academic but it is to emphasize that the functions of organizations charged with industrial-entrepreneurial development are to be clearly demarcated and well defined in order to avoid or reduce overlapping or duplication of activities and ensure a synergetic effect on small industry promotion. A periodic examination of the functions of these organizations, their strengths, needs and shortcomings and the coordination among them is necessary. The whole promotional machinery is to be streamlined to deliver the goods, taking into account the institutional problems that have been listed out earlier. In other words, there is an imperative need to build up functional linkages and relative accountability among the three categories of organizations at the State (provincial), and the district levels, which should finally facilitate a rapid entrepreneurial development.

Infrastructure

We mostly relate infrastructure to physical facilities such as land, site, building, power, water, transport and communication facilities for starting an industry or an enterprise. Some of the infrastructural requirements are enterprise specific and some are of general nature and further we may consider the enterprise-specific infrastructural facilities as primary and other facilities such as schools, hospitals, housing and marketing for day-to-day requirements for the entrepreneurs, their families and workers as secondary. But the latter facilities gradually emerge and get established once the enterprises are started. In the induced and planned entrepreneurial-industrial development provision of infrastructural facilities is a necessary primary condition. Some of the facilities may be managed by the entrepreneurs themselves but some such as power, communications, sometimes, land and work-sheds are beyond the capability and affordability on the part of the small-scale entrepreneurs. Such a provision solely rests on the government development agencies.

Usually, infrastructure as pointed out above is mostly taken to be the physical and material facilities, but it constitutes only a part of the infrastructure in a comprehensive sense. We may think of two kinds of infrastructure for industrial-entrepreneurial development. They are: (a) physical and economic infrastructure; and (b) social infrastructure. The first one comprises the items noted above plus finance and marketing facilities. The social infrastructure consists of clear-cut industrial development policies, political commitment, an able and well-trained, motivated and committed industrial development personnel, a well-coordinated institutional support, positive attitudes, values and preferences of people and an entrepreneurial climate for developing entrepreneurship. Another significant social infrastructure is the entrepreneurial leadership in the target community. One could see that the provision of physical and economic infrastructure is in the hands of and under the purview of governmental agencies. Most of these agencies fall under secondary and tertiary organizations, discussed above. The state regulates the provision of these facilities. Again in a relative sense, the physical and economic infrastructure could be provided by the State with comparative ease. But the question arises: whose responsibility is it to educate the community and the potential entrepreneurs and generate an entrepreneurial climate? It falls largely on the primary set of organizations which have the task of creating the entrepreneurial climate in the communities. The role of other agencies in building up or providing the social infrastructure directly for entrepreneurial development is rather marginal and peripheral. However, it may be noted that the presence or provision of any physical infrastructure is a likely inducement to the population in the area to gradually venture into some enterprises. But there is no denial of the fact that physical and economic infrastructure is a necessary condition but not sufficient for entrepreneurial development. The physical and social infrastructure contributes to the growth of one another and they are complementary to each other, but undeniably it is the social infrastructure which is paramount. Once it is strong, once it is generated both on the part of the development agencies and the people, the physical and economic infrastructure would follow. It is here that the primary industrial development agencies are to play a vital role apprising the client community of what its resources and potentials are, in what direction and ways it could harness and develop its material and human resources, what local consumer needs and external market it could respond to, and the ways and the extent to which the agencies could extend their help to the community in entrepreneurial development.

The approach envisages an intimate and continuous dialogue between the clientele group and the development agencies. It is obvious that some of the material resources (finance, power, transport) are scarce and they are to be allocated judiciously for industrial development, but the more scarce material is the entrepreneur himself. How to identify him, how to motivate, encourage and assure him so that he takes the initiative and ventures into some entrepreneurial activity. What may be called the human-end product (the entrepreneur) in entrepreneurship is the function of the social infrastructure or the entrepreneurial climate. This leads us now to the entrepreneur.

In this context, we may briefly look into the concept and characteristics of successful entrepreneurs as defined and interpreted by social scientists.

Characteristics of Entrepreneurs

When we try to conceptualize the term entrepreneur, we note that though it originated in the west, it has undergone many changes from time to time. In the early 16th century, it was used to denote a dealer who bought a thing at a certain price and sold it at an uncertain price making a profit out of it. A sort of social stigma was attached to this concept. Towards 1961, Schumpeter redefined entrepreneur 'as an agent for change'.... an innovator. Subsequently, it took on the meaning of 'an efficient manager'. In the Indian context and in the context of other developing countries, however, a new concept emerged i.e., 'a person who undertakes to organize, own and run an enterprise'.

Various attempts have been made to understand the emergence of entrepreneurship. Sociologists analyse the phenomenon of entrepreneurship in terms of caste, social status, values, migration, family socialization pattern, etc. Psychologists attempt to explain it on the basis of personality traits or characteristics such as, need for achievement, creativity, propensity to take risk, independence and leadership. Economists consider it from the point of view of occupational background, access to capital, technical experience and insight to exploit economic opportunities and attain economic gains. From these different approaches, it becomes evident that a strict compartmentalized approach will not be of any help in understanding the emergence of entrepreneurship. Since entrepreneur is an individual who lives in a society, both individual and social factors have to be taken into consideration. Similarly, when we talk about a woman entrepreneur, she should be regarded, as an individual who takes up a challenging role in which she wants to adjust her personality needs, family life, social life and economic independence. Such an integrated approach may help us visualize this phenomenon more adequately.[4]

Some of the basic or inherent characteristics may be there in the beginning but as the entrepreneur moves forward with expansion and success in promoting his enterprise other kinds of characteristics are born or emerge in the individual. In a sense, it is a learning kind of thing on the part of the entrepreneur. As he moves forward the essential characteristics which stand for success in entrepreneurial activity emerge and grow over a period of time. The entrepreneur learns on the job, through his success and failure in his venture.

A review of the available literature on the factors contributing to successful entrepreneurship supports the contention that certain personality characteristics are associated with successful entrepreneurs.

McClelland and his associates have reported that entrepreneurs are characterized by (1) unusual creativeness (2) propensity of risk-taking and (3) strong need for achievement. They have also reported that persons high on need for achievement have some specific characteristics. While research has established that achievement motive contributes largely to entrepreneurship, it has also been observed that though achievement helps one to become an entrepreneur, it is not the only factor in making him successful. It is also found that an entrepreneurial manager should have a high need for influencing others (need for power), a low need for affiliation and a large capacity to discipline one's self (inhibition). An entrepreneurial manager is also found to possess flexibility in style and displays high psychosocial maturity. Further, it is also to be noted that entrepreneurs decision to start an industrial unit was not influenced by level of education, income differences, risk-taking ability and need for achievement, but rather an ambition, social prestige, social responsibility, economic gain and perception of demand for a particular product.

The most significant characteristics associated with entrepreneurs are need for achievement, support, independence and leadership. On the basis of the information given by participants of a symposium on Development of Entrepreneurship, the following appear to be the characteristics:

1. Perseverance and hard work
2. Risk-taking ability
3. High aspiration
4. Willingness to learn
5. Dynamic and creative
6. Adoptable
7. Innovative
8. Good Salesmanship
9. Ability to make friends and overcome losses
10. Initiative
11. Self-confidence
12. Will-power
13. Determination to succeed

14. Pleasing personality, composed and tactful
15. High integrity
16. Responsible
17. Excellence in work
18. Perception of time

The research available clearly reveals that an entrepreneur is certainly different from the non-entrepreneur in terms of his psychological and social dispositions. The available evidence only points to some dominant traits in successful entrepreneurs; the optimal combination of characteristics needed for success has not yet been arrived at.

Further, some researchers have come up with another set of characteristics listed below:

1. Drive
2. Self-confidence
3. Long-term involvement
4. Money as a measure
5. Persistent problem-solving
6. Goal setting
7. Moderate risk-taking
8. Dealing with failure
9. Use of feedback
10. Taking initiative and seeking personal responsibility
11. Use of resources
12. Competing against self-imposed standards
13. Internal locus control
14. Tolerance of ambiguity and uncertainty

Further, the following 8 aspects are described as entrepreneurial role requirements.

Eight Entreprenurial Role Requirements

1. Accommodation to venture
2. Total immersion and commitment
3. Creativity and innovation
4. Knowledge of business you want to launch
5. People and team building
6. Economic values
7. Ethics
8. Integrity and reliability

By and large, characteristics that differentiate entrepreneurs from non-entrepreneurs are: confidence, perseverance, determination, hard work,, general knowledge, dynamism, risk taking, optimism, technical knowledge, information gathering ability and initiative.

Entrepreneur

The entrepreneur may be likened to the fourth factor in production-organization (the rest being land, labour and capital). He is as significant as 'organization' in production. Interestingly, these two factors – entrepreneur and organization are intimately associated. What happens when you have the required resources, promotional organizations, physical and economic infrastructure and lack the entrepreneur? To a considerable extent, this is the situation in many of the Asian countries. We are looking for the right kind of entrepreneurs. They are not born as such, but they could be made as such.

There are two kinds of entrepreneurs, the ongoing and the potential ones. The ongoing entrepreneurs are those who are in the field already, some who have taken to entrepreneurship on their own in a spontaneous sense and others who have been induced to this activity. The industrial development agencies in their initial enthusiasm and under pressure of targets for putting a certain number of individuals in the field of entrepreneurship, brought in some entrepreneurs and fulfilled their paper targets. But a considerable number of them are left in the lurch. They are at various stages with varying problems struggling to reach the take-off point in respect to their enterprises. Some are struggling to complete the formalities for final registration of their units, some are held up for want of adequate raw material, working capital, or the requisite machinery and equipment, some waiting for power, some finding it difficult to market their products, and some being tossed over for X or Y licence to go about their business. In a word the entrepreneur who is already in the field faces some problems. Unless the industrial development agencies assess the problems of the ongoing entrepreneur and assist him in ameliorating his condition, we cannot go in for a new entrepreneur. Every satisfied and well-served entrepreneur is a positive force in generating a conducive entrepreneurial climate which in turn motivates, induces and encourages a potential entrepreneur to enter the field.

On the other hand a dissatisfied, not-very-much-cared for left-in-the-lurch-entrepreneur is a potential source of demotivation and discouragement to the new entrepreneur. We do not advocate here that the entrepreneur should be spoon-fed and that he should be a protected child. But he needs a prop in the initial stages in his growth and development. It is not wrong to say that a well-attended to and successful entrepreneur is equal to several professional agents of entrepreneurial development when it comes to motivating people to take to some entrepreneurial activity. If we take care of the ongoing entrepreneurs it would be easy for us to bring the new entrepreneurs into the field.

Identifying, selecting, motivating and training the new entrepreneurs constitute a major task for the entrepreneurial development agency. The promotion or development of entrepreneurship may be undertaken in five phases and we may briefly look into each phase.

Phase I

The first phase relates to the basic physico-psycho-socio-cultural and economic study and understanding of the area where the programme is to be implemented as detailed earlier. Industrial potential survey focusing both on material and human resources of the area will be the basis, based on which feasibility studies are to be prepared for each viable candidate industry covering technical, economic, financial, demand and marketing aspects of the enterprise. Such a study will serve the purposes of developing an action – programme for identifying viable enterprises either resource-based, demand-based or footloose and potential entrepreneurs.

Here the emphasis is to be laid on starting small-scale enterprises where the people are living now, cheap enough so that they can be created in large numbers without calling for an unattainable level of capital formation and imports, with relatively simple production methods, so that the demands for high skills are minimized not only in the production process itself but also in matters of organization, raw material supply, financing, marketing, and the production mainly based on local materials and for local use[4]. With such a purpose, initially to make use of the local resources and the local consumer demands, we are not to look for highly talented, sophisticated entrepreneurs, but people with some interest, with some investment capacity, who are partially unemployed or totally unemployed, people who are looking for some avenues to increase their income, people who are likely to take certain amount of risk in venturing into some entrepreneurial activity. Highly achievement-oriented individuals seek opportunities, create conditions, need less propping and venture into industrial activity. Such people can take care of themselves with minimal support from the development agencies. But our task is to gradually shape the common man into an entrepreneur. Against this objective, potential entrepreneurs in the client community may be drawn from the following segments: (a) artisan groups, (b) high school dropouts, (c) educated unemployed, (d) merchant-trading groups, (e) farmers who are in the process of or likely to partly shift to some enterprise, (f) farm-labourers who are likely to take some small business or enterprise and (g) woman entrepreneurs.

In the first phase as a constructive approach and strategy, the entire client community is to be exposed to the idea of entrepreneurship development. No segment in the community should feel it is isolated or ignored and the programmes are meant only for certain sections. The general exposure of the entire client community to the idea and prospects of entrepreneurship will create awareness, interest among them which will gradually motivate the potential entrepreneurs to move into action.

The creating of awareness, preparing the community, motivating and facilitating some individuals in the community to take decisions, secure the sanction of their families and opinion leaders, that is cutting through the socio-cultural barriers may be done through entrepreneurship-extension education through individual and group methods and through the mass media, always reinforced by personal contacts and counselling. One of the foremost things in the process is raising the aspiration level of the people. They have to be told convincingly of the social and economic advantage inherent in industrial activity. The rise in their standard of living as a result of successfully running an enterprise has to be projected and brought home to them. These ends can be achieved through what is called 'intensive campaign' technique[5]. It is a package of activities comprising an industrial potential survey, publication of the survey findings, holding of small group meetings explaining to people in the community, the kind of enterprises that are feasible in the area, the requirements for starting the recommended enterprises, who can undertake them, the kind of assistance they can expect from the various industrial development agencies and in such a type of campaign, the industrial development personnel and the selected local and political leaders will be involved. The inclusion of influential local and district leadership would build and reinforce confidence and morale on the part of the potential entrepreneurs in the local community.

It may be in order to mention here the steps that may be taken in identifying the viable enterprises and potential entrepreneurs in the client community.

The Steps

1. Identification of the natural resources the community is endowed with.
2. Listing out the ongoing economic and industrial activities carried on by the community based on the resources at its command.
3. Listing out the associated skills available with the members of the community (or the target population).
4. Listing out the kind of new enterprises technically feasible and economically viable that could be promoted based on the available resources and skills.
5. Listing out the existing and required infrastructural facilities in view of the new enterprises suggested.
6. Appraising the client system of:
   - the kind of new enterprises they could take to;
   - the financial, managerial, technical and marketing requirements in respect to each enterprise;
   - the kind of people who can take up the suggested enterprises;
   - specifying in general the qualifications, personal aptitude and abilities and investment

capacity on the part of the prospective entrepreneurs.

7. Appraising the client system of:
   - the kind of help the multiplicity of agencies connected with entrepreneurial development can extend to the prospective entrepreneurs, which may cover questions like What? When? To what extent? How often? To what purpose? etc.
8. Final identification of potential entrepreneurs and matching their interest with the enterprises.

A word on identification of potential entrepreneurs. Depending on the extent of response, the level of candidates, the potential and the capabilities that are sought among the candidates, the optimum number that the resources and schemes could support and sustain, one may go in for psychological tests such as: (a) Achievement Motivation, (b) Risk Taking, (c) Value Orientation, (d) Adoption Propensity, (e) Level of Aspiration, etc. These projective or psychological instruments are rather complementary to the information provided on the application that the candidate fills in, concerning his family background, his educational attainment, work experience, his choice of enterprise, his experience if any in entrepreneurial activity, his investment capacity and his socio-cultural affiliations.

Importantly, the means employed for identification are the application, interview and if need be, the tests mentioned above. One invaluable resource for identifying potential entrepreneurs is the client community itself.

When it comes to identification and selection of potential entrepreneurs, more often, we ignore the local community. The people in the local community may not be conversant with attributes or traits that are contributive to successful entrepreneurship, may not have any idea and understanding of some of the projective techniques used sometimes to measure the strength of need for achievement, value orientation, risk taking and adoption propensity on the part of the prospective entrepreneurs, but they will have a fairly good understanding of the people in the community as to who would do what and to what extent one would fair well and who is innovative and who would manage an activity effectively. This kind of knowledge of individuals is based on the day-to-day observations irrespective of an individual's profession or occupation. And so, one can, to a large extent depend upon and make use of the local community, the small groups in the community for identifying and selecting potential entrepreneurs. As we have pointed out earlier, once the viable enterprises have been identified based on industrial potential survey, one may list out the personal requirements that one is looking for or in other words the kind of people who can answer these requirements in order to respond to the recommended enterprises. Once this information is communicated to the community through individual contact and small group meetings, it is possible for the local community to indicate the names of individuals who are likely to be successful as small entrepreneurs. This could be in addition to individuals themselves coming forward to take to some entrepreneurial activity. The stress here is that the local community could well serve as a source and guide in selecting potential entrepreneurs.

Phase II

It consists of training various categories of personnel who will be involved in locating and developing entrepreneurship in the area under question. A general but comprehensive course of three to four weeks is to be prepared keeping in view the earlier work-experience of the personnel. The participants will be familiarized with the prospects and problems of entrepreneurial development in the area of operation. Further, the programme will include inputs on feasibility studies, techno-economic surveys, preparation of industrial profiles, entrepreneurial development, marketing, etc. (See Appendix for a model training programme). Representatives of financial institutions in the area may be associated with the training programmes. By the end of the second phase, the agency will be in readiness with the knowledge of the area of operation, and also trained personnel to select and train entrepreneurs.

Phase III

It consists of selection and training of potential entrepreneurs in the client community by the agency. The training of the entrepreneurs will be arranged at district or sub-district headquarters. The personnel of the development agency who have already undergone training will conduct the training programme. The duration of this training may range from two to six weeks. It depends on funds and the category of candidates trained. In some cases, inclusive of in-plant studies, the courses are run for 14-20 weeks. The training inputs will include elements that would enable the entrepreneur-trainees acquire basic knowledge, skills and motivation to establish their units and manage them successfully. The training will be both theoretical and practical. Towards the end of their training, the candidates will go back to their villages and make a mini-market survey concerning their enterprises, or prepare project reports. They bring back the field data, and work these into project proposals for securing funds from financial institutions.

Phase IV

It consists of the agency collaborating with other functionally associated agencies to guide and help the trained entrepreneurs in establishing their enterprises, either individually, in small groups or through industrial cooperatives.

Phase V

In the final phase, which will be taken up after a lapse of

six months after the training of entrepreneurs, the training programme will be evaluated. The objective of the evaluation is to find out as to how many of the trained entrepreneurs were able to establish their enterprises and the problems they faced in setting up their ventures. In the light of this experience the training programme for other batches of entrepreneurs will be restructured if necessary.

Support for marketing of products

More often, the entire success of small enterprise promotion in rural-tribal communities hinges on marketing of products of the neo-entrepreneurs. In the initial stages and also, in some cases on the sustained basis, the promotional agencies should help in marketing of the products. The induced and emerging entrepreneurs may be too weak to organize the marketing of their products on their own. The promotional agencies may go in for internal or external export of the indigenous handicrafts and products through a network of marketing channels. Such a support would sustain the ongoing entrepreneurs and also motivate the potential entrepreneurs to ventures into the field.

In sum, we may say that the women constitute a significant segment in the population. Till now, they have not been the focus of entrepreneurial development. The need today to develop entrepreneurship among them is imperative, the development of entrepreneurship among men and women being simultaneous. The question of EDP among women is a question of choice, priority and organization.

REFERENCES

1. Somsak Tambunlertchai and Utis Kaothien, "Thailand's Industrial Transformation and Regional development: Situational Review and Policy Evaluation" (Paper presented at the International Conference on Industrial Transformation and Regional Development in an Age of Global Interdependence, 18-21 September, 1989, Nagoya and Tokyo), p.1.

2. United Nations Economic and Social Commission for Asia and the Pacific (UN/ESCAP), *Entrepreneurship Development for Small and Medium-Scale Industries in Selected Developing Countries* (New York, 1989), pp.2-3.
3. Dr. Asghari Mohiuddin, Entrepreneurship Development Among Women – Retrospects and Prospects, SEDME, Hyderabad, Volume X, Number-1, March, 1983.
4. Medhi Krongkaew, 'The Development of Small and Medium Scale Industries in Thailand" in *Asian Development Review*, Vol.6, No.2, (Manila: ADB, 1988), p.90.

10

Role of Women in Socio-Economic Development

There are two issues of global nature or call them problems or challenges, one currently facing the entire mankind and the other a few societies or distinct cultures; environment and gender development. Environment encompasses what man has done to nature, the way he has exploited, fouled and abused it resulting in threats to the health and survival of future generations of mankind and other species – plants and animals which have been a source of man's survival thus far. The gender question revolves around what man has done or doing to woman, the other half of the mankind. The environment problem is physical, economic, industrial, technological, avarice and senseless short-sightedness on the part of the modern man whereas the gender question is complex steeped deep in history influenced by prejudices, discriminatory religious and social codes of behaviour imposed on women, and man's audacity in arrogating to himself a superior status and treating the woman his subordinate. The status, freedom and respectability accorded to and enjoyed by women in society is a mark of wisdom and civilization of that particular society. We can conceive of a continuum wherein at one end of the continuum women enjoy equal rights, respectability and are equal partners in economic pursuits and social positions and at the other end, one finds women treated inferior to man, deprived of freedom as enjoyed by man. The gender question is a perennial question. The world body may declare equal opportunities and rights for women and men but it is the nation states and the religious and ethnic groups that have to translate such a principle into reality. One is forced to come up with a statement that so long a man does not treat a woman his equal, he is not civilized. Looked at from any angle, political, economic, social, religious, spiritual or moral, woman is an equal partner and should be an equal partner in all pursuits of life.

The purpose here is not to carry on the debate over feminine rights but to look into women's participation in development activities especially in entrepreneurship development. Their participation, the variety, extent, and mode of participation and the activities in which they participate is influenced by religious sanctions (mostly mistaken and misinterpreted by ignorant and selfish men), economic conditions, ethnicity, occupations, professions, social status and personal endowments like literacy, knowledge and skills. Of all the forces that keep women off the economic and social activities as equal partners is religion. Unfortunately and lamentably sanctions and tenets of some religions are unquestionable. That is, you cannot question the logical inconsistency and irrationality in those sanctions and tenets. It is highly sensitive and explosive.

The women in such religious groups, in most of the cases are confined to their homes just to carry their housekeeping, child-bearing and child rearing roles. Quite lamentable, what forces, what authority, what revolution would emancipate the women in these groups so that they contribute economically, benefit socially, grow individually and advance spiritually?

In order to make women as equal participants in all development activities, it is not enough that you bring in constitutional and legislative measures ensuring equal rights and opportunities for women, but what is wanted is creating a right type of awareness and change of attitude both on the part of men and women, and dissolving of age-old arbitrary, deeply crusted prejudices and biases against women.

As democracy is a desirable system of government, women's participation in all development activities is a desirable thing. Everything about women is not dark and dismal. They have been in the forefront in several fields and emerging as substantive partners in economic and social activities. Woman has been an economic, political and ritual partner with man, only in certain designated activities which vary from society to society. We may have a brief historical perspective of women and society.

Women and Society

In the historical evolution of mankind, woman has been an economic partner to man, besides her biological and social roles. It is said that it was the woman who discovered the possibility of domesticating plants for food and beginning the rudiments of hoe-culture. It was so when man was in the hunting and gathering stage. Since then, through agricultural and industrial revolutions, she has been an economic partner in the family of man. She started the enterprise of food cultivation and later adopted bartering the food articles for other necessities of life.

Over a period of time, certain patterns of life and the division of labour changed. She worked on the farm, kept the house and reared the children. Further, in the Indian (Hindu) context, when social stratification (caste-system) and occupations became institutionalized, the womenfolk confined themselves to the chores assigned to them and assumed by themselves in their respective occupations or professions. Again over a period of time, class distinctions emerged, accompanied with restrictions, norms or social sanctions and certain freedoms enjoyed by women. In the general society, high and middle class women tended to confine themselves to the biological and social roles of rearing children and keeping the house. But in the case of economically lower class women, besides their bio-social roles, they had equal or more than equal share in the economic activities of the family.

In the recent past, the increase in women's education, industrialization, urbanization, social and occupational mobility, the emergence of nuclear families, westernization, politico-social movements and changes in the value system, some educated women have taken to certain careers. Some compelled by economic necessity, have taken to small business and trade (Setty, 1985).

Women's Participation in Development

Importance and Role

Historically, women have at all times and in all types of economies made a substantial contribution to the production and distribution of their community's resources. The role of women in the development process has been widely investigated in different cultures of various countries. By now, it has become an established fact that women have been stepping out of their traditional status of being confined to the environment of their homes. They perform dynamic roles in enabling their society to advance towards development and prosperity. Women's productive efforts and their capability to shape family life and thus society have convinced more and more men of the need to recognize women's equal right and status (Shahand *et at.*, 1986).

In an ESCAP document (1989) containing an analysis of the women's contributions to the economy, it is stated that:

"Women's participation" in so-called informal sector activities such as petty trade, brokering, shop-keeping and other small-scale enterprises help to lubricate the developing commercial market economy, performing many functions which are not profitable enough to attract or support larger modern businesses, yet are necessary to serve the local consumption needs of the population at large, particularly lower income groups. It is significant that women are frequently the only members of the indigenous population who can compete with minority immigrant groups in such activities.

Thus women's employment or self-employment in market production makes an important direct contribution to economic growth, and particularly to the development of certain "modern sectors" and industries which could not survive without them and have proved especially important to the balance of payments. But women's non-market activities also play an important though largely unrecognized and unrewarded role.

Women's subsistence agricultural production, for example, subsidizes many rural workers' families and thus lowers the real wage that employers have to pay them, increasing the surplus available for reinvestment and growth. It includes not only the cultivation of staple grains, but also poultry rearing, vegetable farming, collection of forest products and other supplementary activities. Women's craft production for the household use has the same effect. And in many areas, the time-consuming and backbreaking tasks of fetching and carrying water, and gathering firewood, are assigned to women, as is household marketing and the transport of goods often for considerable distances on foot. Child rearing, including the teaching of household and farm production tasks, which largely devolves on women, daily housekeeping and cooking, and general household management, including budgeting and financial management, complete the wide range of activities which comprise women's reproductive duties.

It has become common to describe women as invisible to depict a situation in which planners of development strategies have failed to pay serious attention to the differential roles and functions of women. The differentiation between men and women's role and work may be classified as follows (ESCAP, 1989).

(a) *In agricultural process:* A sexual division of labour assigns to women specific tasks. For instance, in rice cultivation, women are involved to a greater extent than men in transplanting, weeding, harvesting and in some post-harvesting process.

(b) *In industry:* Women have provided the bulk of the labour force in light industries which in many developing countries have spearheaded industrialization programmes, eg., industries such as electronics, textiles and garments, food processing and pharmaceutical. Within this industry there is an uneven distribution of sexes within employment hierarchies, women dominating the lower wage, unskilled or semi-skilled production process. This means that women are vulnerable to particular occupational hazards in the operations in which they are concentrated.

(c) *In domestic roles:* In addition to the unsubstitutable function of child bearing, women are the main providers of basic family needs: food, water, clothing, domestic energy and maintenance of family shelters. They bear the major responsibility of child-care, thus functioning as the principal transmitters to future generations of attitudes and values. In their hands is the burden of the health and well-being of present, past and future generations of the enumerated labour force. The performance of these tasks, particularly in rural areas, is inefficient in the use of resources of time, labour and energy. It is these talks which account for much of women's labour, resulting in an imbalance in which women's work-hours exceed those of men.

In maintaining and nurturing the family, women frequently find ways to add to household income. Their entry or exist from market activities are sometimes flexible, dependent on contingency. This activity occurs mostly in the "informal sector" and is commonly small-scale, requiring low levels of skills, and earning low returns.

In most parts of the developing world, the major benefits of economic growth have failed to reach women. Women have also paid a steep price for the modest glimmerings of modernity that have reached them. In different places around the world, women's labour obligations have multiplied, their independent resources have shrunk, and their autonomy and cultural worth have often diminished as development has unfolded.

Failure to develop women's resources and skills undermines development as a whole. Women's labour, whether paid or unpaid, is essential. Women everywhere are primary caregivers for their families and children. Decisions women make and skills women have materially affect the health, nutrition, attire, cleanliness and emotional equanimity of all family members. With the sharpening recognition that development hinges on the fulfillment of basic human needs and the quality of life, as well as on the transfer of capital and technology, women have at last found their way onto the international development agenda, though the resolution of these problems has barely taken shape (March and Taqqu, 1986).

Manifestation of Women's Problems

Women's special problems manifest themselves across the board but can in large measure be traced to three main areas: the data base for development planning; education and training including extension services; and technological change, not least its social implication.

In the bookkeeping system of development plans, women (and girls) have generally been seen as consumers, not as producers. Moreover, women's work in particular rural women's work, is often not counted statistically.

A primary reason for not including women's work in the computation of the gross national product (GNP) is that so much of it is performed in the family setting. Additionally, it is often of a subsistence nature. On both counts such work, when performed by women, tends to be excluded from official statistics. In many countries such work is recorded, in many others it is not fully recorded or omitted entirely. The reason for non-recording is usually that the societal ideal is that women should not perform such work, in particular, not fieldwork. It should be done by men or, in parts of India e.g., by hired lower-caste women (UNDP, 1980).

Because so much of development efforts has been deficient in its attempts to reach the common people, there is now wide spread agreement that the revised development strategies need to be broad-based and people-oriented. For such strategies to succeed, they must combine two basic principles. On the one hand they must provide for a wide distribution of benefits and services like health care, education and training, productive employment, credit, marketing, fuel, water, sanitation and protection against environmental degradation, in particular the loss of cultivable land through erosion. On the other hand, to make such policies a realistic alternative, a greater mobilization of people as productive agents must be achieved. Their labour, capability, motivation and enterprise in bettering their own conditions must be stimulated. In both respects, women's role in development, not least in rural areas, deserves special attention (UN, 1982).

UNDP (1980) summarized its evaluation of the rural women's participation in development reaching the conclusion:

"If the poor are to be given a fair opportunity to participate in the development effort, there is every reason to consider the participation by women as full and equal partners as a major factor in this effort. In other words, as there are two systems of social stratification, there are two problems of integration, that of the poor and, especially within but also beyond this problem, that of women. No strategy is going to succeed within the foreseeable future".

In India, it has been observed that in Kaira district of Gujarat, where the cooperative movement started, women's status has not improved as a result. While in the past, production and marketing were in women's hands, in the new modern dairy industry management its rewards have been taken over by men.

"Of the more than 2000 persons employed in the Amul (Anand Milk Union Limited) complex, there is only one woman veterinarian and a few telephone operators and secretaries. Not even one woman has been given the mastery over the new technology that has taken over the women's traditional tasks of making butter and cheese". (Brandtzaeg, 1979).

With respect to membership in the cooperative, data from 481 societies show that women only constitute from 2 to 15 per cent of the members. Moreover, the majority of woman members are successors to husbands who have died or are dummy members to enable individual families to control a larger number of shares. With the exception of one all-women society, all the other societies are run by men (Brandtzaeg, 1979).

In the less developed countries the labour force is more evenly distributed among the three categories of workers: employers and own-account workers (self-employed), employees (wage labourers) and unpaid family workers. The distribution of female workers tended to follow this pattern, with the notable variation of a larger proportion of women than of men being employed as unpaid family workers. Indeed, in most cases, including in the more developed countries, females accounted for disproportionate share, often a large majority of the unpaid family workers. Conversely, they accounted for a disproportionately small share of employers and own-account workers. In short, women tend to be underrepresented at the higher and over-represented at the lower levels of the labour force (ESCAP, 1989). Let us look at the situation in India as an illustration.

Experience of Women's Participation in Development in India

India's economy and also the status of her women remained stagnant for a long time. They started to change for the better slowly with the advent of the British education system but women are still victims of the basically exploitative mechanism operating against them. In fact, like the resulting development pattern of the Indian economy, the Indian woman has suffered a dualism in status on her way to play effectively her economic and social role (Sen, 1989).

Shyam (1989) in his study of the India framework for Rural Development stated that:

> "Women labour force constitutes about half of the unorganized labourers in rural areas. In addition to their 10-12 hours per day engagement in household work, women's role in agriculture, animal husbandry and other allied activities is very important. A large number of women labourers are engaged in marginal occupations to supplement the family income. Their contribution, however, is yet to be quantified in terms of working hours as well as in terms of income generated. The green revolution has aggravated the plight of woman labourers in rural areas".

In the history of the country's planned development, women have remained invisible except for the Sixth Plan in which for the first item, a chapter was devoted to the integration of women into the development process. The main challenge in women's development has been the means of mainstreaming women into the development process.

Indian planners (Planning Commission, 1985) have recognized the fact that:

> "The Green Revolution has led to increased demands for casual labour, dispossession of small land holders from their land and consequently, pushing out women from such small land holdings to become wage earners. Though many of the tasks performed by males are mechanized, women continue to toil in labour intensive jobs like rice plantation, cleaning and storage of grain in post-harvest operations, picking of leaves, fruits and hand shelling of groundnut and picking of seeds etc. Women got limited job opportunities in modern occupations / trade as they do not have access to the training required for new technologies. In many areas where multiple crops are grown, the workload of women has increased. In industry, women continue to be employed mostly on unskilled jobs. The average earning of a regular salaried woman worker continues to be less than that of a man".

Conclusion

Empowering, enabling and facilitating women to participate in all development programmes is a stupendous task in view of differential freedom and status enjoyed and the roles performed by women and the importance accorded to them across the diverse societies in the world. It is a task so massive and the efforts should also be multi-dimensional and at multi-level wherein the educational institutions, the media, the writers, leaders of all description, the extension personnel and above all the enlightened public should carry on the job of bringing about a change in the value orientations and the psyche of both men and women that the women are not only biological partners in procreation, but equal partners in social and economic development.

REFERENCES

Brandtzaeg, B.(1979), "Women, Food and Technology: The Case of India", *Economic and Political Weekly*, Vol.XIV, No.47.

ESCAP (1989), *"Status of Women in Asia and the Pacific Region"*, United Nations Economic and Social Commission for Asia and the Pacific, Bangkok, p.113.

March, K.S. and R.L. Taqqu (1986), *"Women's Informal Associations in Developing Countries: Catalyst for Change?"*, Westview Press, Boulder; p.154.

Planning Commission (1985), *Seventh Five Year Plan*, vol.I and III (1985-90), Government of India, New Delhi.

Sen, R.K.,(1989), "The Nature of Women's Role in Economic Development". In Mahajan (ed.) *Women's Contribution to India's Economic and Social Development*, Deep and Deep Publishers, New Delhi; pp.58-73.

Setty,E.D.(1985), "People's Participation in Rural Development: A Critical Analysis", *The Indian Journal of Social Work*, Vol.XVI, No.1; pp.73-85.

Shahand, A., M.A. Tekie and K.E. Weber (1986), "The Role of Women in Slum Improvement: A comparative Study of the Squatter Settlements at Klong Toey and Wat Yai Sri Suphan in Bangkok, Thailand, *Studies on Human Settlements Development in Asia*, HSD Research Report 10, Asian Institute of Technology, Bangkok; p.161.

Shyam, R. (1989), *"India's Framework for Rural Development"*, Commonwealth Publisher, New Delhi, p.112.

UNDP (1980), "Rural Women's Participation in Development", *Evaluation Study No.3*, United Nations Development Programme, New York, p.225.

United Nations (1982), *"Poverty, Productivity and Participation: An Analysis of some Recent Experiences", Bangkok: UNESCAP.*

11

Entrepreneurial Initiatives by Women Self-Help Groups in Andhra Pradesh

The following details speak of some attempts made by the Government of Andhra Pradesh in organizing and helping the women folk below poverty line to collectively venture into some income-generating activities.

This chapter covers programmes under DWCRA and some entrepreneurial initiatives undertaken by some NGOs like Project Shakti of Hindustan Lever Limited, Padmavathi, Rashtriya Seva Samithi, Swayam Krushi, etc.

The main objective of the programme for the Development of Women and Children in Rural Areas (DWCRA) is to improve the lot of rural women through the creation of income-generating activities in a district. It is a programme sponsored by the Government of India. Districts to be covered are selected keeping in view low-literacy rate and high infant mortality rate. It envisages formation of groups of 15-20 rural women each for carrying on income-generating activities. Each group is sanctioned a 'revolving fund' of Rs.15,000/-. In the case of states, the amount is shared equally by the Centre, and State Government and the UNICEF while in the Union Territories, the Central Government bears Rs.10,000/- per group and the balance is borne by UNICEF. UNICEF also bears the expenditure on staff component which is fully reimbursed. The programme has made considerable progress since it was launched in 1982.[1]

Availability of credit is the basic requirement to any citizen, more so, to a poor person. Credit, should be timely as well as easily available. Formal institutions, including nationalized banks are unable to meet the micro credit requirements of the poor people, as normally credit for income generation has been institutionalized rather than micro credit for various purposes. This has left poor persons with no option except to depend on moneylenders for credit. Moneylenders with abundant common sense offer timely – but an exploitative credit, which acts as a poverty trap for the poor. Various studies have shown that in rural India, a person taking credit from moneylender for health or for a marriage sinks down the below poverty line.

Poverty as we understand is a complex phenomena and it cannot be solved only by providing income generating assets but through comprehensive human resource development of poor person enabling him/ her to meet various needs.

Self-Help is the best approach

Experiments in various developing countries proved that the poor can be helped by organizing them into small self-help groups. Hence women self-help groups (SHGs) have become the ray of hope to the development personnel. Government of Andhra Pradesh having realized the power and potential of self-help groups in alleviating the poverty has started mobilizing the poor women into self-help groups. It is a unique step the government has taken in mobilizing the poor into self-help groups.

A typical SHG constitutes 10-15 poor women below poverty line. Members of SHGs save equal amounts as decided in their groups. The movement of SHGs started with a slogan 'save a rupee a day'. Of course there are number of groups who save more than Rs.2/- or Rs.3/- a day.

Starting of SHGs

Once the members come together, they open an account either in a bank or post office in the area of the group. The group authorizes any of the members (elected as group leaders) to operate the group account.

Group processes

Thrift is a good entry point and a binding force for poor women. They see their future in their savings, the savings which meet their immediate needs, and also provide security in their old age.

The meagre savings of an individual may not be sufficient to meet her needs but all the savings of the group members put together can be of great help to one or two members of the group. In any of the best SHGs, the credit operations also start at the end of first month itself wherein the members pool their savings and sanction loan to a needy member. Every group will have its own set of rules and regulations like the amount of savings by members, interest rate on savings, basis on which loans are to be prioritized, interest on loans and penal interest on defaulted amount.

Groups are disciplined

The basic pillar for success of SHGs is its discipline. Every group decides frequency of group meetings, when and where to hold meeting. Best SHGs meet once a week, but normally any SHG should meet atleast once a month. The frequency of meetings strengthens the group processes, higher the frequency better it would be. Best groups maintain their discipline through fining the absentee members and latecomers. The thrift as well as credit operations take place in the group meetings. The meetings have specific agenda and the discussions take place as per the agenda.

A poor woman coming out of her house and attending the meetings as a stakeholder itself is a step towards empowerment.

In the meetings various issues are discussed at length and members decide who should be given the loan. The discussions take place in a democratic and transparent manner. In the best SHGs, each meeting is presided over by members in rotation and this helps to impart leadership qualities to all the members.

Accounts are written in the meeting itself. The standard items of account include attendance register, savings and loan ledger, cash book and individual pass books. The accounts are written either by members themselves or by a person employed by the SHG.

Best practices in SHG are being evolved continuously based on the following factors:-

- Regular meetings.
- Continuous savings
- Internal rotation of savings.
- Conduct of meetings with specific agenda.
- Thrift and credit operations taking place in the group meetings
- Rotation of leaders
- Transparent and democratic decision-making.
- Non-exploitation of members' needs.
- One for all and all for one.
- Urge for increase of corpus.
- Determination for economic and social development

Marketing

The SHGs are assisted in many districts to develop branding of their products ex: Stree Prakasam in Ongole district, Mahila in Adilabad district etc., Women are encouraged to participate in fairs taking place at national level and in other states. Collaboration with Hindustan Lever Ltd., has been secured by SHGs of Nalgonda district where

MACS have been appointed as stockist points and groups as sales points for marketing DWCRA products. Leading super bazaars like Food World, Thrinethra super market have come forwarded to tie up with SHGs to market DWCRA products.

Some DWCRA products have very good demand. Pickle producing SHGs of Guntur district got orders worth Rs 6.00 lakhs, lace groups of West Godavari district got export orders.

SHGs-A Movement in Andhra Pradesh

There are about 3.95 lakhs of women SHGs in Andhra Pradesh covering nearly 53.59 lakhs of poor women. Andhra Pradesh alone has about half of SHGs existing in the Country. Up to 1994, only 10,000 groups were functioning and in the last six years, there was a massive scaling up in SHG activities. The SHGs are not only going in for thrift but also are taking small loans out of the corpus available with the group. The group corpus consists of savings, government assistance and also bank loan. Members use the loan out of group corpus for their personal needs initially. However in the long run such loans are utilized for income generation activities. An amount of Rs. 1043.00 crores is mobilized as corpus with these groups so far and it is estimated that it would increase to Rs. 1,500.00 crores in coming one year. The SHGs are also popularly called DWCRA Groups in Andhra Pradesh. This name became popular after the DWCRA programme (Development of Women and Children in Rural Areas) through which women's groups were assisted initially.

Institutional Building

SHGs are encouraged to come together as Cooperative Societies at the village level and mandal level by federating them under Mutually Aided Cooperative Societies Act 1995. Nearly 250 societies have been formed so far. These societies will be accessing credit from financial institutions, donor agencies, DRDAs and voluntary organizations and help the members of women SHGs in availing bigger loans for economic activities and also help in collective bargaining in marketing of products, purchasing raw materials etc.

Due to this massive Self-Help movement, there is perceptible improvement in socio-economic status of rural women. Due to constant effort of the government, women have become very active, assertive and are concerned with the issues relating to them and their surroundings.

Non-Governmental Organisations' Efforts

Right from the beginning, NGOs in Andhra Pradesh have been working for the cause of women and more than 200 committed NGOs have been involved in facilitating formation of SHGs and in the efforts for their sustenance. NGOs are working in close coordination with DRDAs in training and capacity building, skill development training programmes building SHG centered organizations etc.

STATUS OF DWCRA / SELF-HELP GROUPS IN ANDHRA PRADESH

Total Groups	395233
DWCRA	150414
SGSY (Revolving Fund)	17687
State Matching Grant (Groups)	140833
Groups Formed In 200-01	60441
Eligible SHGs For Assistance	86299
Women Covered (In Lakhs)	53.59
Women Savings (Rs. In Crores)	550.00
Govt.Assistance (Rs. In Crores)	493.00
Total Corpus (Rs. In Crores)	1043.00

LIST OF PRODUCTS MADE BY SHGS IN ANDHRA PRADESH

SRIKAKULAM	Mesta Products, Food items, Handlooms, Candles, Agarbarthis, Wooden toys, Home toys, Grooms, Brass, Bell metal, Pappads, Tamarind, Groundnut Kernel, Cashewnut, Dry Fish, Pottery
VIZIANAGARAM	Mango jelly, Leather & Rexene Bags, Wire Bags,

	Embroidery, Bobbili Veena, Banyans, Adda Leaf, Honey, Wool, Lace, Khadi, Soft Toys
VISAKHAPATNAM	Food items, Mesta, Etikoppaka Wooden Toys, Palm Leaf, Handlooms, Pickles, Coir, Tamarind, ginger, Mirabulum, Brass, Leather, Detergent Powder, Mango jelly, woollen Carpets
EAST GODAVARI	Kalankari, Coir Products, Wooden Toys, Sea Shells, Zari Sarees, Handloom Sarees, Lace Products, Dry Fish, Pickles, Coconut Products, Coir, Soft Toys, Seakoi, Soap Nut, Cane Products, Plaster of Paris, Non Veg. Pickles, Cloth bags, Candles, Croatia bags
WEST GODAVARI	Lace products, Food items, Pickles, Lungies, Blankets, Carpet, Kalankari, Soft toys, Mats, Printed sarees, Paper sweet (pootarekulu), Coconut brooms, Coconut oil, Readymade garments, Wire bags
KRISHNA	Dry Fish, Kalankari, Pickles, Wool items, Banians, Detergent powders, Palm Leaf, Rexene Bags, Ties, Pop corn, School Bags, Ready made Dresses
GUNTUR	Eatable items, pickles, Note books, Pads, Detergent Powder, Paper pulp toys, Leather Lampshades& Puppets, Peteru Sarees, Kalankari, Rold Gold Ornaments, Wire bags, Honey, Ghee, Wool items, Decorative articles, Hair Oil, jute bags, Khuresha wire bags
PRAKASAM	Leather bags, Pickles, Sarees, Dress material, Eatables, Crotia bags, Eatables, Fish & prawn, Readymade garments, Masala powders, Agarbathi, Dry Fish, Crotia wire bags, Zukad Sares, Chilli Power
NELLORE	Zari Sarees, Sea shells, Modern dress making, Kalankari, Croatia bags, Banana wire bags, Palm leaf, Cushion covers, Leather & Rexene bags, Leather chappals, Wooden cutlery, Carpets, Agarbathi, Masala powder, Pickles, Paturi sarees, Readymade garments, Soft toys
KURNOOL	Eatable, Soft toys, Embroidery, Wool items, Leather goods, Wool blankets, Sculptures, Furniture, Leather goods, Kalankari, Khadi, Fabri printed sarees Dyeng & Painting sarees, Silk sarees, Pickles, Bed sheets & towels, Rexene bags

ANANTAPUR	Leather lampshades & Puppets, Readymade garments, Dress material, Pickles, Masala powders, Gem stones, Agarbathi, Bamboo products, Eatables, unit cases, Nylon mats, Bags, Sarees, Soft toys, Kalankari products, Wool products, Silk cloth, Dress material
CUDDAPAH	Basket making, Wire bags, Broom sticks, Sweets, Ghee, Wooden sculptures, Pickles, Masala powder, Mosquito net, Towels, Cotton Sarees, Handlooms
CHITTOOR	Terrakota pottery, Kora toys, Leather goods, Wire bags, Zaree sarees, Lungies, Agarbathi making, Ariveni Handicrafts, Sea shells, Pen refill making, Copper vessels, Brass idols, Plaster of Paris, Furniture (windows), Wooden toys, Readymade dress material
RANGA REDDY	Banjara needle work, Pochampalli sarees, Dress material, Soft toys, Pot painting & wood painting, Palm leaf, Eatables, Pickles, Detergent powder, Napkins, Bed sheets, Petticoats, Photo lamination & paints, Decorative articles, Agarbathis, Candles
NIZAMBAD	Soft Toys, Food items, Readymade Dresses, Leaf plates, Ornaments, Pottery, Embroidery, Gollabhama Sarees, Chappals, Blankets, Toys, Medicine, Papads, Wool products, Jute items, Lambadi ornaments, Banjara toys, Eatables, Dry Fish, Cow Therapy medicines
MEDAK	Embroidery, Wool, Leather, Rexene item, Blankets, Toys, Medicine, Papads, Pearls, Jute items, Readymade garments, Camphor, Naphthalene, Incense sticks, Hindi crafts, Eatables, Detergent powder, Chappal, Leaf plates
MAHBUBNAGAR	Cotton & Silk sarees, Gadwal Sarees, Towels, Pickles, Hats, Kalankari bed sheets & towels, Soft toys, readymade garments, Eatables
NALGONDA	Bed sheets, Handlooms, Chudidars, Pillow covers, Diwan sets, Frocks, Cushion cover, Petti coats, Blouses, Plaster of paris toys, Lambadi ornaments, Fish Pickle, Leather chappals, Brass items, Turmeric, Chilli powder, Cloth bags, Bakery products, Food items
WARANGAL	Lungies, Towels, Kalankari, Sarees, Carpet,

	Chappals, Durries, Banians, Candles, Turmeric powder, Leather bags, Greeting cards, Honey, Ghee, Bakery products, Detergent powder
KHAMMAM	Handlooms, Sarees, Carpets, Brass items, Leaf Plates, Greeting cards, Dry Foods, Mats, Pickles, Readymade Garments, Kalankari, Candles, Eatables, Pickles
KARIMNAGAR	Silver Filgree items, Rexene bags, Velvet bags, Decorative items, Petti coats, Sarees, Shirts, Eatables, Pickles, Soft toys, Rexene Bags, Luggage bags, Papads, Bamboo products, Pillow covers, Purses, Towels, Banians, Detergent powders
ADILABAD	Handlooms, Agarbathi, Bamboo items, Brass articles, Mondas, Pickles, Adda Leaf Plates, Chappal, Toys, Paints, Cement products, Wooden furniture, Baskets, Petty coats, eatables, Lace items, Leather Chappals, Wool products, Chilli & Turmeric powder

Opportunities

- Channeling various development schemes particularly concerning women and children – Convergence of development activities
- Networking amongst the group - Mahila Banks
- Provides a platform for women to discuss common problems
- Improve awareness level of rural women – on various
- Development schemes and government agencies implementing them.
- Improve socio-economic well-being of the rural women through micro credit.
- Marginalizing the role of moneylenders in the rural areas through access to credit.
- Instill a sense of self-confidence among rural women

Policy Initiatives

Entrustment of Civil works SHGs

- Execution of civil works were entrusted to SHGS
- SHGs were given necessary technical trainings on execution of works and they were provided detailed booklets.
- About 562 works worth of Rs. 376.00 lacs were entrusted from Panchayat Raj Department to the self-help groups
- In the same way Roads and buildings department entrusted 20 works worth of Rs. 3.29 lacs and Irrigation department entrusted 3 works worth of Rs. 3.70 lacs to the self-help groups

Supplies to welfare hostels entrusted to SHGs

- All the welfare hostel supplies like provisions and commodities were entrusted to SHGs.
- There are 243 government hostels (SC-122, ST-70 and BC-50) in the district; the SHGs are carrying out business worth of 27.16 lakhs per month towards supplies to the hostels and generating an income of Rs. 3.00 lacs per month.

Raising of nurseries entrusted to SHGs

- 68 groups presently raising about 40 lac plants and earn ing Rs. 9000/- per group/season

Fair price shops entrusted to SHGs

- 140 appointments were issued to SHG to run fair price shops

Punt service contract was entrusted to SHGs

- At Mattampally on river Krishna 3 groups are managing and earning 1.5 lacs per year by providing punt services i.e. carrying passengers from Nalgonda district side to Guntur district side across the river.

Non Timber Forest Produce – contracts entrusted to SHGs

- In 7 mandals 21 groups are collecting NTFP and earningRs. 5000/- per group/season. Eg. Custard apple.

Other Income Generating Activities

SHGs managing HLL rural distributorship

- Five MAC Societies are distributing HLL products to entire Nalgonda district rural retailers and to SANGHAMITHRA super bazaars managed by 10 MAC Societies. The profit margin is about 13%.

MACS managing Nirodh vending machines

- At 82 places covering 48 mandals SHGs & MACS are managing NIRODH vending machines. Net profit is Rs. 300/- per pack of 500 condoms.
- They are selling oral pills, while encouraging spacing methods the SHGs earn 15% profit on sales

Cement bricks

- 69 SHGs have taken up manufacturing of cement solid bricks and selling to DM (Housing) through NIRMITHI KENDRA

Super bazaars

- 10 MAC Societies have started income generating activity under SANGHAMITHRA super bazaars. Each unit established with an outlay of Rs. 2.00 lakhs. The profit margin is 10% i.e. Rs. 4000/- to 5000/- per month

Sanitary Napkins:

- To improve health and hygiene of rural women sanitary napkin units at places were established with an outlay of Rs. 7.00 lacs. The product is sold at a profit of Rs. 5/- per pack under the brand name "SWETCHA MAHILA"

Wealth from the waste:

- 9 charcoal units were established in 9 mandals with an outlay of Rs. 1.00 lakh by using prosophis species and earning Rs. 5000/- per 10 Mt.

Agro services:

- SHGs running a unit at Nakrekal with an outlay of Rs. 5.00 lakhs. Monthly income is at Rs. 5000/-

Land lease:

- 15 groups have taken about 100 acres of land on lease and raised vegetables, commercial crops etc.

Formation of new SHGs with poorest of the poor

Eligible women population

- Scheduled castes: 156893
- Scheduled tribes: 82855
- Total: 239748
- No. of groups can be formed : 15983
- Women already covered: 60126
- Groups already formed: 4008

The initiative

- New groups formed: 1948
- Women now covered: 29175

(Please see Appendix-IV for details of schemes for woman entrepreneurs offered by Govt. of India & State Governments and governmental agencies)

MUTUALLY AIDED COOPERATIVE THRIFT SOCIETIES (MACTSS)

Introduction

The Government of Andhra Pradesh is marching forward towards social and economic empowerment of women through better access of women to economic resources, increased

DWCRA EVENTS IN 2003

Sl. No.	*Exhibition*	*Place of Exhibition*	*Particulars*	*Period of Exhibition*	*Total No. of Groups Participated*	*Total Sales (Rs. in lakhs)*
1.	All India Industrial Exhibition	Exhibition Grounds, Hyderabad	Organized by Exhibition Society, Exhibition Grounds, Nampally, Hyderabad-CWE&SE Organised DWCRA Bazar in the site allotted by Exhibition Society in 63rd AIIE	01.01.2003 to 15.02.2003 (45 days)	75 groups	145.00 upto 10.02.2003
2.	Kakatiya Kalamahotsa-valu,	Karimnagar	Organised by District Administration, Karimnagar - DRDA arranged DWCRA Bazar in the event	18.01.2003 to 20.01.2003 (3 days)	170 groups	100.00
3.	Kadapot-savam	1) Muncipal Stadium, Cuddapah, 2) JR Memorial Hall, Proddutur 3) MPDO office, Rajannapet	Dist Admn. Organized Kadapotsavam in three places i.e. Cuddapah, Proddutur & Rajannapet, DRDA arranged DWCRA Bazar in three places	29.01.3002 to 01.02.2003 (5 days)	88 groups	50.00
4.	India International Travel Mart	Neckalce Road, Hyderabad	AP Tourism organized India International Travel Market Necklace Road, Tank Bund, Hyderabad and allotted 3 stalls to DWCRA/SHGs	01.02.2003 to 03.02.2003 (3 days)	6 groups	15.00

Cond...

5.	Grama Sree Mela	Bhvaneswa Orissa	CAPART organized Exhibition through DRDA Bhuvaneswar and allotted 2 stalls to DWCRA/SHGs from A.P.	03.01.2003 to 12.01.2003 (10 days)	2 groups	1.60
6.	Heritage Health Festival	Lalitha Kala Thoranam, Public Gardens, Nampally, Hyderabad	AP Tourism Dept. organized Heritage Health Festival at Lalitha Kala Thoranam, Public Gardens, Nampally, Hyderabad and allotted stall to DWCRA/SHGs food products	07.02.2003 to 09.02.2003 (3 days)	3 groups	1.50
7.	Flemingo Festival	Sullurpet, Nellore	Dist. Admn.Nellore organized Flemingo Festival at Sullurpet, Nellore Dist – DRDA arranged DWCRA Bazar in the event	10.02.2003 to 12.02.2003 (3 days)		
8.	Krishna Mahotsavam	Vijayawada	Dist. Administration, Krishna Dist. organized Krishna Mahotstav at Vijayawada and DRDA arrange DWCRA Bazar in the event	12.02.2003 to 16.02.2003 (5 days)		

Source:- www.ap.nic.in/dwcra

mobility, awareness, assertiveness, confidence, self-respect, self-esteem and gender equality. Net-working of SHGs at village, cluster and mandal level are emerging with the pro active role taken by the Government by way of introduction of MACTS Act, 1995 which is encouraging Women's Cooperative Thrift Societies. In the last 5–6 years the Government has been involving the women as active partners in the development process. Due to the best efforts and facilitation of State Government at present 350 MACTS are functioning successfully in A.P., consisting of 4.31 lakh members, having share capital of Rs.580.48 lakhs. The total corpus of 350 MACTS is Rs.1777.28 lakhs.

Savings and credit or income generation requires a holistic approach to human development, which ultimately leads to community development. The approach towards policy alleviation should be self-help. Savings plus credit is a good starting point for group formation. Now in Andhra Pradesh the Self-Help Groups (SHGs) have become a forum for the collective unit of the poor against common expression and explanation, to understand individual and common problems and to improve their skills and capabilities to manage resources. These groups are highly cohesive entities. All members of the group conform strictly to the group standards and its leaders represent the feelings of the members.

Hence, it has become necessary to federate the groups bringing them under a statute, making them an economic group into a Cooperative Society, which can manage their own affairs, systematically follow the principles of cooperation formally. The groups in A.P. not only thrift-oriented but involved in several social and political activities at various levels.

In A.P. such groups are federated under the provisions of A.P. Mutually Aided Cooperative Societies Act, 1995. MACTSs vary from 1 village to 15 villages covering of 50 to 100 groups consisting of 200 to 2000 women members. A

MACTS is a community development financial institution with development consciousness and focus on poverty alleviation and empowerment of women. These MACTSs are also popularly called as 'Mahila Banks in Andhra Pradesh'.

Credit is an effective instrument of Social change and most critical need for survival. The Women's Thrift Credit Mutually Aided Cooperative Societies are voluntary, formed by the members of the SHGs. Both shareholders and directors belong to the women members of the society. These institutions are self-reliant business enterprises based on thrift and self-help and one controlled by the members for their economic and social betterment and is accountable to the members.

MACTSs provide easier, faster and higher access of credit to poor women at low rate of interest (Rs.1/- to Rs.1.50). Responsibility is placed on the groups to select the needy beneficiaries, disburse the loans and to ensure prompt repayments. An Executive Committee of 7 to 13 consisting of the representatives of the women helps to administer the bank.

Objectives

The Objectives of MACTS are:

- Providing credit to poor women without security.
- Reducing moneylender exploitation at low rate of interest.
- Assets creation.
- To improve economic status of women.
- Creation of micro enterprises.
- Avoiding long loan sanction procedure and delay.
- To undertake sustainable employment generation activities.
- Generate livelihood to poor women.

Guidelines

The MACTS is formed with the following guidelines:

1. Thrift/DWCRA group Members only.
2. Minimum age of the members is 18 years and married women only.
3. Group savings of minimum 1 year.
4. Permanent Resident of the village.
5. Regular savings habit among all the group members.
6. Regularity in conduct of monthly meetings by the group.
7. Maintenance of Ledgers, Registers.
8. Internal lending among the Members.
9. Resulting by the Thrift/DWCRA group to pay share capital of Rs.500/- or Rs.1000/-.
10. Entry fees Rs.20/- to Rs.100/- each member.

Requirements to Join a Macts Are

- Seniority of the groups – minimum 1 year.
- Regular thrift.
- Level of internal lending.
- Level of repayment.
- Regularity of group meetings.
- Regular in maintenance of group records.
- Functional literacy level of groups.
- Family planning status of members.
- Participation in community programmers.

Key activities of these institutions

1. Cultivating the habit of thrift and savings among the members. Loan to members with or without security for productive and asset formation and for consumption purpose.
2. Offer Credit and non-credit services in pursuit of

women's economic prosperity through loan and credit.

3. Arrange for storage, grading, processing, value addition, packing, transportation and sale of the produce of the members.
4. Assist for enhancing the economic productivity and income of women and for asset formation.
5. Assist programmes promoting women self-employment, income generation, health, and education.
6. Gain collective wisdom in financial matters in organizing and managing their own finance and distributing the benefits among themselves.
7. Promote group production activities for gainful employment of women.
8. Providing technical and imparting training for its members.
9. Procure, pool, purchase, utilize and distribute inputs required for women in I.G.A. and consumer articles and articles required for household requirements.
10. Undertake any activity, which is incidental and essential for the attainment of the objective of the society.

Eligibility for Sanction of Loans

The criteria for sanction of loans are:

- Only for members in the MACTS.
- Loan application should be recommended by the group
- Leader and by the director at the village level.
- They should not be loanees or defaulters for large amounts through any other sources as certified by group leader.
- Registers, passbooks should be regularly updated.
- Urgency, need and viability of loans.

Types of Loans

	Income Generating (60%)		*Assets Consumption Purposes (40%)*
1.	Purchase of agrl. Land	1.	Education
2.	Milch animals	2.	Health needs
3.	Electric motors	3.	Marriages
4.	Petty business	4.	Accidents
5.	Flour mills	5.	Festivals
6.	Grinders	6.	House constructions
7.	Sewing machines	7.	House repairs
8.	Cloth business	8.	
9.	Fruit business	9.	
10.	Land on lease	10.	

Recovery of Loans

100% Loan Recovery is identified in all the MACTS.

Beneficiaries

The Beneficiaries are all women, who are engaged in income generating activity and saving a min-amount of Rs.30/- per month regularly. They form into small self-help groups and in a group, on average as mentioned earlier, there are 15-20 members from different households, but residing in the some area. They are either SCs, STs, BCs and other caste members but basically they are all below poverty line. Occupation-wise they may be:

- Agricultural Labourers.
- Marginal and small farmers
- Non-farm wage farmers
- Unemployed or any disadvantaged groups, such as fisher women, petty traders and crafts women.

These people are made aware of their condition and importance of savings and credit and rotate the group's savings as their corpus and lend to their own group members to meet their immediate credit requirements. The external funding may be revolving fund provided to the women groups, grant-in-aid provided by the state Government for doing small business.

The group members are homogenous in terms of members' income, sex, social status, and place of residence and like-mindedness. Only one person or household is a member of the group. A member should attain the age of 18 years but not more than 60 years. Each member should be willing to accept the objective of the group. The group shall elect a representative/leader for a period of 3 years and she will be a member in the representative General Body of the Cooperative Society.

The groups conduct regular meetings – fortnightly or monthly and attendance of all members is compulsory. The time and place of the meeting is fixed and in the meeting members share their savings. All transactions are approved in the group meeting through resolution. At the group level, the group savings and loans issued to members will be maintained. The documents are in their simplest form and easy to write by a member who has simple numerical and writing abilities.

The self-help groups or DWCRA groups existing for more than one year and vibrant in doing credit and savings operations and who can manage them on their own independently can federate into a cooperative society under the provisions of A.P. Mutually Aided Coop. Societies Act. Byelaws also are formulated to send the local requirements and got them registered.

Among other things, all the members of the group, will become members of the society. The committee is elected democratically and there is continuity of the elected management. The elected management consists of committee members.

Implementing Agency:

The implementing agency at the state level is the Commissionerate of Women Empowerment & Self-Employment, Hyderabad. The Commissioner, Women Empowerment & Self-Employment will release the funds as per project outlay to the societies through the Project Directors of the concerned districts. The managing committee of the society in turn ground the scheme with and reports compliance. The unit for grounding the scheme is ultimately the cooperative society at the village or cluster of the villages level.

Role of Commissionerate

On receipt of funds pass on the funds to the societies through the Project Directors of DRDA. Takes every step that the funds are strictly utilized for the purpose for which they were released. Obtain quarterly reports in a format and obtain utilization certificates. Besides quarterly reports, evaluates independently the working of the society. Provides guidance to the DRDA and evolves a strategy for good working of the society.

Commissionerate will see to writing and maintenance of accounts uniformly following standard formats' and procedures. Obtain statutory returns and audit reports and evaluate the working of the society. This evaluation work may be taken up by independent agencies also.

At the District level, the Collector and ROs implement the scheme. The societies are supervised and they submit reports to the Commissioner, Rural Development. The DRDA basing on the local needs provides assistance and guidance for getting credit through banks and marketing their products of the members of the society. The training is provided to both members, group leaders, committee members of the society both in financial management. Accounting and capacity building. If necessary the DRDAs may arrange field visits to the group members to upgrade their skills.

Training and Capacity Building

Special programmes have been designed for training and capacity building of the Presidents, Secretaries and members of MACATS. Trainings on management and Maintenance of Accounts, Micro Credit etc., is organized for the members of MACTS. In addition to the above exposure visits are organized for awareness generation.[2]

In a relative vacuum and rarity of interest, initiative, knowledge, skills and resources material and human on the part of the downtrodden women folk, the Self-Help Groups function as educational and enabling instruments to gradually elevate the life of the poor to minimum meaningful standard of life. This development is a journey and the destination will be moving forward on and on. The way in which the programmes are being carried on serves as training for the women folk. Entrepreneurial activities being carried cn with assistance from different quarters, it is hoped that it would play a contagious role drawing people from other segments of the population. Here, we may presume though, the self-help groups are functioning collectively, over a period of time, individuals within the group are likely to graduate into successful independent entrepreneurs.

While speaking of entrepreneurial initiative on the part of the women, the district of Warangal in the State of Andhra Pradesh presents an interesting and successful case as to how the woman members of SHGs were mobilized, encouraged and assisted to collectively carry on manufacturing and marketing of chilli powder.

Empowering Women Through Self-Help Groups

Andhra Pradesh Government has been vigorously pursuing the micro finance agenda for empowering poor women. DRDA, Warangal has made very conscious efforts to thoroughly internalize this new paradigm of development. As a result, organization of women into SHGs had really taken the shape of a movement in the district. Indeed it is a conscious path chosen by women to shape their own destiny. It is also believed that promotion of non-farm related micro enterprises is an integral part of planned strategy for securing balanced development of economy of the poor women. Steadfast efforts in this direction gave birth to some very spontaneous innovations of women in the district. In this regard, Chilli Processing Unit of 514 women is surely an inspiring story.

Of late, there is a paradigm shift in development process by incorporating the gender concerns as an important element of development strategy. Duly recognizing the importance and involvement of women in participatory model of development, Andhra Pradesh Government has taken up the theme of women's empowerment as one of the main agenda items to tackle rural poverty and socio-economic issues. With over 700 million women living in poverty globally, micro finance programming is seen as an essential tool in poverty alleviation. In recent years, micro finance programmes have been used as not only a tool for economic upliftment but also as an effective way to meet women's practical and strategic needs. In coherence with globally emerging development perspective, Andhra Pradesh Government has also been vigorously pursuing the micro finance agenda for empowering poor women. DRDA, Warangal has made very conscious efforts to thoroughly internalize this new paradigm of development and operationalise the same. As a result, organization of women into SHGs had really taken the shape of a movement in the district. Indeed it is a conscious path chosen by women to shape their own destiny. Concomitantly, several challenges emerged in terms of a variety of capacity building and further growth demands from women SHGs.

In Warangal District, 22836 groups are functioning with 3.10 lakh women with a corpus of Rs.85 crore. Out of 22836 groups, about 15000 groups are linked with various banks to avail credit facilities for production and consumption needs. Obviously, this is a clear indication of the quality and growth potential of SHGs.

As a logical step towards further development of women SHGs in the district, concerted and coordinated efforts are being made to sensitize and motivate women to undertake micro enterprises. Further, the interest in enterprise building is necessitated from the following local processes: (a) poor or dependent extremely on exploitative markets and have no control on their produce; (b) being non-enterprising, the poor are not well placed to take advantage of non-farm employment opportunities; and (c) lack of resource, capacities and opportunities. Hence are unemployed for several months. It is also believed that promotion of non-farm related micro enterprises is an integral part of planned strategy for securing balanced development of economy of the poor women. Our perseverance in this regard gave birth to some very spontaneous innovations of women in the district. In this regard, Chilli Processing Unit of 514 women is surely an inspiring story.

Chilli Processing Unit

Genesis of the Idea:- Senior women self-help groups in Parvathagir Mandal have graduated to the stage of looking out for opportunities for profitable micro enterprises. Through a participatory process, opportunities available within the area were meticulously scanned and a list of feasible micro enterprises was prepared. Chilli being one of the major crops in the area, some women have started looking into the possibilities of setting up a Chilli Processing Unit (CPU). The proposal was further scrutinized and deeply analysed and found that it is a quite profitable venture. The local NGO and DRDA enabled the women SHGs to come together and develop necessary institutional linkages for putting their idea into concrete action form.

Favourable Conditions

Following conditions enabled women to set up their Chilli Processing Unit.

- Warangal district has about 62,500 acres of land under chilli crop.
- Warangal chapatta is a special chilli variety locally cultivated and which has high commercial value due to it's colour and moderate pungency.
- A project for organic production of chillies in 300 acres is already under implementation in close vicinity to these groups.
- Financial support available from the Spices Board for any spices promotion enterprises.
- Leadership and managerial capacity developed by SHGs by virtue of their experience.
- Financial capacity of the women SHGs to invest in-group enterprises.
- Good working relationship between SHGs and local service area bank.

Financial Sources

	The unit has been set up with	Rs.23.33 lakhs as under
1.	Share capital from members (514)	Rs.05.14 lakhs
2.	Grant from Govt. of India (Spices Board, Kochi)	Rs.10.28 lakhs
3.	Grant from Infrastructure Fund of DRDA, Warangal	Rs. 07.91 lakhs
	Total	Rs. 23.33 lakhs

4. Working capital loan: Rs.20.00 lakhs from Indian Overseas Bank, Parvathagiri.

NABARD has also extended managerial & technical support

Organizational Process

Through an intensive process, women SHGs have reached an understanding that chilli processing unit is worth attempting to enhance their income and livelihood opportunities. The idea has been communicated to all the senior groups in a cluster of 10 villages in Parvathagiri Mandal and women SHGs which were strongly convinced came forward to invest and initiate this group enterprise.

Profile of the Chilli Processing Unit

- 2.3 acres of land with good water facility by the main roadside with all conveniences for transportation and future expansion.
- Building with good space for work shed, store, packing unit, rest & change room, office room, security outpost and toilets.
- Pulverizes (20 & 30 HP), Automatic pouch packing machine, electronic weighing equipment suitable for high quality of chilli powdering with installed capacity of 3 tons production per 24 hours.
- Roaster for quick removable of moisture from chillies.
- 500 square metres drying yard for hygienic chilli processing and drying.
- Electricity connection with 60 HP dedicated transformer.
- Agmark quality certification.
- Quality testing full-fledged laboratory available within the unit premises.
- Vermi and Nadep Compost units to convert bio-waste into compost.

514 women organized themselves into 'Srujana Mahilabhivridhi Upadhi Mutually Aided Cooperative Society (Srujana Women Development & Employment Mutually Aided Cooperative Society). This society legally came into existence

with 35 SHGs hailing from 12 villages. Total members are 514 of which 73 are from SC, ST, and BC communities. Each group has raised a share capital of Rs.15,000/- and demonstrate their conviction in the idea. This further enabled them to access financial support from the Spices Board, Govt. of India and DRDA, Warangal.

This has now become an example for women entrepreneurship on the one hand and demonstration of collective strength and wisdom of women on the other. It has become a model for *"Harvesting women's collective strength for poverty alleviation"*.

Organizational Set-up

I. General Body: All the 514 women who have paid share capital and membership fee constitute the general body of 'Srujana'. It meets atleast once in a year and is the supreme body to decide on the affairs of the society.

II. Representative General Body: 35 women SHGs which are part of this 'Srujana' elected one representative from each group and they constitute the representative general body. They act as link between individual shareholders and the Board of Directors. On all critical issues they consult their respective group members and represent their opinion to the managing committees.

III. Board of Directors: Nine board members are elected from the representative general body. President, Vice-President and Treasurer and six board members constitute board of directors and this board is responsible for day-to-day decision-making and overall management.

IV. Manager: He/she is a full time employee paid by the society and responsible for the job chart delegated by the governing body.

The unit has extended into a land area of 2.5 Acres with abundant facilities. The unit consists of Machinery Hall, Packing room, Storeroom and an office room. In addition to this, chemical and quality testing laboratory is also set-up with a Rs.10.00 lakh grant from the Spice Board, Kochi.

The Project proved that women have developed abundant self-confidence and self-esteem through SHG movement. Not only economic poverty but also social and gender issues can be tackled effectively through this process. Government and Non-Government agencies can play a proactive role in mobilizing, organizing and sustaining SHGs. Necessary managerial, technical and marketing skills can be imparted to groups to enhance their livelihood opportunities.

A drying yard is also constructed and Mango and Lemon plantation is done in unused area to derive additional income from the land apart from adding beauty and greenery to the area.

A vermin compost unit is also established to treat the waste material and converting it into organic manure.

Facilitation & Process Moderation

An NGO, MARI has played a vital role in mobilizing women and forming Srujana MACTS and bringing governmental agencies together to access financial and other resources for establishing the unit. This has also become a model for Government and Non-Government organization partnership in development process. NGO can mobilize and motivate people to come together and Government Agencies can extend necessary financial, technical, managerial and marketing support to establish an enterprise.

Procurement, Production: The chilli is procured from shareholders as well as from other farmers. Parvathagiri, Narsampet, Nallabelli, Duggondi, Parkal, Eturunagaram and Mangapet Mandals are identified as having good production of Warangal Chapata Chilli. G4 and Sannam Chilli variety production is abundant in 50 kms radius of the unit. Primary processing of whole chilli is done by the members at their houses. The processed whole chilli is procured in bulk and the same is kept in cold storage. As per the production demand material is transported to the unit. Powdering of chillies can be done meeting highest quality standards. Per shift (8 hours) one-ton chilli can be powdered. Packaging machine for automatic pouch filling of 50 and 100 grams pouches and electronic weighing and packing of higher quantities can be done ensuring the best quality and hygiene standards.

Quality:- This unit is linked to a project of organic cultivation of chilli in 300 acres. Thus, the product of the unit is very safe in terms of pesticide residues levels. Samples of raw material will be analysed in the laboratory to ensure required oleoresin, pungency and colour value. Laboratory analysis also helps in eliminating dust and filth particles in the final product. Work force is educated and provided with necessary hygiene & safety ware for ensuring product quality. Storage of raw material in cold storage also helps in protecting the quality. The producers have already been provided with tarpaulin sheets and drying yards to protect quality in post harvesting processing.

Marketing Strategy:- Multi pronged strategy including local marketing to export has been contemplated. The product will be thoroughly popularized among all the SHGs in the district and channels for distribution of product to all the strategic marketing locations will be developed. Networking with other marketing enterprises of SHG women in neighbouring districts will be established. Consumption points under the control of Government like hostels, Devastanams (temples) would be approached for bulk orders. Product will also be marketed through PDS and Gruhamithra supply channels. For exporting Chapata Chilli product, opportunities would be explored through Spices Board, Kochi. Private marketing agencies will be involved for pushing the product into the mainstream market. Cleaned and Dried whole mirchi will be supplied to the oleoresin extracting units in Kerala.

Uniqueness of the Project

1. First women SHG's initiative and entrepreneurship in the state.
2. Quality product with Agmark from Government of India.
3. Participation by SHGs, Government organization, NGO & Bank. A successful intervention by all the development partners.
4. Total construction of the project is done by women groups only.
5. An innovative project to utilize the local resources to create sustainable employment opportunities and providing reasonable market rates to producers of chillies and spices commodities of the area.
6. Transforming the consumption based SHGs into entrepreneurship oriented SHGs leading to employment generation and empowerment of women.
7. Value addition to the agriculture products.

Experience in the Project

The project proved that women have tremendous energies to start their own enterprises given the right opportunities. They have developed abundant self-confidence and self-esteem through SHG movement. Not only economic poverty but also social and gender issues can be tackled collectively through this process.

Government and Non-Government agencies can play a proactive role in mobilizing, organizing and sustaining SHGs. Necessary managerial, technical and marketing skills can be imparted to groups to enhance their livelihood opportunities.

This is a classic example of convergence of all stakeholders for achieving the anticipated common goal. The differences, if any, between Government organizations and NGOs may be resolved for further development agenda and then we can expect our energies becoming synergies.

Further, Govt. of India/financial institution, while releasing any grant to NGOs can also involve stake-holding institutions for achieving better results. NGO, alone cannot achieve substantially without the active support from Government agencies.

This is a successful experiment but the requisite coordination and convergence is required in marketing the products and making it a viable enterprise.

SOURCES

1. *India, 1991,* Publications Division, Ministry of Information & Broadcasting, Govt. of India.
2. *www.ap.nic.in/dwcra*
3. T. Chiranjeevulu, "Empowering Women through Self-Help Groups", *Kurukshetra,* New Delhi, March, 2003, pp.16-19.

12

Efforts of NGOs in Promoting Mini-Enterprises Among Women

Compared to the government, NGOs have several advantages in terms of decision making, planning and implementing their programmes and activities. They are not burdened by any bureaucratic rigidity. We find in most of the NGOs women employees. They have close interaction with the clientele system and the pattern of communication among the employees in NGOs is rather intimate and friendly. They are selective in their approaches choosing smaller groups and working with them intimately and intensively. They do play and could play a significant role in promoting entrepreneurship among the women groups in rural and urban areas. They are good at the grassroots level and could be effective partners in entrepreneurship development among women. The following case studies are illustrative of the role that is played by private organizations.

Apart from the consistent efforts made by the government through several programmes especially organising Self-Help Groups under national programme DWCRA, some of the NGOs have initiated helping women groups enter into mini entrepreneurial activities. The spur for this movement is provided by the NGOs and in the case of Hindustan Lever Limited (HLL) though on one hand it may look like boosting their products in rural areas, it has created employment and considerable earning to the women more especially who fall under below poverty line (BPL).

Project Shakti

Hindustan Lever Limited (HLL) and its constituent companies have been in India since 1931. Over these decades, HLL has benefited from the developments in the country. The company equally, in its own way, has contributed to these developments. HLL has consciously woven India's imperatives with the company's strategy and operations. These areas have been developing and using relevant technology, stimulating industrialisation, exports, adding value to agriculture and generating productive employment and income opportunities.

Project Shakti is HLL's latest initiative, in keeping with this purpose of integrating business interests with national interests.

The objectives of Project Shakti are to create 'Income generating capabilities' for underprivileged rural women by providing a sustainable micro enterprise opportunity, and to improve rural living standards through health and hygiene awareness.

HLL's vision for Project Shakti is to scale it up across the country by 2010, creating about 11000 Shakti entrepreneurs, covering 100,000 villages and touching the lives of 100 million rural consumers.

Following the pioneering work carried out by Grameen Bank in Bangladesh, several institutions, NGOs and governmental bodies have been working closely over the last 4 to 5 years to establish Self-Help Groups (SHGs) of rural women in villages across India. Their experiments clearly show that micro-credit, when carefully targeted and well-administered, can alleviate poverty significantly. Importantly, success depends not only on infusion of credit, but on investment opportunities.

This is where HLL is playing a role in creating such

profitable micro enterprise opportunities for rural women. For the SHG women, this translates into critically needed sustainable income contributing to better living standards and prosperity. For HLL, it provides access into hitherto unexplored rural hinterlands. Armed with micro-credit, women from SHGs become direct-to-home distributors in rural markets. This micro enterprise is relatively risk-free and high on return. HLL provides the necessary training inputs to these groups on the basics of enterprise management, which the women need to stabilise their enterprises. Under the project, HLL offers a range of mass-market products to the SHGs, which are relevant to rural consumers.

This model was piloted in Nalgonda district of Andhra Pradesh in 50 villages in 2001. The Government of Andhra Pradesh took the pioneering step of supporting the initiative by enabling linkages with the network of DWCRA groups of ruiral women, set up for women development and self-employment. It has since been extended to over 5000 villages in 52 districts in Andhra Pradesh, Karnataka, Gujrat and Madhya Pradesh. Project Shakti, as of date, has 1000 woman entrepreneurs in its fold. HLL is being assited in the rollout by Marketing & Research Team (MART), an organization engaged in the social sector.

State Governments as well as NGOs are actively involved with HLL in the implementation of this project. The response has been encouraging. Most SHG Women have seen this as a powerful business proposition and are enthusiastically participating in it. A typical Shakti entrepreneur conducts business of around Rs.15,000 per month, which gives her an income in excess of Rs.1000/- per month on a sustainable basis. As most of these women are from below the poverty line, and live in extremely small villages (less than 2000) population), this earning is very significant, and is almost double of their past household income. For most of these families, Project Shakti is creating opportunities to live in conditions of dignity, with real freedom from want.

The most powerful aspect about this model is that it creates a win-win partnership between HLL and its consumers, some of whom will also draw on the organization for their livelihood, and builds a self-sustaining virtuous cycle of growth for all.

To improve the business skills of the SHG women, extensive training programmes are being held. Such workshops have already covered over 1000 woman entrepreneurs in Andhra Pradesh and Karnataka.

Additionally, as a part of their training programme, HLL Management Trainees are spending over 4 weeks in rural areas, providing business consultation to nascent SHG enterprises engaged in the manufacture of various products such as spices, hosiery items, etc.

HLL is now in the process of piloting 'i-Shakti' an IT-based rural information service that will provide solutions to key rural needs in the areas of agriculture, education, vocational training, health/hygiene, etc. in Nalgonda district. Plans are being drawn up to bring in partners involved in agriculture, health, insurance and education to catalyse overall rural development.

Step by step, Project Shakti is unleashing the potential of rural women and thus changing their lives. It is ushering in prosperity and, more importantly, self-respect. As one of the Shakti entrepreneurs, Rojamma, says, 'It is more important than money. When they see me, they crowd around me and call me 'Shaktiamma'. I am someone today.'

Fast-moving consumer goods (FMCG) major, Hindustan Lever Ltd, is picking up where the Grameen Bank of Bangladesh left off. Leveraging the micro-credit model to expand its rural market, it is piloting 'Project Shakti'—its five-month-old marketing initiative involving women belonging to micro-credit self-help groups (SHGs) in the Nalgonda district of Andhra Pradesh.[2]

Willing to experiment, the company followed the growth initiative suggested by HLL's Project Millennium last year that drew upon the Grameen Bank concept.

The project, with an obvious 'win-win' partnership potential, involves women from SHGs turning into direct-to-home distributors for HLL in their area, thus helping the company expand its rural market from its existing 40 per cent penetration in villages with population of over 2,000.

For the women, it means income generation without the headache of starting their own venture and becoming vegetable vendors, fish vendors, pan shop owners, etc., which has generally been the micro-credit model to date.

The products being sold through this unique direct marketing initiative are HLL's leading brands including Clinic Plus shampoo, Lifebouy, Wheel, A1 tea and Nihar coconut oil.

In fact, due to customer demand for other HLL products, Three Roses tea, Fair And Lovely cream and Pond's talcum powder have been added to the inventory. At the grassroots level, the project is being coordinated and implemented by Marketing and Research Team (MART).

Andhra Pradesh was obviously chosen for the pilot project as 20 per cent of its rural population is covered by the micro-credit model. The micro-credit concept, that impacts 45 lakh women belonging to 3.33 lakh SHGs in the State, creates wealth for the members of the groups and helps them better their lives and alleviate poverty. The micro-finance collected in the State, through savings as well as institutional loans, is around a whopping Rs. 800 crore.

For the project, 50 SHGs closest to the highway in Nalgonda district were identified. These are covered by three Mutually-Aided Credit Thrift Societies (MACTS), which act as semi-distributors in the project. MACTS, which generally consist of 14 to 15 SHGs, are federated into a co-operative and work in close tandem with the SHGs.

In fact, the project has had several interesting spin-offs. One of the MACTs distributing HLL products has started its own supermarket, while another is shortly purchasing a vehicle for its distribution network.

"The investment opportunity is relatively risk-free and high on return. HLL is committed to providing the necessary training inputs to these groups on the basics of enterprise management which the groups can then use to enlarge their initiatives," says an HLL spokesperson. But it plans to upscale the pilot only after its analysis and evaluation is completed.

"The challenge has been to move from micro-finance to micro-enterprise," says Mr Kashyap whose organization has also carried out a feasibility study for the Andhra Pradesh Government on the micro-enterprises that can be taken up by SHGs. It is, in addition to, training of district functionaries and the women themselves on how to run such micro-enterprises.

Some of the ventures being implemented are superbazars run by the women, sanitary napkin units and the traditional dairy and handloom initiatives. But for the corporate world, it's Project Shakti to look out for.

While speaking of the success of the efforts made by HLL in organising and providing opportunities to women to become self-employed and also emerge as mini-entrepreneurs, here we have in brief a few interesting profiles of individual women who had the benefit of support from the HLL.

1. **Ms. Rojamma**

   Village: Kurumurthy

   District: Mahabubnagar, Andhra Pradesh

Ms. Rojamma was married off when she was 17. After two daughters were born, her husband abandoned the family.

She heard of Project Shakti, at a meeting at the District Rural Development Authority's office, and took a loan of Rs.10,000 from her Self-Help Group (SHG).

Today, the turnover of her enterprise is about Rs.20,000 a month. Her net earning is approximately Rs.1500 a month, which is double what she earned before becoming a Shakti entrepreneur.

Ms. Rojamma says that today she has the confidence of educating her two daughters ... and she has self-respect. 'When they see me, they crowd around me and call me 'Shaktiamma'. I am someone today – It is more important than money," adds Ms. Rojamma.

2. **Jella Sujathamma**

   Village:- Peddakaparthy

   District:- Nalgonda

Ms. Sujathamma's spouse is a weaver. But the income was not enough for the family, including their daughter and two sons.

Five years back, she joined a Self-Help Group (SHG), formed under the aegis of the District Rural Development Authority. She came to know about Project Shakti in January, 2001, and became one of the first Shakti entrepreneurs of the State.

Ms. Sujathamma did not have enough funds of her own. So, she took a loan of Rs.10,000 from her SHG to start the enterprise. Today her turnover has grown from Rs.10,000 a month to Rs. 25,000. Besides, she now also sells staples, sugar, edible oil and a variety of other household items.

Her income over the past two years has brought about a sea change in her family's standard of living. Ms. Sujathamma now wants to buy a moped to extend her coverage area and increase the scale of her enterprise.

3. **Ms. Jayamma**

   Village:- Basireddypalem

   District:- Prakasam

Ms. Jayamma is a widow, with two daughters and a son. Her son has dropped out from school, while the two daughters are students of Class X and V respectively.

Her son used to be engaged in agriculture, but stopped work some time back as the earnings were poor. She was finding it difficult running the household, and meeting the educational expenses of her daughters.

It was at such a stage that she heard about Project Shakti, and decided to become a Shakti entrepreneur. She was trained by the Company on how to run her own business. Today she runs a successful micro-enterprise and is happy with her earnings. She hopes that the future will see her enterprise expanding.

4. **Ms. Pogaku Anitha**

   Village:- Areypally

   District:- Warangal.

Ms. Anitha used to be a part-time anganwadi teacher but lost her job. Her father's income is just about Rs.1400 a month, which was not enough to run the household.

The potential of Project Shakti attracted her to join the initiative. Today she does a business of Rs.18,000 to 20,000 a month, and her personal earning is over Rs.1500 a month. She says that she and her family are very happy with her new business and the regular monthly income generated.

Her dream is to grow her enterprise beyond Rs. 50,000 per month.

5. **Ms. Sundaramma**

   Village:- Bhimanapalli

   District:- East Godavari

Ms. Sundaramma is 50 years old. Marrying the three daughters left the family in deep debt. The couple's only son has separated from them. Her age did not permit her to engage in hard labour and there was not much else that she could do.

She heard about Project Shakti through a meeting at the MDO office. She became a Shakti entrepreneur and today, she has expanded her operations to her village and neighbouring villages. Her income out of the enterprise is about Rs. 1200 to Rs. 1500 per month. In addition, she prepares and sells pickles.

She says that though she is 50 years, Project Shakti has ensured that she is not dependent on anyone. Rather it is she who is helping out her children. She believes that if the bank were to increase the loan, she can expand the enterprise.

6. **Ms. Narayanamma**

   Village:- Mangapatnam

   District:- Kadapa.

Ms. Narayanamma's husband is a farmer. They have two children, studying in Classes IV and III.

There was a pressing need for Ms. Narayanamma to supplement her husband's income, as agricultural earnings were poor due to vagaries of rainfall. It was at this point that she came to learn of Project Shakti from the Assistant Gram Sevika.

Ms. Narayanamma says that her earnings have not only

helped the family tide over present financial difficulties, but also that they are now able to save some money for the future.

Ms.Narayanamma wants to build her Shakti enterprise further. With the confidence that she has gained from the initiative, she also wants to take up new projects.

7. **Ms. Padmavati**
   Village:- Chirumarri
   District:- Khammam.

Ms. Padmavathi's husband is a carpenter, but earnings have been sparse in the last one year. Though a housewife, she wanted to support the family with additional income. That is when she heard of Project Shakti at a meeting at the Mandal Development Office. She decided to become a Shakti entrepreneur, and took a loan of Rs. 10,000 from her SHG. With a helping hand from Hindustan Lever through the initial days of transition into an entrepreneur, her turnover today is about Rs. 15,000 a month, and her net earning out of it about Rs. 1000 a month.

With her confidence and her acquaintance with the wider world, she is now starting an entirely new enterprise — an Internet Kiosk in her village. HLL is helping her in this pursuit. She says she has herself become self-reliant and has endowed her family with greater financial strength, all because of Project Shakti.

Case Study of Two Successful NGO's in Andhra Pradesh

Further, the initiatives taken by the Mahila Abhyudaya Podupu Sangam, Tirupati, Rashtriya Seva Samithi (RASS) and Swayamkrushi Mutually Aided Cooperative Thrift Society Limited in Andhra Pradesh are quite interesting. The contribution by the NGOs mentioned above is really paving the way and motivating other non-governmental organizations to work towards developing entrepreneurship among women. The role played by the NGOs in this respect is rather a stimulant and an encouraging factor to the government to further their schemes and efforts to cover larger population of women help themselves become self-employed as entrepreneurs.

The 'Padmavathy' Experience

The women in Tirupati were mostly migrants from nearby areas backed by illiteracy, poverty and lack of basic amenities. They were involved in odd activities with fluctuating incomes. Against this background, women had major responsibilities of maintaining their families. This necessitated the need for a regular source of credit. The efforts were to identify and promote income-generating activities among women through a credit delivery system. The banks were initially persuaded to provide loans at Differential Interest Scheme. Despite good repayments, banks could not meet the growing demands for credit on a continuous basis and there was no scope for repeat loans.

The Mahila Abyudaya Podupu Sangam is a self-managed group which generates financial resources through their own savings. Each sangam consists of 10 to 15 members belonging to a particular slum. The primary source of funds is from the savings of members and interest earned on loans extended. Each sangam creates a common fund in order to meet the operational cost. The repayment rate is 100 percent because of individual responsibility of each member. Apart from financial functions, sangam is a platform for women to interact and address many of their day-to-day problems. The interactions between sangams resulted in the formation of an association called 'Cluster Association'. Each sangam became a member of the same. The activities of the Association include; promotion of new sangams, resolution of conflicts within and between sangams, address to the common issues etc.

The 'Padmavathy' which is a legal entity has certain objectives:

- To mobilize funds from formal financial institutions to meet the larger credit needs of its members.
- To promote formation of new sangams.
- To motivate the members to manage financial requirements independently without external subsidies.
- To promote unity among women of different sangams to give them collective identity for collective action.

Besides the above objectives, 'Padmavathy' functions as a forum for information and exchange of ideas among different sangam members. It also has the responsibility of reaching out to more and more of poor women by expanding its activities.

Impact of 'Padmavathy'

'Padmavathy,' which started its operations a decade ago, had 221 sangams and 2647 members by July 1996. The sangams have mobilized Rs. 38.58 lakhs as savings 'and Rs. 8.31 lakhs as common fund after having met their operational costs. The sangam members with their own savings have a sense of security and confidence.

'Padmavathy' sangam is the first organization linked under the informal banking programme of SIDBI. Initially, It availed a soft loan of Rs.4 lakhs from SIDBI with the purpose of promoting micro enterprises by women. This assistance had encouraged 200 women to start their own income generating activities. Because of a good repayment experience, SIDBI had sanctioned a second loan of Rs.5 lakhs also a grant for training members for better credit utilization.

It is true that sustainability of any development initiative is possible only when the participants change their role from passive recipients to active own managers. The 'Padmavathy' experience has proved it through commitment to work, sincere efforts to share the benefits of development and active involvement of several sangam members. The model further proves the fact that poor are bankable and the timely access to credit can bring about changes in the lives of thousands of poor women. The sangams have been successful in obtaining loans on reasonable terms with simple procedures. They have also been instrumental in motivating many members who were earlier idle, in taking up some economic activity. Thus, the experience of this model is a source of inspiration for many other poor women with similar socio-economic conditions.

The Rashtriya Seva Samithi (RASS)

Background

The RASS was established in 1981 at Tirupati. The activities and programmes of RASS were designed for the development of poor in the drought prone Rayalaseema districts of Andhra Pradesh. This region has a high percentage of population who belong to scheduled castes and the backward castes. The region does not have any major industries except a few agro-processing units. It also lags behind other regions of the State in terms of basic amenities. The rapid growth of population has aggravated poverty, unemployment and environmental degradation in the Rayalaseema region. Some of the anti-poverty programmes proved ineffective, as it was more on target achievement rather than human development. Moreover, the rural poor were not involved from the stage of planning to the stage of implementation and evaluation of programmes meant for their upliftment.

Objectives

The main objective of RASS was to adopt such a strategy, which would bring into fold the poor in the development process .The RASS, believes in the following:

1. Involvement of poor in the entire process of development from planning to monitoring.
2. Identification of priorities by the poor themselves.
3. Empowerment of women as a key to self-sustained development of the poor.
4. Provision of community infrastructure as an essential pre-condition for self-sustained growth.
5. Development of agriculture and related activities using local knowledge and local resources apart from modern techniques to reduce the incidence of poverty and unemployment.

The RASS considers the following four interventions as crucial for the poor to reach a stage of social consciousness and empowerment.

Human resource development (by way of massive education, skill upgradation, health services, safe drinking water, sanitation etc. for the disadvantaged groups)

Economic development (through propagation of modern agriculture and technology, family based asset creating activities and waste land development)

Attitudinal changes (to promote greater gender equality, self-reliance and environmental sensitivity)

Self-management and momentum (for the promotion of saving and credit, community management of infrastructure, leadership and self-help).

Area of Operation and Growth

The core area of operation of RASS includes the districts of Cuddapah, Anantpur, Kurnool and Chittoor. The initial activities of RASS were concentrated in Chittoor district, which accounts for an estimated population of 4.3 million. Subsequently, these activities were spread to other districts of Rayalaseema.

Over a period of eighteen years, RASS has been successful in building up a large administrative infrastructure and reaching out to the rural poor in the backward areas within Andhra Pradesh and in the States of Orissa and Tamil Nadu. Because of its involvement in multi-faceted activities, several funding agencies at the national and international level have shown interest and confidence in RASS. Starting with three program activities in eight villages with 15 staff members, RASS has acquired the status of a national level organization. During 1997-98, RASS had 32 programme activities with 3695 programme staff in 3540 villages operating in three States. The budget of RASS which was Rs.0.08 million 1981 had gone up to Rs.72.08 million during the year 1998. Thus, RASS has recorded a phenomenal growth for the past eighteen years.

Women Centered Activities

To tap the potentialities and managerial capacities of rural women RASS has implemented several activities. RASS has been instrumental in organizing rural women to show their strength and defend themselves for their rights with the formation of Mahila Mandals. These Mandals work under the direct supervision and guidance of RASS and also, get regular information about Government programmes, bank financing, marketing trends etc. The successful working of Mahila Mandals has resulted in the formation of a large number of Self-Help Groups (SHGs).

For women to get gainful employment especially belonging to SC, ST and BCs, RASS provides training facilities and generates innovative programmes. The vocational skills, thus acquired, help women to be self-reliant.

Growth and Performance of SHGs

The successful working of Mahila Mandals has resulted in the formation of a large number of Self-Help Groups (SHGs).

In 1990 with the help from RASS, 30 SHGs were formed involving 10-15 women members. Within a year, there were 123 SHGs with a total membership of 1559 women. A significant feature of this system was that a large number of women shifted their borrowing from traditional moneylenders to SHGs at reasonable rates of interest. Moreover, RASS has linked with Rasthriya Mahila Kosh (RMK) and NABARD to mobilize funds. RASS has borrowed about Rs.7million from RMK and lent it to informal women groups. Along with the loan from RMK and their own savings, women groups have generated credit to the extent of Rs.11million. Some of the notable features of this scheme are a high percentage (96) of repayment, utilization of funds for income creating activities and generation of savings by women members in the SHGs.

Constraints

- Lack of support from male members (of the families) as well as banks
- Large magnitude of the target group of poor people
- Attitudinal rigidities
- Difficulty in creating awareness among people
- Limited resources with the NGOs
- Large requirements of training and sensitization of issues
- Limited number of experienced intervention agencies
- Diversities of situations due to wide coverage

Overall Impression

- Use of resources (credit) for income generating activities
- Adoption of non-traditional activities
- Improvement in the income levels of SHGs members
- Nearly 100% recovery of loans

- Generation of small savings in the rural sector among women
- Use of local knowledge and resources in productive activities
- Reduction in transaction cost for both banks as well as SHGs
- Maintenance of minimum records in the form of registers.
- Maintenance of proper accounts by the SHGs.
- Regular meetings of the SHGs members to tackle problems among themselves.
- Healthy relation and coordination between SHGs, NGOs and banks.
- Grant assistance by banks to NGOs for capacity building (towards strengthening and monitoring of SHGs, training, computerization, etc.).
- Support services to NGOs by banks for networking with other smaller NGOs.

Swayamkrushi Mutually Aided Cooperative Thrift Society Limited[4]

The formation of a women's savings and credit system...

Swayamkrushi was formed for women. Poor women generally need small amounts of credit at frequent intervals. Repayment schedules have to be adjusted to their earning cycle. There is a need to build a micro-credit system, as the poor in the area are otherwise wholly dependent on private moneylenders. To understand the formation of Swayamkrushi it is important to understand the history of another organization—the Youth Charitable Organization (YCO). Revolving loan schemes and team action groups. In 1984 YCO worked with 15 villages to establish a revolving loan programme to finance income generation activities through women's savings and credit groups (known locally as TAGs). Each TAG has an average of 10 members and the TAGS in each village made up a Mandal. At this stage loans were extended with no interest rate and no fixed repayment time.

The loans were used to purchase dairy animals and to invest in agriculture, fish vending, sheep rearing, palm fibre processing and other small businesses. The use of a revolving loan fund motivated the women's TAGs to increase their saving activities. Between the TAGs a decision was made to save on a uniform basis. These savings were used to support further lending and also helped the groups, via YCO, to access external lines of credit. In particular external credit was received, via local banks and YCO, from NABARD, a national agricultural credit programme run by the Government, and from RMK a department of the government focused specifically on supporting women's economic activities. By 1993, 90 villages were involved.

The development of Swayamkrushi

By 1996 it was clear that some TAGs were able to save at faster rates than others were. Groups therefore established their own monthly savings targets. At the same time the groups' capacity to record and manage savings and loans had improved. A decision was made by YCO to support the formation of an independent mutual cooperative which would be fully owned by the women who were members of the savings and credit groups. As a result Swayamkrushi (self-help) Women's Development Mutually Aided Cooperative Credit Society came into existence. Swayamkrushi currently has 5,450 members each of whom has paid a Rs. 10 membership fee and provided Rs.10 share capital. The way Swayamkrushi works and the women who are members of Swayamkrushi and who save on a regular basis for 6 months are eligible for loans financed by the members' savings.

Each time a member takes a loan, she must provide 10% of the loan amount as additional share capital. If a woman wants to leave Swayamkrushi she must first ensure that her loan is fully repaid. Her savings and share capital are returned to her although she has the option to leave her share capital with Swayamkrushi if she wants to. In this case she remains eligible for payment of share dividends. All members also pay an annual premium of Rs. 100 towards a group life insurance scheme. At the moment external lines of credit are still managed by YCO at the request of external financiers. However it is anticipated that Swayamkrushi will begin managing external credit during the next 12 months and that there will be a gradual transfer of savings and credit management responsibilities from YCO to Swayamkrushi. YCO has committed personnel support to Swayamkrushi for the first three years of its operation but the organization is expected over this time to gradually begin to provide partial remuneration for the staff involved and to be fully self-sufficient in a couple of years.

Legal status of Swayamakrushi

The Cooperative is legally constituted under the 1995 Andhra Pradesh Mutually Aided Cooperative Societies Act. There are currently 8900 members. The Cooperative is managed by a Board that meets monthly and is composed of 9 individuals elected by the Membership. The Chief Executive Officer attends Board meetings as an ex-officio member but with no voting rights.

Swayamkrushi loans

Current outstanding short and medium term loans amount to Rs. 15,930,208 (US $ 331,879) out of the total loans of Rs. 44,433,900 (US $ 925,706). All payments are made in cash. The current sources of capital used by the Cooperative to support its loan portfolio are shown in the table below. All members are required to save a minimum of Rs. 30 per month. Where lines of credit are provided by agencies such as RMK, that restrict the interest rate at which funds can be on lent, additional savings are required from members taking out loans from these lines. The additional savings are used, in effect, to harmonise the interest rates applied to medium term loans and ensure a consistent charge of 18% across this part of the loan portfolio. A 24% interest rate is applied to short-term loans (12 months or less).

However to date only 2 of these have been taken out. Housing loans attract a 12% interest rate with terms ranging between 5 and 12 years. Members of the Cooperative receive 6% on their savings, a rate that is competitive with other local financial agencies (commercial banks 3.5%, other local cooperatives 4.5% - 5%). If a member wishes to resign from the Cooperative she must provide one month's notice.

Members receiving loans have an option to pay back the loans sooner than the term agreed (i.e. to prepay). 10 people have done this in order to be able to take out a further loan. However, no payments lower than the monthly repayment are allowed. If a member has problems in repayment this has to be dealt with at TAG and/or Mandal level. Under the Co-operative Act there is provision for default to be dealt with rapidly in the court.

Criteria for Short & Medium Term Loans

The borrower must be a member of the Cooperative. (i.e. Have contributed Rs. 100 for 10 shares, paid a membership fee of Rs. 10).

The borrower must have saved regularly for at least 6 months. (Minimum monthly savings currently set at Rs. 30/- month).

The borrower must provide 2 guarantors who are also members of the Cooperative.

Criteria for House Loans

Rs.35,000 for 10 years repayments of Rs. 400 per month. As for short and medium term loans but also:

Land deed or patta in the applicant's own name or House or land deed in the name of the member's father or brother together with a letter authorizing transfer in the case of default. In the case of land or house being used as collateral valuations and lien searches are carried out by the Government sub-registrar in the relevant area and appropriate certification provided to the Cooperative.

Dividend

Members have agreed that the Cooperative should retain all dividends for the first 3 years of its operation.

The Future Development of Swayamkrushi Developing Autonomy

Over the next 2 years it is anticipated that the Cooperative will take over entire responsibility for management of the savings and loan portfolio associated with the village Mahila Mandals. Major external credit lines will be managed during this time by YCO, until Swayamkrushi has established a financial management record. Staff who are currently on secondment from YCO will be permanently employed by the Cooperative by the end of the period at which time their salaries will be the sole responsibility of Swayamkrushi. A three-year business plan has been developed for the Cooperative along these lines.

Increasing the House Loan Portfolio

At the moment the number of house loans extended by the Cooperative is extremely limited. It should be noted that at the moment, in theory, families with title deeds could apply for house loans directly from commercial banks. In practice this would be extremely difficult. The standard term for individual mortgage financing from these agencies is 3 to 4 years and the repayment structure means that repayments in the early stages only reduce the capital loan marginally. Processing time is also much shorter in the case of the cooperative - 15 days compared to 3 or 4 months in the case of the commercial lenders. In any case few families in the area could, at the moment afford commercial house loans delivered outside of the Guarantee initiative which offers considerably longer repayment terms.

One of the ideas being explored at the moment is the establishment of a separate house savings scheme within Swayamkrushi with provision being made for investment in share capital specifically linked to house loans. The aim is to encourage families to save 5%-10% of the house loan they will require and for this amount to be maintained as a hedging fund, reducing the vulnerability of the Cooperative to defaults on house loan repayments.

Increasing the Capital Base by Attracting Richer Villagers

Swayamkrushi is considering offering larger loans to better off villagers in order to increase its capital base and hence its long term financial viability. However security in the form of land and/or gold and jewelry would have to be provided. At the moment gold cannot be accepted as security as the offices are not sufficiently secure. The intention is to require gold to the value of four times the loan size.

Keeping Swayamkrushi in Women's Hands

The Cooperative has considered the issue of men's participation in the savings and loan scheme. In some villages there are men's associations but no mahila mandals as the men have resisted their formation. The co-operative has taken a clear decision to exclude men's associations from Swayamkrushi. They believe that men's inclusion would only strengthen the exclusion of women from financial management at village level.

REFERENCES

1. Hindustan Lever Limited – Project Shakti Brochure
2. http://www.blonnet.com/businessline/2001/05/21/stories/14210204.htm
3. http://www.gdrc.org/icm/wind/rass.html

- RASS, 1998. 'Partners in Progress—Organizing Communities for Development'
- RASS, 1998. Awakening Gender Potential—The SHGs Way.
- SIDBI, 1999. Annual Report 1998-99'.
- SIDBI, 1997. Development Report, October 1997.
- Sri Padmavathy Mahila Abyudaya Sangam, 1996. Community Banking—Our Gurthimpu.
- Sri Padmavathy Mahila Abyudàya Sangam, 1996. Training Manual for Community Banking.

4. http://www.ycongo.org/women's_coop_.htm

Appendices

APPENDIX -I

ENTREPRENEURSHIP DEVELOPMENT TRAINING PROGRAMMES (EDTPs)

Introduction

Entrepreneurship is the human side of industrial development and for that matter economic development. In any society, now and then motivated individuals emerge as entrepreneurs, launch their enterprises, learn the secrets of their business and acquire managerial skills through their entrepreneurial activities. In other words, it is self-learning on the job. But the emergence of such spontaneous entrepreneurs is small in number against the number that is required for speedy and wider spread of small industry in predominantly agrarian societies in the developing countries. Most of these countries are engaged in inducing entrepreneurship among different segments of their society, who have the potential to venture into some entrepreneurial activity. Potential or motivation, though a necessary condition, is not sufficient for the individuals to start and run their enterprises successfully and so training in entrepreneurship in its multi-facets is imperative and runs as a corollary in the promotion and development of small-scale industry.

Objectives of EDTPs

The objectives of a training programme in entrepreneurship development are to develop the motivation of potential entrepreneurs, help them in taking up suitable enterprises, enable them to prepare economically viable and technically feasible bankable projects and enhance their enterprise-building skills. The training programmes basically funnel down to the understanding of three key elements and in a measure, they are interrelated.

Entrepreneur as a Person

In regard to the first element, the entrepreneur as a person, the objective is to facilitate understanding of himself or herself, his or her motive strength, value orientation, adoption propensity, risk-taking ability, level of aspiration and capabilities in inter-personal relationship. This understanding of oneself and others is provided through psychological exercises and games. The very climate that is created in this part of the training and the training group situation (the participant amongst his fellow participants) is to a considerable degree a revelation of oneself to oneself and a motivating factor for entrepreneurial activity.

Enterprise

Here it is an understanding of all the aspects of an enterprise: the choice of an enterprise, comparative advantages, the product, the product design, its economic viability, the technical imperatives, the process, scale of investment, financial implications, extent of profitability, its potential marketability and its sustainability over a period of time in terms of availability of raw materials and other inputs.

Environment

The environment mainly comprises understanding the prospects of a particular line of enterprise, its location, the government's industrial policy, the institutions, technical and financial support extended to the sources of raw materials, machinery and equipment, and the prospects of marketing of products within and outside the country.

Further, the EDTPs in general focus upon various aspects of management, financial, production, material and marketing and labour laws and taxation.

The Clientele of EDTPs

The clientele or the target groups that enter or induced to enter the threshold of entrepreneurship are of diverse background and so the training curricula may have to be formulated and offered to suit their background, especially, keeping in view their educational background, technical training, previous experience and the broad spectrum of enterprises they are likely to venture into. The target groups of EDTP participants may be categorized as follows:

(i) General Entrepreneurs
(ii) Science & Technology Entrepreneurs
(iii) Women Entrepreneurs
(iv) Educated Unemployed Entrepreneurs
(v) Ex-Servicemen Entrepreneurs
(vi) Rural Entrepreneurs including the Weaker Sections
(vii) Artisan Entrepreneurs
(viii) Tribal Entrepreneurs
(ix) Handicapped Entrepreneurs

Besides the above, the EDP trainers, managers and administrators constitute a special category of participants who undergo a Trainers Training Programme with a coverage of core EDTP modules plus a comprehensive theoretical and practical training in methodology and skills.

Though, there will be target specific topics in each of the above training programmes, the core body of the areas that would be common to all the programmes may include:

(a) Entrepreneurship Quality/Motivation Development;
(b) Enterprise Launching & Resourcing;
(c) Enterprise Management; and
(d) Entrepreneurship Discipline / Social Responsibility.

What we have mentioned above in terms of categories of target groups and the core body of areas that may be incorporated in all the training programmes is illustrative and suggestive and the EDP training faculty, in a given situation, may formulate their curricula in a manner they think appropriate to the target group.

A model syllabus for general entrepreneurs is provided here.*

SYLLABUS FOR GENERAL ENTREPRENEURS

The EDTP endeavours to change, educate and equip a person to become a successful entrepreneur. The whole process envisages developing the participant's latent qualities and skills as also equipping him with other capabilities. By the end of the programme, the participant is expected to be in a position to crystallize his vision into action and launch and manage his enterprise with competence.

Coverage

The significant phases of the programme in entrepreneurship training should be seen as a continuum. The objectives, duration, methodology and coverage etc., can be examined as one cohesive package for Entrepreneurship Training. The syllabus for the general entrepreneur, therefore, should be understood as guidelines wherefrom all the specific modifications and variations can be made, depending upon the target group.

The four fundamental areas which a comprehensive programme should cover can be identified as follows:

---

* *Adopted from "Model Syllabi for Entrepreneurship Development Training Programme" developed by the National Institute for Entrepreneurship & Small Business Development, New Delhi, 1985. Please see the above source for the syllabi for the other categories of target groups listed above.*

A. Entrepreneurial quality and identify development;
B. Enterprise launching including resourcing;
C. Enterprise management; and
D. Social responsibilities and entrepreneurial discipline.

The word "Motivation" has to be understood the way one interprets this word which shapes one's goal and behaviour. Historically, achievement-motivation has been equated with entrepreneurial motivation. Over a period of time experiments revealed that only achievement-motivation was not sufficient to help a person to become an entrepreneur. The concept of entrepreneurial motivation, therefore, assumed significance. Entrepreneurial coping ability, tolerance to ambiguity, persuasiveness and search for emotional support for sustaining a sense of purpose are generally beyond the purview of achievement motivation and these form a core component of entrepreneurial motivation.

The focus in EDP is on the person entrepreneur. His potentialities have to be tapped, energized and ultimately his vision has to be translated into action.

The Entrepreneur Motivation Development Laboratory provides experiential learning situations to the entrepreneurs to help them examine their outlook and attitude towards entrepreneurship and help practice newly learnt behaviour.

Earlier it was believed that people would respond to the opportunities automatically and therefore, alleviate themselves out of poverty; this view does not hold good. The second assumption was that people are, by birth either inclined to or against entrepreneurial functions. This view also has already been dispelled.

During the early sixties some professionals (McClelland and his associates) engaged in this task started investigating the possibilities and their finding revealed that:

(a) people can acquire motives and develop through education.

(b) the newly aroused motives are more likely to influence future thoughts and actions.

Experiments conducted in India in mid-sixties supported the observations mentioned above.

An attempt is made in the Laboratory to work on the "Motives and emotive" determinants of individual behaviour, achievement-motivation and its associated network for entrepreneurship, risk-taking and concept of moderate and calculated risk, perception of personal and environmental risks for achieving goal, achievement planning and goal setting behaviour of the entrepreneur. The EMT laboratory can be devised as a continuous programme spread over 6 days preferably in the first week of the programme. EMT relevance and linkage to remaining part is the most crucial aspect in the design of the EDTP. To help develop entrepreneurial identity, the duration may have to be extended up 10 to 12 days with interventions of additional days appropriately linked with project launching and management phase.

A. Entrepreneurial quality and identity development

It must be noted that while EMT is specialized training programme, it is a significant and integrated component of the entire Entrepreneurship Development Programme package. Certain unique feature distinguishes this module from the rest. Firstly, the programme is experiential in nature. Secondly, the programme touches the hard core of the individual motivation, perception and his goal, which sows the seeds of change process that we intend to develop in the person.

The basic objective in this phase is to enable the entrepreneur to have a good look at himself. He starts assessing his potentialities, confidence and entrepreneurial spirit and learns to match them with his options and alternatives in entrepreneurial pursuits. The specific objectives of the phase, however, can be listed as follows:

(a) to increase entrepreneurial spirit.
(b) to reduce participant's psychological resistance to change.
(c) to effect positive attitudes towards entrepreneurship among participants.
(d) to build up confidence among participants in their ability to achieve.
(e) to train each participant to apply reasonable standards of excellence to his own performance.
(f) to set attainable goals for himself.
(g) to improve inter-personal relations and influence competence of participants.
(h) to make participants aware of relationship between need for achieving, thinking and action.
(i) to form the EMT Group into a cohesive reference group for each other.

This phase is conducted right in the beginning of the programme to unfreeze the ground and to generate a sense of learning among the participants about the entrepreneurial venture. Their desire to know further, their plans and decision to crystallize their ambition into action is attained during the first week of the programme itself. The participant's receptivity of learning increases commitment to himself and his goal. Further, change and development in the attitude of the person may lead to a change and development in his knowledge and skill at a much faster pace.

It is in this context that this phase helps him crystallize his ideas to enable him launch his project. The subsequent phase on enterprise launching deals with these aspects in detail.

B. Enterprise launching including resourcing

Having changed the person in first phase we should help the entrepreneur crystallize his thoughts and translate his dream into a reality. The topics suggested in the syllabus have, therefore, been included more for their practical utility rather than their academic significance. While the overall objective of the EDTP syllabus is to develop selected trainees into confident and successful entrepreneurs by imparting systematic and comprehensive training, this phase is designed to encourage technological upgradation wherever possible. To be more precise the objective of this phase is to equip the participants with appropriate techniques for:

(a) Product Selection;
(b) Preparation of Project Report; and
(c) Launching the Enterprise.

The contents recommended have been so chosen, as to help build healthy units and avoid industrial sickness. The would-be entrepreneur has to learn to relate himself with the environment. The skills needed for this process shall be acquired during the course of training. The success of this phase can be evaluated only if it assists the entrepreneur in becoming the self-developer.

To enable the participants to identify opportunities where others do not, 17 sessions have been recommended for Environment Analysis and Project Selection. It is realized, information itself is a tremendous factor of production. On product selection, 6 sessions have been recommended of which two are expected to provide the theoretical input in a classroom situation and four sessions should be for guided field work/audio-visual presentation/panel discussions. The particular methodology can be chosen by the trainer to suit the specific requirements. Quite possibly, the trainers may prefer to devote more time on market survey so that during the EDTP itself they are able to finalize a product. In case the batch is such, it is suggested that 4 to 6 days can be exclusively devoted for this work and accordingly the programme may be stretched.

Flexibility rather than rigidity should be the password. The curriculum has been designed not to restrict the trainers to the classroom activities but to enable them to bring the participants as near to reality as is possible. Thus, appropriate methodology, like lectures, reading material, Technical notes, Guided fieldwork, Audio-Visual aids, panel discussions, Case Studies, Industrial Exercises, Checklists etc., have been suggested.

More than training it is the interaction of certain local factors which fosters the entrepreneurial goal. Such local factors, quite clearly shall not be available in all parts of the country. Hopefully enough, a correct blend of the methodologies suggested should assist in providing the three critical inputs of knowledge, Skill and Attitudes, which are very necessary for resourcing and enterprise launching.

Within this phase of 2-1/2 weeks, trainers may like to condense or expand certain area depending upon specific needs. Topics such as "Foreign Collaboration" can be dropped, while others may be abridged. Where the need is for providing still more comprehensive inputs certain topics could be discussed in greater detail for durations more than specified. Some topics for example "Procedure for Raw Material Inputs" may be added.

An ideal situation would be where the potential entrepreneurs actually launched the enterprise simultaneously with their training. But as this may not be always feasible, this syllabus does not specifically deal with such a situation.

The entrepreneur needs to be exposed next to managerial competence and skill. This phase aims at enhancing his functional skills.

C. Enterprise management

Entrepreneurs of Small Industry will generally have to manage their enterprises themselves. It is, therefore, essential to train potential entrepreneurs in various management techniques, so as to make them effective in the managerial process of combining men, machines, materials, money and market to accomplish specified entrepreneurial objectives.

The content and coverage of Enterprise management in EDTP will depend upon the level of the participants and the length of the course. While the EDP Training schedule will take several weeks, essentials of entrepreneurial management could be covered in 2 weeks consisting of 58 sessions each of 1-1/2 hrs. duration. This excludes field visits. The basic objective of this phase is to acquaint participants with the essentials of:

(a) Personnel Management;
(b) Production Management;
(c) Materials Management;
(d) Financial Management including Cost & Accounting Practices;
(e) Marketing Management;
(f) The basic management concepts and applications of industrial laws.

This course is designed to create an awareness and appreciation of basic management concepts and tools in order to build participants' capability to deal with real-life work situations which will enable them to internalize the knowledge and skills imparted during the course of training. This, it is hoped will sensitize the participants enough to identify problems and arrive at appropriate solutions.

D. Social responsibilities and entrepreneurial discipline

It is important that business ethics and social responsibilities of the entrepreneur be considered throughout the training modules. Inculcating an apt value system will surely generate fruitful results for the entrepreneurs and the society in the ultimate analysis. Needless to add, compliance with the obligations arising from the laws of the land, expectations of the social set-up and care for ecology and environment are indispensable in any planned developmental efforts for entrepreneurship.

Methodology

Training methodologies are wide ranging. The assimilation and its extent, would however depend upon the methodology used and its specificity in any training situation. It is important that the trainer be equipped in an approach adequate to the level of the participants and the depth of training required. The trainer should continuously be keeping in mind the appropriateness of methodology to be used in the training module. Depending upon the target group, he may draw from the syllabus recommended and decide upon the depth to be covered. The trainer may select any combination of the following methods:

(i) Lecturers.
(ii) Case Studies.
(iii) Business games.
(iv) Problem-oriented exercises and projects.
(v) Syndicate methods.
(vi) Films.
(vii) T-Group.
(viii) Role Play
(ix) Shop floor lectures.
(x) Experiential learning.

The suitability of a method or combination of methods, however, has been indicated against each topic.

The detailed structured outline, coverage, objectives and durations are presented in the tables A1-A4.

Duration

The distribution of sessions to different aspect of training are as follows:

Entrepreneurial quality/identity development	31
Enterprise launching and resourcing	48
Enterprise management	58
Social responsibility and Entrepreneurial discipline	4
	141

Besides these sessions there may be field visits of 4-6 days, and another inplant study of 4-6 days duration.

Another 1 to 2 weeks time may be required if the actual project report on selected topics need to be developed.

Taking all these together, the total EDTP may be for 6-10 weeks duration. This calculation is based on 4 sessions in a day and 6 working days in a week. The duration however, will be changed if training is to be conducted as part time.

Important Guidelines

A. Entrepreneurial quality and identity development

1. Number of sessions range from 20-30 covering 4 sessions a day upto a maximum 6 days.
2. It varies with number of participants because EMT Lab demands individual attention.
3. The above sequence has been largely in a chronological order: However, certain areas need to be spread over a number of days as indicated above.
4. In case of rural entrepreneurship activity data may be generated in the beginning at stretches followed with TAT. Analysis need not precede activity exercise.
5. Session on coping mechanism, influencing ability

and other aspects of entrepreneurial behaviour can be incorporated during enterprise launching or afterwards fitting it with the language of enterprise.

6. In order to develop identity of entrepreneur, EMT trainer can not be just concerned with the first week's input or behaviour input; trainer has to provide a linkage and integrate with entire syllabus. Entrepreneurial process integration can emerge with appropriate interventions at various points in different programmes. Trainer has to use his own discretion in this.
7. Goal-setting and action plan may need more time.
8. Public statement on proposed action plan may enhance the commitment to entrepreneurial goal.

B. Enterprise launching and resourcing

1. Each session would be of 90 minutes duration.
2. Lecture notes may be based on the lectures delivered.
3. Reading material would be additional literature.
4. Wherever available appropriate films may be shown.
5. Audio-visual aids to be used wherever necessary.
6. All exercises related to enterprise launching should be related to the selected enterprise. In case the entrepreneurs have not selected a project during training, a separate one-week period may be allotted for preparing actual project report after field visit.

C. Enterprise management

1. Additional session can be added depending on the entrepreneurs' background, size and type of enterprises introducing to computer/information management.

2. Production planning, systematic control etc., can be included accordingly.

D. Social responsibility and entrepreneurial discipline

1. The topics indicated under this, may be treated simultaneously with other topics or may be taken up separately at one place.

   This can also be done by discussing pros and cons of entrepreneurial career or need and scope of entrepreneurship in present economic context.

Field Visit and Inplant Study

Depending on the level of enterprises both the field visits and inplant studies of 4-6 days duration each can be organized as a part of the EDTP. However, a field study of 4-6 days duration will always help provide practical experience and is recommended as part of the general entrepreneurs course.

TABLE-A1

ENTREPRENEURIAL QUALITY AND IDENTITY DEVELOPMENT (EM/LAB)

	Subject and Coverage 1	*Method* 2	*No. of Sessions* 3	*Remarks* 4
1.	Programme Clarity-Sharing Expectations and Unfreezing	Micro-lab	1	Micro-lab may have some impact on quality of TAT stories that participants later on write; choice of using ML after TAT is however left to the trainer.
2.	Data Collection about Self	Imagination exercise instrument (thematic apperception test) "Who am I"? Write up.	1	Proper care needs to be taken in administering TAT to stimulate their thoughts.
3.	Introduction to Need System and Motivational pattern of Entrepreneur - Conceptualizing Entrepreneurial skill and behaviour.	Lecture-cum-discussion	1	It can also be conducted after assessing the achievement imagery. However, as per the trainer's choice conceptual linkage to forenoon session may be meaningful here.
4.	Risk Taking Behaviour - - Hope for success and fear of failure - Learning from feedback Ring toss exercise	Ring toss exercise	2	It may extend to third session, in case group size exceeds 20.
5.	Analysing Motive Strength; - Locating achievement imageries; intensity of motives.	Analysing TAT stories. (Group and individual)	4	It may be continuous sessions or distributed over 2 to 3 days to reinforce the concepts.
6.	Personal efficacy - remaining individual life goal; - its linkage to entrepreneurship - locus of control.	Analysing who am I (in small groups/ individual)	1	Can be discussed in-depth individual level when the trust is very high in the group.

TABLE-A2

ENTERPRISE LAUNCHING AND RESOURCING

	Subject and Coverage	*Method*	*No. of Sessions*	*Remarks*
	1	*2*	*3*	*4*
(I)	**Environmental Analysis**			
1.	Entrepreneurial processes and enterprise building - Characteristics & contents - Decision making in enterprise building - Types of enterprises	Lecture/Discussion	2	—
2.	Environmental scanning and analysis - Government Policy, i.e., industrial policy - Reservation of products for development of SSI Sector - Government purchase - Promotional policy	Lecture/Discussion	2 6 Field Study)	
3	Institutions and their role - Statutory and promotional - Role and functions	Lecture/Discussion	2	—
4.	Government assistance and incentives - Scope - Benefits	Lecture/Discussion	2	—

Table - A2 (Continued)

	1	2	3	4
5.	Sources of information			
	- Classification, documentation and use.	Lecture/Discussion	1	—
6.	Procedures for setting up SSI			
	- Formalities to be completed of checklist.	Lecture/Discussion	1	—
(II)	**Project Selection/Formulation**			—
1.	Project Identification	Lectures cases		—
	- Generating project ideas			
	- Short listing			
	- Final selection			
	- Broad project category, specific sector and sub-sectors.			
2.	Project selection	Lectures, reading material, and technical notes	6	—
	- Market segmentation			
	- Market survey, market alternatives, an overview of the future product development, marketing strategy over time.	Guided field work audio-visual. Panel discussion (experiences of entrepreneurs).	2	—
	- Methodology of updating market survey.			
	- Product selection			
3.	Feasibility			
	- Industry and firm level feasibility	Lectures, case studies	2	—
	- Study of typical project report			
	- Of financial institutions	Group & individual exercises	2	—

Table - A2 (Continued)

	1	2	3	4
4.	Determining size - Manageability - Future investment opportunities - Implications of pre-break-even level of output.	Lecture	1	—
5.	Choosing appropriate technology - Criteria of selection of technology - Alternatives to optimal choice - Selection of plant and machinery - Skill involved for technology - Labour and raw material requirement	Lecture check list	2	—
6.	Estimation of Cost - Project cost estimates - Production costs	Group and individual exercise	1	—
7.	Time scheduling - Project monitoring and review techniques.	Illustrations case studies	2	—
	- Summary sessions of project selection.	Lecture	2	—
III	**Project Appraisal**			—
1.	Technical, economic, financial	Technical notes, group work.	2	—
2.	Managerial and marketing feasibility	Lectures, panel discussion		

Table - A2 (Continued)

	1	2	3	4
(IV)	**Financial Analysis**			
1.	Means of Finance, Concept of Risk Capital; Long-Term and Short-term Loans; Leasing Hire-Purchase; Expectations of Banks/ Financial Institutions; Precautions and Procedures for Preparing Projected Balance Sheet, Profit and Loss A/C, Cash Flow Statement; Ratio Analysis, Rate of Return, etc.	Lectures and Lecture notes. Exercise	4	—
2.	Financing of Working Capital Requirement, Cost, Volume, Profit Sensitivity Analysis	Case studies Differs with change in capacity utilization of the enterprise and its level	2	—
(V)	Forms of Enterprise			
1.	Proprietary			
2.	Private Limited Company	To be discussed before the project is finalized.	2	—
3.	Partnership etc.,			
(VI)	**Foreign Collaboration**			
	- Alternatives available - Financial, technical - Outright purchase of know-how, guidelines for collaboration.	Lectures Reading material	1	—

TABLE-A3

ENTERPRISE MANAGEMENT

	Subject and Coverage 1	*Method* 2	*No. of Sessions* 3	*Remarks* 4
(I)	**Basic management Concepts**			
(a)	Functions of Management, Planning, Organizing, Directing, Controlling, Coordinating	Lectures, Discussion, Films	2	Provides an overview of the various aspects of organizations and Management in brief. Provides a feel of Business Management Audit, Time Management.
(b)	Principles of Sound Organization, Span of Control, Authority, Responsibility, Accountability.	Lectures, Discussion, Films	2	
(c)	Introduction to Business Mathematics and Statistics	Lectures, Discussion, Films	1	Calculation of interest and personnel values of Borrowings, Ratio & Proportion. Moving Averages for Costing. Trend Analysis, Histogram. Pie Chart. Data Presentation.
(d)	Business Communication Barriers to Communication, Written Analysis, Oral and Written Communication.	Lectures, Discussion, Films	1	
(II)	**Personnel Management**			
	Work motivation, Labour relations, Wages administration, incentives etc.	Lectures, Discussion, Films	2	To train for handling work force. The focus will be Entrepreneurial Management. Film on personnel management may be screened and discussed.

Table - A3 (Continued)

	1	2	3	4
(III)	**Production Management**			
a)	Production Planning and Control Routing, Scheduling, Dispatching, Expediting and Evaluating; Production Scheduling Techniques Methods and Procedures in Production.	Lectures, Discussion, Film	4	To equip the participants with managerial skills for planning, formulation of targets, procedures, systems and optimum utilization based on production control techniques and practices.
b)	Quality Control – Inspection Standards and Specifications – ISI	Lectures, Discussion, Film	2	Improvement of quality, use of quality raw material and equipment accuracy in measurements, operation and processes, quality consciousness.
c)	Systematic Plant Maintenance and Lubrication	Lectures, Discussion, Film	2	
d)	Methods improvement, Work Measurement, and Value Analysis	Lectures, Discussion, Film	2	
e)	Industrial Safety	Lectures, Discussion, Film	2	
(IV)	**Materials Management**			
a)	Inventory Control; Definition of Inventory, Types of Inventory, Storage and Issues, Records Inventory Case.	Lectures	6	
b)	Materials Handling Equipment (Analysis and Selection)	Discussion		

Table - A3 (Continued)

	1	2	3	4
c)	Economic Order Quantity, maximum safety stores, recorder points; -Make or buy decision - Purchase policies & procedures	Film		
d)	Classification and modification; Standardization, substitution, simplification			ABC control analysis; VEL-analysis, VIEN Analysis, Store Management
(V)	**Financial Management Including Costing and Accounting Practices**			To develop analytical skills for dealing with financial management in small industry. To train the participants in the maintenance of accounts and compilation of financial statements.
a)	Tools of Financial Analysis; - Ratio analysis relating to liquidity, leverage, activity & profitability, funds flow/cash flows analysis.	Lectures, Discussions, Exercises	2	
b)	Effects of Income Tax	Lectures, Discussions, Exercises.	1	
c)	Management of Working Capital; - Size of Working Capital, Risk Factor, Management of Cash including Bank Credit, Management of Accounts, Receivables, Management of Inventory, Effects of Inflation on Working Capital Management.	Lectures, Discussions, Exercises	2	

Table - A3 (Continued)

	1	2	3	4
d)	Financial Accounting; - Double entry system, books of accounts, accounting principles, concept of business income, depreciation accounting profit and loss appropriation and preparation of balance sheet.	Lectures	4	
e)	Cost Accounting; - Cost of goods sold, direct cost-labour, material, overheads, price determination, profit margins, cost control, budgeting as a means of cost control, marginal costing.	Lectures, Discussions, Exercises, Films	4	
f)	Risk Taking and Insurance - Essentially against fire, theft, destruction, natural calamities, strikes, law & order, etc.	Lectures, Discussions, Exercises, Films.	1	
(VI)	**Marketing Management**			To develop essential skills in marketing arrangement: To provide practice in qualitative and quantitative analysis to make decisions in the market situation.
a)	Role of Marketing in Small Industry and Business	Lectures, Discussion, Exercises	3	
	- Importance of consumer's point of view, consumer's behaviour, buying habits.	-do-		

Table - A3 (Continued)

1		2	3	4
	- Marketing	-do-		
	- Product policies, Brand	-do-		
	- Policies	-do-		
b)	Packaging	-do-	1	
c)	Channels of distribution government purchases	-do-	1	
d)	Role of Government Agencies in Marketing	-do-	1	To give an insight to legislation related to Small Industry and Business, labour and taxation laws, and procedures and regulations covering exports and imports
e)	Pricing Policies and Practices	-do-	1	
f)	Product Mix-Segmentation	-do-	1	
g)	Sales, Control, Appraisal of	-do-	1	
h)	Management of Receivables	-do-	1	
i)	Advertising and Sales Promotion	-do-	1	
j)	Introduction to Import/Export Procedures	-do-	1	
(VII)	**Problem Solving and Innovation** -Problem Identification, Analysis, Diagnosis	Lectures Case Study	2	
	Repayment Behaviour Meeting Stationery Requirement, to care for Ecology, Environment & Society	Lectures, Discussions	4	Sensitization to Social responsibility and entrepreneurial discipline can be done through reference at different stages of training or can be done at one point preferably towards the end of the training. The intensity and relevance may be as per the style and size of enterprises. This may be done for reinforcing commitment.

APPENDIX – II(A)

SOME IMPORTANT RESOURCES AND THEIR INDUSTRIAL USES*

A. AGRO-RESOURCES

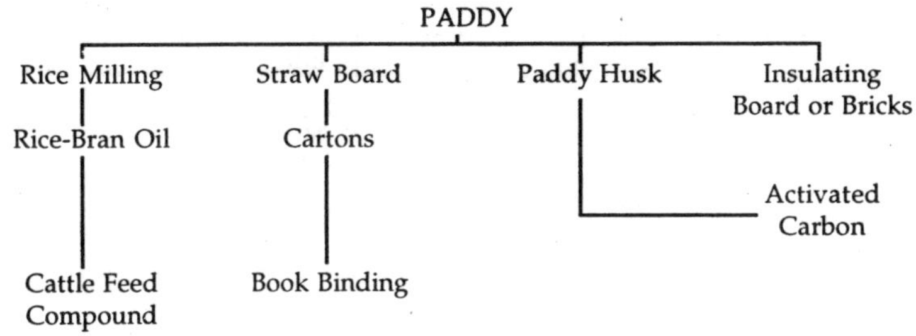

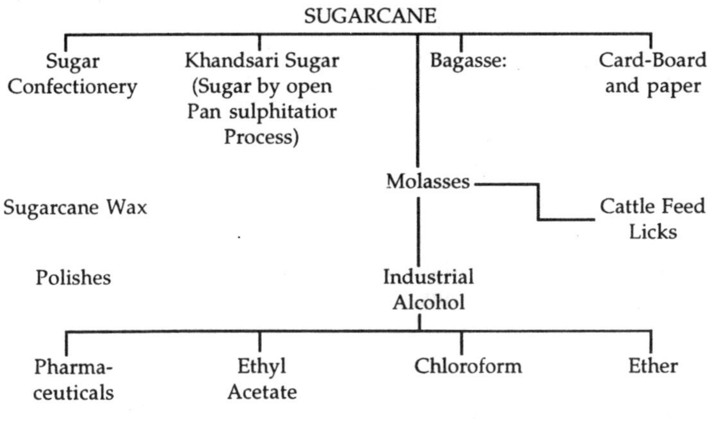

* *Source*: National Institute of Small Industry Extension Training (NISIET), Hyderabad, India, as cited by Setty,E.D., 1991, in Rural Industrialization, Small Scale and Cottage Industries in Asia, UNCRD Working Paper No.91-2, United Nations Centre for Regional Development, Nagoya, Japan

Appendix – II (A) (contd.)

FRUITS AND VEGETABLES

- Squashes
- Juices
- Jams
- Jellies
- Custard Powder
- Canning

- Cashew
  - Cashew Kernels
  - Cashew Shell Oil
  - Cashew Apple-Wine
- Orange
  - Orange Peel Oil
- Banana
  - Banana Powder
  - Banana Figs
  - Banana Chips
  - Starch from Banana Stem
- Mango
  - Mango Cereal Flakes breakfast food and flavouring agent)

COCONUT

- Copra
  - Oil Mills
    - Oil
    - Cake
- Dessicated Coconut
- Fibre
  - Coir Mats, Mattings, Etc.
  - Rubberised Coir
- Activated
- Shell Powder

TAPIOCA (CASAVA)

- Starch
  - Dextrine
    - Glucose
- Sago

Appendix – II(A) (contd.)

GROUNDNUT

- Husk
  - Hard Board
- Oil Mills
  - Cake
    - Solvent Extraction Of Oil
      - Proteins
      - Carbohydrates
      - Cattle Feed
  - Oil
    - Refining
    - Hydro-generation
      - Soap Stock & Washing Soap

OTHER OIL SEEDS

Castor Seed	Cake Oil	Lubricants Hydrogenerated Castor Oil Hydraulic Brake Fluid Dehydrated Castor Oil	
	Paints	Detergents Soaps	Synthetic Yarn
Linseed (Linum Usitatissimum lin)	Oil Mills	Double Boiled Linseed Oil	— Paints
Sunflower seed- (Cartharmus Tinctorius)	Oil Mills —	Refined Edible Oil	
Mowha Seed (Madhuca indica) Neem Seed (Melia Azadiracta	Oils —	Washing Soap	

Appendix – II (A) (contd.)

RUBBER

Rubber	- Rubberized Fibre - Rubber Gloves - Rubber-moulded Goods - Rubber-Dipped Products - Tyres and Tubes - Foam Rubber

(VII)	Papaya	- Pectin and Papain

FIBRES

Jute	- Jute Twine - Bags

SPICES AND CONDIMENTS

Chilli Pepper	.... =	Powder — Oleoresin	Curry Powders Hot Chutneys Pickles
Garlic Turmeric	.... =	Powder	
Ginger	.... =	Crystallized Ginger Dried Ginger	
Tamarind	.... =	Tamarind Concentrate	

Appendix – II (A) (contd.)

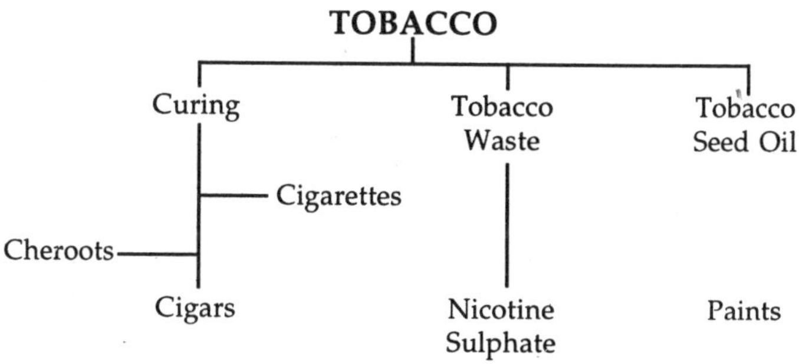

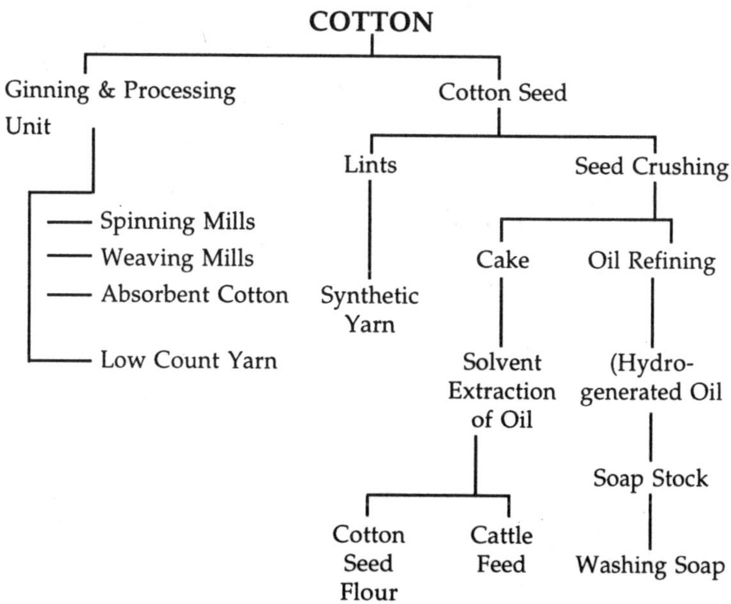

B. FOREST RESOURCES

1. TIMBER

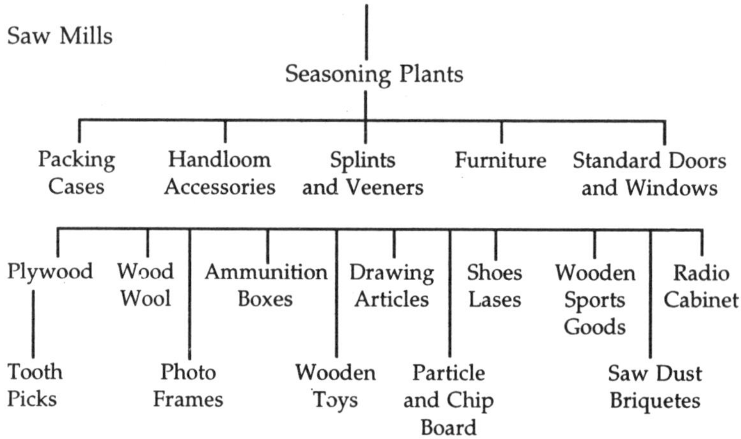

II. MINOR FOREST PRODUCTS

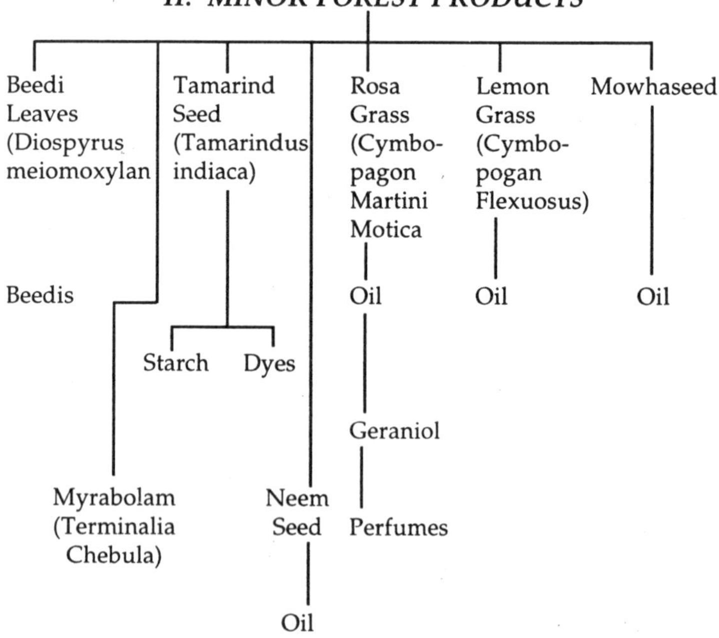

Minor Forest Products (contd.)

- Sisal (Agave Sisalana
  - Fibre
  - Wax
- Shellac
  - Sealing Wax
  - Colours
- Sundrawood (Acacia sundra)
  - Katha (Cactechu)
- Gum Arabic (Acacia Arabicca)
  - Liquid Gum
- Soap Nuts (Saplnous Emaginatus)
  - Soap Nut Powder
- Nuxvomica (Strychonu Nux Vomica)
  - Medicine
- Konnum and Barks
- Avaram (Cassiafistula And Auriculata)

C. MARINE RESOURCES

I. Fish

- Fish Canning
- Fish Freezing
- Fish Curing
- Fish Oil
- Fish-meal

II. Salt

- Table Salt
- Dairy Salt
- Industrial Salt
- Mineralized Salt

III. SEA BITTERNS

- Mixed Salt
  - Potassium Sulphate
  - Potash Alum
- Potasium Chloride
- Magnesium Sulphate
- Magnesium Carbonate
- Magnesium Trisillicate

- Gypsum
  - Hydrated Calcium Sillicate

D. LIVESTOCK RESOURCES

I. HIDES & SKINS

- Tanning
- Finished Leather
- Industrial Leather
- Leather Footwear
- Leather Goods
- Cycle Saddle Tops

II. WASTES

- Castings For Sausages from Intestines
- Guts from Animal Intestines
- Glue from Tannery Wastes
- Wool Rugs
- Bone Meal and Powder
- Gelatine

III. OTHERS

i). Caracass utilization plants

ii). Meat – Canning Sausages

iii). Bristles (hog hair)

iv). Egg powder

APPENDIX – II (B)

LIST OF AGRO-BASED INDUSTRIES SUGGESTED FOR IMPLEMENTATION IN DEVELOPING COUNTRIES*

Absorbent Cotton
Agricultural discs
Agricultural Implements
Agricultural Implements, Chaff cutters
Agricultural Implements, Conventional & Imported
Agricultural Implements, Power Tiller
Agricultural Machinery
Agricultural Plough
Agro-service centre
Ajowan Oil
Alcohol
Aloe Fibre Ropes
Bakery
Bal-Ahar
Banana Figs
Banana Powder
Banana Pseudostin
Caffeine from Tea Waste
Card Board
Cashew Kernels
Cashew Liquor
Cashewnut
Cashewnut Shell Liquid
Cashew Processing Factory
Casava Processing
Cattle Feed
Furfural
Ginger & Ginger Products
Ginger Oil
Grape Products Processing
Groundnuts Processing
Huller Modernisation
Ice Cream & Ice Cream Powder/Candy
Jute Stick Powder
Jute Sutali & Rope
Khandasari Sugar
Lemon Grass Oil, Ionone
Maize – Corn Flakes
Malted Food
Mango Processing
Mini Sugar Plant
Oil Crushing
Oil Mill
Oil Seeds
Oil Seed Crushing & Refining of Oils
Oleoresin
Orange Oil
Oxalic Acid
Paddy Processing
Palm Fibre
Palmarose Oil
Papain & Pectin from Raw Papaya

Chicory Powder
Chimney Powder
Coconut Desicated Processing
Coconut Oil
Coconut Shell Flour
Coconut husk, Decorticating
Coir
Condensed Milk
Confectionery & Chocolate
Cotton Seed Processing
Cotton Seed oil
Corrugated Paper Board
Dall Mill
Dehydrated Castor Oil
Dehydrated Fruits, Vegetables
& Soap Powders
Dehydrated Vegetable Plant
Double boiled linseed oil
Extraction of oil from Neem Seed
Farm Machinery
Fruit Juice Fruit Pulp
Fruit Preservation & Canning
Fruit Processing
Fruit & Vegetable Canning
Fruit & Vegetable Preserving
Fruit & Vegetable Processing
Peanut Butter
Pineapple Fibre
Pine Oil
Power Tiller
Poultry Feed
Protivita
Ragimalt
Rice Bran Oil
Rice Mil! Huller Screen
Rope & Ban Manufacturing
Rubber Seed Oil
Saw Dust Briquetting
Sago unit
Saponio from Soap Nuts
Solvent Extraction,
Oil Cake
Soup Masoor Dal
Splints and Veneers
Starch from Maize
Starch from Potato
Starch from Tapioca
Straw Board
Sugar Cane Wax, Bleached
Surgical Bandages
Synthetic Cryolite
Tamarind Seed Starch
Vermicellic
Vegetable Milk Curd from
Groundnuts

* *Source*:- NISIET, Hyderabad, India, as cited by Setty, E.D., 1991, in *Rural Industrialization, Small-Scale and Cottage Industries in Asia*, UNCRD Working Paper, op.cit.

APPENDIX-II (C)

Illustrative list of Small Scale units that could be set up under the scheme of Integrated Infrastructure Development (IID) depending upon local requirements and resource endowments*

I. Agro-Forest Based and Food Preservation

1. Fruit and Vegetable Preservation/Processing/ Dehydration
2. Oil Mills/Expellers
3. Animal/Poultry Feeds
4. Processing of Spices
5. Cereal Processing
6. Bakery and Confectionary Products
7. Dairy Products Processing
8. Hatcheries/Nurseries
9. Cold Storage
10. Meat and Fish Processing
11. Pickles/Squashes/Juices etc.
12. Leaf Plates/Cups
13. Soap Nut Powder
14. Handmade Paper
15. Extraction of Essential Oils
16. Herbs Collection/Processing
17. Mushroom Production/Processing
18. Potato/Tomato Products
19. Starch
20. Brushes/Brooms
21. Silk Worm Rearing & Silk Processing
22. Papad & Vadi
23. Bee-keeping

II. Chemical/Plastic/Rubber Products

1. Soap & Detergents
2. Dhoop & Agarbatti
3. Paints/Varnishes/Distemper
4. Chalk Crayons
5. Candles
6. Hydrated Lime
7. Allopathic/Ayurvedic Medicine Formulations
8. HDPE/PVC Rigid Pipe/Polythene Pipes
9. Plastic Sheets
10. Plastic Bags
11. P.P. Granules
12. Plastic Container/Storage Tanks
13. Consumer Plastic Products
14. Plastic Shoes/Chappals/Hawai Chappals
15. Rubber Footwear
16. Thermoplastic Rubber Products
17. FRP Products
18. Injection Moulding Plastic Products
19. Consumer Rubber Products
20. Hair Oils
21. Gums/Resins
22. Charcoal
23. Plastic Ropes

III. Leather Products

1. Leather Shoe Uppers Closed
2. Leather Shoe (Indian type-Desi jute)
3. Leather Sandals/Chappals
4. Leather-cum-Rubber Chappals/Sandals
5. Leather/Rexin Hand gloves
6. Leather Suitcases and other products

7. Handbags & Purses (Leather/Rexin)
8. Leather Straps/Belts
9. Chrome Tents/Sole
10. Village Leather Processing
11. Leather Garments
12. Leather Washers and Laces
13. Leather Travel Goods

IV. Mechanical Engineering Industries

1. Agriculture/Horticulture Implements
2. Fabrication Unit
3. Storage Bins/Sheet Metal Products
4. Ploughs
5. Hoes
6. Mowers
7. Hand Pumps
8. Hand Shovels
9. Kudalis
10. Persian Wheels
11. Chaff Cutters
12. Disc Harrows
13. Levellers
14. Insecticides Sprayers
15. Seed Bins
16. Wheat & Rice Threshers
17. Seed Drills
18. Winnowers
19. Ghamelas
20. Seed Cleaners
21. Harvester Grader
22. Oil Crusher
23. Shell Huskers
24. Dal Mill

V. Electronics and Electrical Products

1. AM/FM Radio
2. Audio Tape Recorder and Combination with Radio
3. Public Address Amplifier
4. Assembly of Loud Speakers
5. TV Booster Amplifiers
6. Electronic Fan Regulators
7. Electronic Gas Lighter
8. Electronic Lantern/Emergency Lamp
9. Battery Eliminator/Power Packs
10. Electronic Calculators
11. Assembly of Audio Cassette (Blank)
12. Monochrome T.V. Receivers
13. Colour T.V. Receivers
14. Assembly of Blank Video Cassette
15. Invertors & Convertors
16. Solid state Voltage Stablizers
17. Moisture Meter (Electronics)
18. Soil Testing Meter
19. Water Analyser
20. Electronic Milk Analyser
21. CRT, DATA/Display Monitor (Monochrome/Colour)
22. G.L.S. Lamps
23. Auto Lamps
24. Lamp Fittings
25. Miniature Lamps
26. Conductors, Cables & Wires
27. Electrical Measuring Instruments
28. Small Transformers
29. Household Electrical Appliances
30. Room Coolers/Desert Coolers

31. Electrical Wiring Accessories
32. Plugs, Sockets and Switches

VI. Hosiery and Textile

1. Powerloom
2. School Bags/Holdals/Shopping Bags
3. Cotton Durries
4. Ready made Garments
5. Cotton Hosiery:
   (i) Vests/Knitted
   (ii) Socks
   (iii) Under Garment
6. Woollen Hosiery:
   (i) Socks, Shawls, Muffler, Pullovers, Blankets
7. Nylon Socks
8. Rain Coats
9. Bed Sheets
10. Canvas Shoes
11. Shoe Laces
12. Tags/Wicks
13. Surgical Bandage
14. Canvas Shoes
15. Pranda/Ribbon
16. Cotton Nawar

* *Source*:- Comprehensive policy package for Small Scale Industries and Tiny Sector, Ministry of SSI, Govt. of India, 2000, http://www.smallindustryindia.com/policies/policypkg.htm

APPENDIX-III (A)

INDIA'S INDUSTRIAL POLICIES FROM 1948 TO 1991 OFFICE OF THE DEVELOPMENT COMMISSIONER (SMALL SCALE INDUSTRIES) MINISTRY OF SMALL SCALE INDUSTRIES GOVT. OF INDIA NEW DELHI

1. Industrial Policy Resolution New Delhi, 6 April, 1948
2. Industrial Policy Resolution New Delhi, 30th April 1956
3. Industrial Policy Statement 23rd December, 1977
4. Industrial Policy Statement July, 1980
5. Industrial Policy 1990
6. Statement of Industrial Policy New Delhi, July 24, 1991

1. INDUSTRIAL POLICY RESOLUTION NEW DELHI, 6 APRIL, 1948

No. 1(3)-44(13)/48-The Government of India have given careful thought to the economic problems facing the country. The nation has now set itself to establish a social order where justice and equality of opportunity shall be secured to all the people. The immediate objective is to provide educational facilities and health services on a much wider scale, and to promote a rapid rise in the standard of living of the people by exploiting the latent resources of the country, increasing production and offering opportunities to all for employment in the service of the community. For this purpose, careful planning and integrated effort over the whole field of national activity are necessary: and the Government of India propose to establish a National Planning Commission to formulate programmes of development and to secure their execution. The present statement, however, confines itself to Government's policy in the industrial field.

2. Any improvement in the economic conditions of the country postulates and increase in national wealth: a mere redistribution of existing wealth would make no essential difference to the people and would merely mean the distribution of poverty. A dynamic national policy must, therefore, be directed to a continuous increase in production by all possible means, side by side with measures to secure its equitable distribution. In the present state of the nation's economy, when the mass of the people are below the subsistence level, the emphasis should be on the expansion of production. Both agricultural and industrial; and in particular on the production of capital equipment of goods satisfying the basic needs of the people and of commodities the export of which will increase earnings of foreign exchange.

3. The problem of State participation in Industry and the conditions in which private enterprises should be allowed to operate must be judged in this context. There can be no doubt that the State must play a progressively active role in the development of industries, but ability achieve the main objectives should determine the immediate extent of State responsibility and the limits to private enterprise. Under present conditions, the mechanism and the resources of the State may not permit it to function forthwith in industry as widely as may be desirable. The Government of India are taking steps to remedy the situation; in particular, they are considering steps to create a body of men trained in business methods and management. They feel, however, that for some time to come, the State could contribute more quickly to the increase of national wealth by expanding its present activities wherever it is already operating and by concentrating on new units of production in other fields, rather than on acquiring and running existing units. Meanwhile, private enterprise, properly directed and regulated, has a valuable role to play.

4. On these considerations the Government have decided that the manufacture of arms and ammunition, the production

and control of atomic energy, and ownership and management of railway transport should be the exclusive monopoly of the Central Government. Further in any emergency, the Government would always have the power to take over any industry vital for national defence. In the case of the following industries, the state which in this context, includes Central, Provincial and State Governments and other Public Authorities like Municipal Corporations will be exclusively responsible for the establishment of new undertakings, except where, the national interest, the State itself finds it necessary to secure the cooperation of private enterprise subject to such control and regulation as the Central Government may prescribe:

1. Coal (the India Coalfields Committee's proposals will be generally followed).
2. Iron and Steel.
3. Aircraft manufacture.
4. Shipbuilding.
5. Manufacture of telephone, telegraph and wireless apparatus, excluding radio receiving sets.
6. Mineral oils.

While the inherent right of the State to acquire any existing industrial undertaking will always remain, and will be exercised whenever the public interest requires it, Government have decided to let existing undertakings in these fields develop for a period of ten years, during which they will be allowed all facilities for efficient working and reasonable expansion. At the end of this period, the whole matter will be reviewed and a decision taken in the light of circumstances obtaining at the time. If it is decided that the State should acquire any unit, the fundamental rights guarantee by the Constitution will be observed and compensation will be awarded on a fair and equitable basis.

Management of State enterprise will, as a rule, be through

the medium of public corporations under the statutory control of the Central Government, who will assume such powers as may be necessary to ensure this.

5. The Government of India have recently promulgated a measure for the control by the State of generation and distribution of electric power. This industry will continue to be regulated in terms of measures.

6. The rest of the industrial field will normally be open to private enterprise, individual as well as cooperative. The State will also progressively participate in this field; nor will it hesitate to intervene whenever the progress of an industry under private enterprise is unsatisfactory. The Central Government have already embarked on enterprises like large river valley developments which are multipurpose projects of great magnitude, involving extensive generation of hydro-electric power and irrigation on a vast scale, and calculated in a comparatively short time to change the entire face of large areas in this country. Projects like the Damodar Valley Scheme, the Kosi Reservoir, the Hirakud Dam, etc. in a class by themselves and can stand comparison with any of the major schemes in America or elsewhere. The Central Government have also undertaken the production of fertilizer on a very large scale, and have in view other enterprises like the manufacture of essential drugs, and of synthetic oil from coal; many Provincial and State Governments are also proceeding on similar lines.

7. There are certain basic industries of importance, apart from those mentioned in paragraph 4, the planning and regulation of which by the Central Government is necessary in the national interest. The following industries whose location must be governed by economic factors of All-India import, or which require considerable investment of a high degree of technical skill, will be the subject of Central regulation and control:

1. Salt
2. Automobiles and tractors
3. Prime movers
4. Electric engineering
5. Other heavy machinery
6. Machine tools
7. Heavy chemicals, fertilizers and pharmaceuticals and drugs
8. Electro-chemical industries
9. Non-ferrous metals
10. Rubber manufactures
11. Power and industrial alcohol
12. Cotton and woolen textiles
13. Cement
14. Sugar
15. Paper and Newsprint
16. Air and Sea transport
17. Minerals
18. Industries related to defense.

The above list cannot obviously be of an exhaustive nature. The Government of India, while retaining the ultimate direction over this field of industry, will consult the Governments of the Provinces and States at all stages and fully associate them in the formulations and execution of plant. Besides these Governments, representatives of Industry and Labour will also be associated with the Central bodies which they propose to establish, as recommended by the Industries Conference.

8. Cottage and small-scale industries have a very important role in the national economy. Offering as they do scope for individual, village or cooperative enterprise, and means for the rehabilitation of displaced persons. These industries are particularly suited for the better utilization of local resources

and for the achievement of the local self-sufficiency in respect of certain types of essential consumer goods like food, cloth and agricultural implements. The healthy expansion of cottage and small scale industries depends upon a number of factors like the provision of raw materials, cheap power, technical advice, organized marking of their produce, and where necessary, safeguards against intensive competition by large scale manufacture, as the education of the worker in the use of the best available technique. Most of these fall in the Provincial sphere and are receiving the attention of the Governments of the Provinces and the States. The Resolution of Industries Conference has requested the Central Government to investigate how far and in what manner these industries can be coordinate and integrated with large-scale industries. The Government of India accept this recommendation. It will be examined, for example, how the textile mill industry can be made complementary to, rather than competitive with the handloom industry, which is the country's largest and best-organized cottage industry. In certain other lines of production, like agricultural implements, textile accessories, and parts of machine tools, it should be possible to produce components on a cottage industry scale and assemble these into their final product at a factory. It will also be investigated how far industries at present highly centralized could be decentralized with advantage.

The Resolution of the Industries Conference has recommended that Government should established a Cottage Industries Board for the fostering of small scale industries. The Government of India accept this recommendation and propose to create suitable machinery to implement it. A Cottage and Small Scale Industries Directorate will also be set up within the Directorate General of Industries and Supplies.

One of the main objectives will be to give a distinctly cooperative bias to this field of industry. During and before the last war, even a predominantly agricultural country like

China showed what could be done in this respect and her mobile industrial cooperative units were of outstanding assistance in her struggle against Japan. The present international situation is likely to lessen to a marked degree our chances of getting capital goods for large-scale industry and the leeway must be made up by having recourse to small-size industrial cooperative throughout the country.

9. The Government, however, recognise that their objective, viz. securing the maximum increase in production will not be realised merely by prescribing the respective spheres of the State and of Private enterprise in Industry. It is equally essential to ensure the fullest cooperation between labour and management and the maintenance of stable and friendly relations between them. A resolution on this subject was unanimously passed by the Industries Conference which was held in December last. Amongst other things, the resolution states:

> "... The system of remuneration to capital as well as labour must be so devised that, while in the interest of the consumers and the primary producers excessive profits should be prevented by suitable methods of taxation and otherwise, both will share the product of their common effort, after making provision for payment of fair wages to labour, a fair return on capital employed in the industry and reasonable reserves for the maintenance and expansion of the undertakings."

Government accept this Resolution. They also consider that labour's share of the profits should be on sliding scale normally varying with production. They propose, in addition to the overall regulation of industry by the State, to establish machinery for advising on fair wages, fair remuneration for capital, and conditions of labour. They will also take steps to associate labour in all matters concerning industrial production.

The machinery which Government propose to set up will function at different levels, central regional and unit. At the centre, there will be Central Advisory Council, which will cover the entire field of industry, and will have under it Committees for each major industry. These Committees may be split up into sub-committees dealing with specific questions relating to the industry eg. Production, industrial relations, wage fixation and distribution of profits. The regional machinery under the Provincial Governments will be Provincial Advisory Boards which like the Central Advisory council, will cover the entire field of industry within the Province; they will have under them Provincial Committees for each major industry. The Provincial Committees may also be split up into various sub-committees dealing with specific questions relating the production, wage fixation and industrial relations. Below the Provincial Committees will come the Works Committees and the Production Committees attached to each major industrial establishment.

The Works Committees and the Production Committees will be bi-partite in character, consisting of representatives of employers and workers only, in equal numbers. All other Committees will be tri-partite, with representatives of Government, employers and workers.

Government hope that the machinery proposed will substantially reduce the volume of industrial disputes. In the case of unresolved conflicts. Government trust that management and labour will, in their own interests and in the larger interests of the country, agree to settle them through recognised channels of conciliation and arbitration, which will be provided by Government. The Industrial Relations Machinery, both at the Centre and in the Provinces, is being strengthened, and permanent industrial tribunals are being established for dealing with major disputes.

The Government of India are also taking special steps to improve industrial housing as quickly as possible. A scheme for the construction of one million workers' houses in ten years is under contemplation, and a Housing Board is being constituted for this purpose. The cost will be shared in suitable proportions between Government, employers and labour, the share of labour being recovered in the form of a reasonable rent.

In order to ensure quick decisions on the various matters arising out of Industrial Truce Resolution, Government are appointing a special officer.

10. The Government of India agree with the view of the Industries Conference that, while it should be recognised that participation of foreign capital and enterprise, particularly as regards industrial technique and knowledge, will be of value to the rapid industrialisation of the country, it is necessary that the conditions under which they may participate in Indian industry should be carefully regulated in the national interest. Suitable legislation will be introduced for this purpose. Such Legislation will provide for the scrutiny and approval by the Central Government of every individual case of participation foreign capital and management in industry. It will provide that, as a rule, the major interest in ownership, and effective control, should always be in Indian hands; but power will be taken to deal with exceptional cases in a manner calculated to serve the national interest. In all cases, however, the training of suitable Indian personnel for the purpose of eventually replacing foreign experts will be insisted upon.

11. The Government of India are fully alive to their direct responsibility for the development of these industries which they have found necessary to reserve exclusively for State enterprise. They are equally ready to extend their assistance to private or cooperative enterprise in the rest of the industrial field, and in particular, by removing transport difficulties and by facilitating the import of essential raw-materials to the maximum possible extent. The tariff policy of Government

will be designed to prevent unfair foreign competition and to promote the utilisation India's resources without imposing unjustifiable burden on the consumer. The system of taxation will be reviewed and readjusted where necessary to encourage saving and productive investment and to prevent undue concentration of wealth in a small section of the population.

12. The Government of India hope that this elucidation of their intentions on fundamental aspects of industrial policy will remove all misapprehensions, and they are confident that a joint and intensive effort will now be made by labour, capital and the general public, which will pave the way for the rapid industrialisation of the country.

2. INDUSTRIAL POLICY RESOLUTION NEW DELHI, 30TH APRIL 1956

No.91/SF/48-The Government of India set out in their Resolution dated 6.4.48 the policy which they proposed to pursue in the industrial field. The Resolution emphasized the importance to the economy of securing a continuous increase in production and its equitable distribution, and pointed out that the State must play of progressively active role in the development of industries. It laid down that besides arms and ammunition, atomic energy and railway transport, which would be the monopoly of the Central Government, the State would be exclusively responsible for the establishment of new undertaking in six basic industries except where, in the national interest, the State itself found it necessary to secure the cooperation of private enterprise. The rest of the industrial field was left open to private enterprises though it was made clear that the State would also progressively participate in this field.

2. Eight years have passed since this declaration on industrial policy. These eight years have witnessed many important changes and developments in India. The constitution

of India has been enacted, guaranteeing certain fundamental rights and enunciating Directive Principles of State Policy. Planning has proceeded on an organised basis, and the first Five Year Plan has recently been completed. Parliament has accepted the socialist pattern of society as the objective of social and economic policy. These important developments necessitate a fresh statement of industrial policy, more particularly as the Second Five Year Plan will soon be placed before the country. This policy must be governed by the principles laid down in the Constitution, the objective of socialism, and the experience gained during these years.

3. The Constitution of India, in its preamble, has declared that it aims at securing for all its citizens:

"JUSTICE, social, economic and political;

LIBERTY, of thoughts, expression, belief, faith and worship;

EQUALITY of status and of opportunity; and to promote among them all;

FRATERNITY, assuring the dignity of the individual and the unity of the Nation."

In its Directive Principles of State Policy, it is stated that –

"The State shall strive to promote the welfare of the people by securing and protecting as effectively as it may a social order in which justice, social, economic and political, shall inform all the institutions of the national life."

Further that-

"The State shall, in particular, direct its policy towards securing:

a. that the citizens, men and women equally, have the right to an adequate means of livelihood;
b. that the ownership and control of the material resources of the community are so distributed as best to subserve the common good:

c. that the operation of the economic system dies not result in the concentration of wealth and means of production to the common detriment;
d. that there is equal pay for equal work for both men and women;
e. that the health and strength of workers, men and women, and the tender age of children are not abused and that citizens are not forced by economic necessity to enter vocations unsuited to their age of strength:
f. that childhood and youth are protected against exploitation and against moral and material abandonment."

4. These basic and general principles were given a more precise direction when Parliament accepted in December 1954, the socialist pattern of society as the objective of social and economic policy. Industrial policy, as other policies, must therefore, be governed by these principles and directions.

5. In order to realize this objective, it is essential to accelerate the rate of economic growth and to speed up industrialization and, in particular, to develop heavy industries and machine making industries, to expand the public sector, and to build up a large and growing cooperative sector. These provide the economic foundations for increasing opportunities for gainful employment and improving living standards and working conditions for the mass of the people. Equally, it is urgent, to reduce disparities in income and wealth which exist today, to prevent private monopolies and the concentration of economic power in different fields in the hands of small numbers of individuals. Accordingly, the state will progressively assume predominant and direct responsibility for setting up new industrial undertakings and for developing transport facilities. It will also undertake State trading on an increasing scale. At the same time, as an agency for planned national development, in the context of the

country's expanding economy, the private sector will have the opportunity to develop and expand. The principle of cooperation should be applied wherever possible and a steadily increasing portion of the activities of the private sector developed along cooperative lines.

6. The adoption of the socialist pattern of society as the national objective, as well as the need for planned and rapid development, require that all industries of basic and strategic importance, or in the nature of public utility services, should be in the public sector. Other industries, which are essential and require investment on a scale which only the state, has, therefore, to assume direct responsibility for the further development of industries over a wider area. Nevertheless, there are limiting factors, which make it necessary at this stage for the state to define the field in which it will undertake sole responsibility for further development, and to make a selection of industries in the development of which it will play dominant role. After considering all aspects of the problem in consultation with the Planning Commission, the Government of India have decided to classify industries into three categories, having regard to the part which the State would play in each of them. These categories will inevitably overlap to some extent and too great a rigidity might defeat the purpose in view. But the basic principles and objectives have always to be kept in view ad the general directions hereafter referred to be followed. It should also be remembered that it is always open to the State to undertake any type of industrial production.

7. In the first category will be industries the future development of which will be the exclusive responsibility of the State. The second category will consist of industries, which will be progressively State-owned and in which the State will, therefore, generally take the initiative in establishing new undertakings, but in which private enterprise will also be expected to supplement the effort of the State. The third category will include all the remaining industries, and their

future development will, in general, be left to the initiative and enterprise of the private sector.

8. Industries in the first category have been listed in Schedule A of this Resolution. All new units in these industries, save where their establishment in the private sector has already been approved, will be set up only by the State. This does not preclude the expansion of the existing privately owned units, or the possibility of the State securing the cooperation of private enterprise in the establishment of new units when the national interests so require. Railways and air transport, arms and ammunition and atomic energy will, however, be developed as Central Government monopolies. Whenever cooperation with private enterprise is necessary, the State will ensure, either through majority participation in the capital or otherwise, that it has the requisite powers to guide the policy and control the operations of the undertakings.

9. Industries in the second category will be those listed in Schedule B. With a view to accelerating their future development, the State will increasingly establish new undertakings in these industries. At the same time, private enterprise will also have the opportunity to develop in this field, either on its own or with State participation.

10. All the remaining industries will fall in the third category, and it is expected that their development will be undertaken ordinarily through the initiative and enterprise of the private sector, though it will be open to the State to start any industry even in this category. It will be the policy of the State to facilitate and encourage the development of these industries in the private sector, in accordance with the programmes formulated in successive Five Year Plans, by ensuring the development of transport, power and other services, and by appropriate fiscal and other measures. The State will continue to foster institutions to provide financial aid to these industries, and special assistance will be given to enterprises organised on cooperative lines for industrial and

agricultural purposes. In suitable cases, the State may also grant financial assistance to the private sector. Such assistance, especially when the amount involved in substantial, will preferably be in the form of participation n equity capital, though it may also be in part, in the form of debenture capital.

11. Industrial undertakings in the private sector have necessarily to fit into the framework of the social and economic policy of the State and will be subject to control and regulation in terms of the Industries (Development and Regulation) Act and other relevant legislation. The Government of India, however, recognise that it would, in general, be desirable to allow such undertakings to develop with as much freedom as possible, consistent with the targets and objectives of the national plan. When there exists in the same industry both privately and publicly owned units, it would continue to be the policy of the State to give fair and non-discriminatory treatment to both of them.

12. The division of industries into separate categories does not imply that they are being placed in watertight compartments. Inevitably, there will not only be areas of overlapping but also a great deal of dovetailing between industries in the private and the public sectors. It will be open to the State to start any industry not included in Schedule A and Schedule B when the needs of planning so require or there are other important reasons for it. In appropriate cases, privately owned units may be permitted to produce an item falling within Schedule A for meeting their own requirements or as by products. There will be ordinarily no bar to small privately owned units undertaking production, such as the making of launches and other lightcraft, generation for power for local needs and small scale mining. Further, heavy industries in the public sector may obtain some or their requirements of lighter components from the private sector, while the private sector in turn would rely for many of its

needs on the public sector. The same principle would apply with even greater force to the relationship between large scale and small-scale industries.

13. The Government of India would, in this context, stress the role of cottage and village and small-scale industries in the development of the national economy. In relation to some of the problems that need urgent solutions, they offer some distinct advantages. They provide immediate large-scale employment; they offer a method of ensuring a more equitable distribution of the national income and they facilitate an effective mobilization or resources of capital and skill which might otherwise remain unutilized. Some of the problems that unplanned urbanization tends to create will be avoided by the establishment of small centres of industrial production all over the country.

14. The State has been following a policy of supporting cottage and village and small-scale industries by restricting the volume of production in the large-scale sector by differential taxation or by direct subsidies. While such measures will continue to be taken, whenever necessary, the aim of the State Policy will be to ensure that the decentralized sector acquires sufficient vitality to be self-supporting and its development is integrated with that or large-scale industry. They State will, therefore, concentrate on measures designed to improve the competitive strength of the small-scale producer. For this it is essential that the technique of production should be constantly improved so and modernized the pace of transformation being regulated so as to avoid as far as possible, technological unemployment. Lack of technical and financial assistance, of suitable working accommodation and inadequacy of facilities for repair and maintenance are among the serious handicaps of small-scale producers. A start has been made with the establishment of industrial estates and rural community workshops to make good these deficiencies. The extension of rural electrification, and the availability of power

at prices, which the workers can afford, will also be of considerable help. Many of the activities relating to small-scale production will be greatly helped by the organization of industrial cooperatives. Such cooperatives should be encouraged in every way and the State should give constant attention to the development of cottage and village and small-scale industry.

15. In order that industrialization may benefit the economy of the country as a whole, it is important that disparities in levels of development between different regions should be progressively reduced. The lack of industries in different parts of the country is very often determined by factors such as the availability of the necessary raw materials in certain areas has also been due to the ready availability of power, water supply and transport facilities which has been developed there. It is one of the aims of national planning to ensure that these facilities are steadily made available to areas which are at present lagging behind industrially or where there is greater need for providing opportunities for employment provided the location is otherwise suitable. Only by securing a balanced and coordinated development, of the industrial and the agricultural economy in each region, can the entire country attain higher standards or living.

16. This programme of industrial development will make large demands on the country's resources of technical and managerial personnel. To meet these rapidly growing needs for the expansion of the public sector and for the development of the village and small-scale industries, proper managerial and technical cadres in the public services are being established. Steps are also being taken to meet shortages at supervisory levels, to organise apprenticeship schemes of training on a large scale both in public and in private enterprises, and to extend training facilities in business management in universities and other institutions.

17. It is necessary that proper amenities and incentives should be provided for all these engaged in industry. The living and working conditions of workers should be improved and their standards of efficiency raised. The maintenance of industrial peace is one of the prime requisites of industrial progress. In a socialist democracy labour is a partner in the common task of development and should participate in it with enthusiasm. Some laws governing industrial relations have been enacted and a broad common approach has developed with growing recognition of the obligations of both management and labour. There should be joint consultation and workers and technicians should wherever possible, as associated progressively in management. Enterprises in the public sector have to set an example in this respect.

18. With the growing participation of the State industry and trade, the manner in which these activities should be conducted and managed assumes considerable importance. Speedy decisions and a willingness to assume responsibility are essential if these enterprises are to succeed. For this wherever possible, there should be decentralisation of authority and their management should be along business lines. It is to be expected that public enterprises will augment the revenues of the State and provide resources for further development in fresh fields. But such enterprises may sometimes incur losses. Public enterprises have to be judged by their total results and in their working they should have the largest possible measure of freedom.

19. The Industrial Policy Resolution of 1948 dealt with a number of other subjects which have since been covered by suitable legislation or by authoritative statement of policy. The division of responsibility between the Central Government and the State Government in regard to industries has been set out in the Industries (Development and Regulation) Act. The Prime Minister, in his statement in parliament on 6th

April 1949, has enunciated the policy of the State in regard to foreign capital. It is, therefore, not necessary to deal with the subjects in this resolution.

20. The Government of India trust that this statement of their Industrial Policy will receive the support of all sections of the people and promote the rapid industrialisation of the country.

SCHEDULE A

1. Arms and ammunition and allied items of defence equipments.
2. Atomic energy.
3. Iron and Steel.
4. Heavy castings and forgings of iron and steel.
5. Heavy plant and machinery required for iron and steel production, for mining, for machinery tool manufacture and for such other basic industries as may be specified by the Central Government.
6. Heavy electrical plant including large hydraulic and steam turbines.
7. Coal and lignite.
8. Mineral oils.
9. Mining of iron ore, manganese ore, crome-ore, gypsum, sulphur, gold and diamond.
10. Mining and processing of copper, lead, zinc, tin, molybdenum and wolfram.
11. Minerals specified in the Schedule to the Atomic Energy (Control of Production and Use) Order, 1953.
12. Aircraft.
13. Air transport.
14. Railway transport.
15. Shipbuilding.

16. Telephones and telephones cables, telegraph and wireless apparatus (excluding radio receiving sets).
17. Generation and distribution of electricity.

SCHEDULE B

1. All other minerals except 'minor minerals' as defined in Section 3 of the Minerals Concession Rules 1949.
2. Aluminum and other non-ferrous metals not included in Schedule A.
3. Machine tools.
4. Ferro-alloys and tool steels.
5. Basic and intermediate products required by chemical industries such as the manufacture of drugs, dye-stuffs and plastics.
6. Antibiotics and other essential drugs.
7. Fertilizers
8. Synthetic rubber.
9. Carbonisation of coal.
10. Chemical pulp.
11. Road transport.
12. Sea transport.

3. INDUSTRIAL POLICY STATEMENT NEW DELHI, 23rd DECEMBER, 1977

For the past 20 years, Government Policy in the sphere of industry has been governed by the Industrial Policy Resolution of 1956. While some of the elements of that Resolution in regard to desirable pattern of industrial development still remain valid, the results of actual policies in the industrial field have not been upto the expectations or declared objectives. The growth of per capita national income during the last 10 years has been about 1.5 per cent per annum and is clearly inadequate to meet the needs of a developing economy. Unemployment has increased, rural-urban disparities have widened and the rate of real investment has stagnated. The growth of industrial output in the last decade has been no more than 3 to 4 per cent per annum on an average. The incidence of industrial sickness has become widespread and some of the major industries are the worst affected. The pattern of industrial costs and prices has tended to be distorted; and dispersal of industrial activity away from the larger urban concentration has been very slow.

The new Industrial Policy must, therefore, be directed towards removing the distortions of the past so that genuine aspirations of the people can be met within a time-bound programme of economic development.

The close interaction between the agricultural and industrial sectors of our economy cannot be over-emphasised. Much of our industrial production is based on agricultural raw materials. Similarly, in order to increase our agricultural productivity by adaptation of modern technology and agronomic practices to our own conditions, important inputs have to come from our industrial sector. The highest priority must be accorded to generation and transmission of power. Our recent experience demonstrates that lack of adequate power availability has become one of the most important constraints in the development of agriculture and industry. Similarly, cement and steel required to build our irrigation projects, the implements for ploughing and preparing the land, the equipment for processing high quality seeds, fertilizers and pesticides, oil and power, a wide range of industrial products are essential for increasing the level of our agricultural production. The prosperity and the distribution of income arising from a broad-based growth of agriculture and related activities in the countryside has to provide the basic demand for a wide range of industries producing articles of consumption. It is only by such a process of reinforcing interaction of the agricultural and industrial sectors that employment can be found for the large number of the rural population who cannot be absorbed in the agricultural sector.

Today, our assets in terms of foodgrains and foreign exchange reserves are considerable. But much more importantly our most valued asset is the willing hands of our rural manpower and the technicians who today from the third largest group of skilled manpower in the world. Great opportunities and great challenges are open to us now; but they cannot be seized by timid and hard-hearted policies. A new approach is called for in several areas of our national life. This new approach should reflect not only our vast resources and special endowments but should show particular concern for the utilisation of these resources and endowments for the amelioration of the living conditions of the majority of our people, the new industrial policy should and will hereafter place man as the centre of planning and implementation of projects and schemes.

Small-Scale Industries

The emphasis of industrial policy so far has been mainly on large industries neglecting cottage industries completely relegating small industries to a minor role. It is the firm policy of this Government to change this approach.

The main thrust of the new Industrial Policy will be on effective promotion of cottage and small industries widely dispersed in rural areas and small towns. It is the policy of the Government that whatever can be produced by small and cottage industries must only be so produced. For this purpose an exhaustive analysis of industrial products, has been made to identify those items which are capable of being established or expanded in the small scale sector. This list of industries which would be exclusively reserved for the small-scale sector has been significantly expanded and will now include more than 500 items as compared to about 180 items earlier. However, it must also be ensured that production in this sector is economic and of acceptable quality. The list of industries reserved for the Small Scale Sector has to be continually reviewed so that capacity creation does not lag behind the requirements of the economy. An annual review of reserved industries will be undertaken in order to ensure that reservation accorded to the small scale is efficient and is also continually expanded as new products and new processes capital of being manufactured in the small scale are identified.

Tiny Sector

While the existing definition of small scale industries will remain, within the small scale sector special attention will be given to units in the tiny sector namely those with investment in machinery and equipment upto Rs One lakh and situated in towns with a population of less than 50,000 according to 1971 census figures, and villages. Schemes will be drawn up for making available margin money assistance especially to tiny units in the small-scale sector as well as to cottage and household industries.

Legislation for Cottage Industries

While there has been reservation for the small scale sector, there has been no special protection for cottage and household industries sector, Government will consider introducing special legislation for protecting the interest of cottage and household industries with a view to ensuring that these activities which provide self-employment in large numbers get due recognition in our industrial development.

District Industries Centres

In the past, there has been a tendency to proliferate schemes, agencies and organisations which have tended more to confuse the average small and rural entrepreneur than to encourage and help him. The focal point of development for small scale and cottage industries will be taken away from the big cities and State capitals to the district headquarters. In each district there will be one agency to deal with all requirements of small and village industries. This will be called the District Industries Centre. Under the single roof of the District Industries Centre, all the services and support required by small and village entrepreneurs will be provided. These will include economic investigation of the district's raw materials and other resources, supply of machinery and equipment provision or raw material, arrangements, for credit facilities, and effective set-up for marketing and a cell for equality control, research and extension. The Centre will have a separate wing for looking after the special needs of cottage and household industries as distinct from small industries. The Centre will establish close linkages with the Development Blocks on the one hand with specialised institutions like Small Industries Service Institutes on the other. It is the intention of the Government to extend this important organisational pattern to all the district in the course of the next four years. Suitable financial and organisational support will be provided to the State Governments to achieve this objective. The financial assistance given to small and cottage industries under the Rural Industries Programme will also be extended to all the districts in the country with in the next four years.

Effective Financial Support

In order to provide effective financial support for promotion of small village and cottage industries, the Industrial Development Bank of India (IDBI) has taken steps to set up a separate wing to deal exclusively with the credit requirements of this sector. It will coordinate, guide and monitor the entire range of credit facilities offered by other institutions for the small and cottage sector, for whom separate wings will be set up in these institutions particularly nationalized banks. Banks will also be expected to earmark a specified proportion of their total advances for promotion of small, village and cottage industries. It is the policy of Government to see that no worthwhile scheme of small or village industry is given up for want of credit.

The growth of the scale and cottage industries sectors has been tardy mainly for want of satisfactory marketing arrangements for their products. The marketing of goods of these sectors with its concomitant of product standardization, quality control, maximum support for these activities on a priority basis. Measures such as purchase preference and reservation for exclusive purchase by Government Departments and Public Sector Undertakings will also be used to support the marketing of these products.

Khadi and Village Industries Commission

At present 22 village industries are within the purview of the Khadi and Village Industries Commission. The promotional work in this area has, however, been haphazard and progress has been slow. The Khadi and Village Industries Commission will work out detailed plans for development of these village industries by adopting modern management techniques. Especially for the production of footwear and soaps, special programmes would be drawn up to increase progressively their share in the total production of these items in the country. The list of items currently under the purview of the Commission will be revamped so that it can more effectively fulfill the role assigned to it. In the programme for development of village industries, the promotion of Khadi has a special place. A breakthrough in the field of Khadi is in sight with prospects of spinning and weaving polyester fibre along with cotton fibre. The preliminary work done so far holds out the hope of developing a large market of polyester khadi spinners and weavers. The Khadi and Village Industries Act is being amended to permit the implementation of a large scale programme in "Nai Khadi". The Government is committed to providing maximum financial and marketing support that is needed for promotion of the khadi programme.

Along with khadi, the clothing needs of the masses can be progressively met through development of the handloom sector, which provides employment to the bulk of people engaged in the production of textiles. Government will not permit any expansion in the weaving capacity in the organised mill and powerloom sector. In order to provide adequate supply of yarn for the handloom sector, the Government will ensure that the handloom sector has priority in the allocation of yarn spun in the organised sector. In case there is any shortage, Government will ensure that steps are taken to increase spinning capacity. Further, in order to provide a ready market for handloom products, it will be ensured that the organised mill sector does not provide unfair competition to the handloom sector. Certain items of textiles are already reserved for production in the handloom sector. However, such reservation has not been very effective. The Government will enforce the existing reservation and further extend it to other items.

Appropriate Technology

The development and application of technology appropriate to our socio-economic conditions have so far not received adequate attention. It will henceforth be an integral part of policy and Government will ensure that this important area gets adequate attention special arrangements will be made to ensure an effective and coordinated approach for the development and widespread application of suitable small and simple machines and devices for improving the productivity and earning capacity of workers in small and village industries. It will further be Government's endeavor to fully integrate such appropriate techniques of production with the broader programme of all round rural development.

Role of Large Scale Industries

In addition to small and village industries, there is also a clear role for large-scale industry in India. However, the Government will not favour large-scale industry merely for demonstration of sophisticated skills or as monuments of irrelevant foreign technology. The role of large scale industry will be related to the programme for meeting the basic minimum needs of the population through wider dispersal of small scale and village industries and strengthening of the agricultural sector. In general, areas for large scale industry will be: (a) basic industries which are essential for providing infrastructure as well as for development of small and village industries, such as steel, non-ferrous metals, cement, oil refineries; (b) capital goods industries for meeting the machinery requirement of basic industries as well as small scale industries; (c) high technology industries which require large scale production, and which are related to agricultural and small scale industrial development such as fertilizers, pesticides, and petro-chemicals etc; and (d) other industries which are outside the list of reserved items for the small sale sector, and which are considered essential for the development of the economy such as machine tools, organic and inorganic chemicals.

Large House

Past experience shows that Government policies have not succeeded in restraining the disproportionate growth of large Houses. While a certain measures of growth of existing enterprises is inevitable and also necessary for continued health of these enterprises, the growth of large House has been disproportionate to the size of their internally generate resources and has been largely based on funds borrowed from public financial institutions and banks. This process must be reversed.

In future, expansion of Large House will be guided by the following principles:-

1. The expansion of existing undertakings and establishments of new undertakings will continue to be subject to the provisions of the Monopolies and Restrictive Trade Practices Act. The provisions of this Act including those relating to dominant undertakings would be effectively implemented;

2. Except in the case of industries eligible for automatic growth of capacity, the expansion of existing undertakings into new lines and establishments of new undertakings by large House will require specific approval of Government; and
3. Large Houses will have to rely on their own internally generated resources for financing new or expansion projects. While an appropriate debt equity ratio will be permitted in the case of industries like fertilizers, paper, cement, shipping, petrochemicals, etc. which are relatively more capital intensive in nature, the debt equity ratio in the case of other less capital-intensive or less sophisticated industries will be so fixed as to reflect the greater use of their own internally generated resources by the large houses.

In its licensing policy, Government will regulate the activities of the large houses to bring them in line with the country's socio-economic goals, where large scale units, whether belonging to large houses or not are already engaged in the manufacture of items since reserved for the small scale sector, there will be no expansion in their capacity. On the other hand, the share of these units in the total capacity for these items will be steadily reduced and that of small scale and cottage Sector increased. In licensing other activities of large-scale industry, particularly of units belonging to large houses, Government would pay due regard to the existing share of these units in the total domestic production of these items. It will be the policy of government to ensure that no unit or business group acquires a dominant or monopolistic position in the market. The present industrial activities of the large houses will be scrutinised so that unfair practices arising out of manufacturing inter-linkages are avoided.

In order to ensure social accountability, the financial institutions whose support is vital for setting up and running of large scale enterprises will be expected to assure a more active rule in overseeing the activities of undertakings financed by them in order to ensure that management is increasingly professionalism and conforms to national priorities.

Public Sector

The public sector in India has today come of age. Apart from socialising the means of production in strategic areas, public sector provides a countervailing power to the growth of large houses and large enterprises in the private sector. There will be an expanding role for the public in several fields. Not only will it be the producer of important and strategic goods of basic nature, but it will also be used effectively as stabilising force the responsibility essential supplies for the consumer. The public sector will be charged with the responsibility of encouraging the development of a wide range of ancillary industries, and contribute to the growth of decentralised production by making available its expertise in technology and management to small scale and cottage industry sectors. It will also be the endeavour of Government to operate public sector enterprises on profitable and efficient lines in order to ensure that investment in these industries pays an adequate return to society. The Government attaches high priority to the building up of a professional cadre of managers in the public sector who would be given the necessary autonomy and entrusted with the task of providing dynamic and efficient management to such enterprise.

Indigenous and Foreign Technology

The country has well-developed infrastructure of scientific establishments. Future development of industries in India must be based on indigenous technology as far as possible. Full scope will be given to the development of indigenous technology. It is also essential that development of indigenous technology is responsive to the objective of efficient production in increasing quantities of goods that society urgently needs. Science and technology must contribute to the improvement in the living standards and the quality of life of the large mass of our people.

In order to promote technological self-reliance, the Government recognises the necessity for continued inflow of technology in sophisticated and high priority areas where Indian skills and technology are not adequately developed. In such areas, the Government's preference would be for outright purchase of the best available technology and then adapting such technology to the country's needs. Indian firms which are permitted to import foreign technology would be required in appropriate cases to set up adequate Research and Development facilities so that imported technology is properly adapted and assimilated. The Government will also set up a national registry of foreign collaboration in the Secretariat of the Foreign Investment Board so that there is continuous monitoring of these efforts.

Foreign Investment

The Government would also like to clarify its policy regarding participation of foreign investment and foreign companies in India's Industrial development. So far as existing foreign companies are concerned, the provisions of the Foreign Exchange Regulation Act would be strictly enforced. After the process of dilution under this Act has been completed, companies with direct non-resident investment not exceeding 40 per cent will be treated on par with Indian companies, except in cases specifically notified, and their future expansion will be guided by the same principles as those applicable to Indian companies.

Foreign investment and acquisition of technology necessary for Indian's industrial development would be allowed only on such terms as are determined by the Government of India to be in the national interest. In areas where foreign technological know-how is not needed, existing collaborations will not be renewed and foreign technological know-how is not needed, existing collaborations will not be renewed and foreign companies operating in such fields will have modify their character and activities in conformity with national priorities within the framework of the Foreign Exchanges Regulation Act. To guide entrepreneurs, Government will issue a revised illustrative list of industries where no foreign collaboration, financial or technical, is considered necessary since indigenous technology has fully developed in this field.

For all approved foreign investment, there will be complete freedom for remittance of profits, royalties, and dividends as well as repatriation of capital subject, of course, to rules and regulations common to all. As a rule, majority interest in ownership and effective control should be in Indian hands though Government may make exceptions in highly export-oriented and/or sophisticated technology areas. In hundred per cent export-oriented cases, Government may consider even a fully owned foreign company.

Indian Joint Ventures Aboard

A number of have been set up in joint ventures many developing countries by Indian Entrepreneurs in collaboration with local associates. At the present stage of the country's industrial development, substantial export of capital from India will neither be feasible nor desirable. The contribution of the Indian entrepreneur to the joint ventures abroad shall, therefore, have to be mainly in the form of machinery and equipment, structurals and also technical know-how and management expertise. In cases where, in addition, some cash investment is found necessary, Government will be willing to consider such investment up to a maximum limit to be prescribed for this purpose.

Import Liberalization

Self-reliance must continue to be a paramount objective of country's industrial and economic policy. Recent events in the international economy have demonstrated that the main burden of adjustment to external shocks and changing international environment has to be borne by the Country itself. Our industrial strategy, therefore, must respond to the objective of creating an industrial base, which is sufficiently diversified and sufficiently strong to withstand the vagaries of international trade and aid relationship. The creation of a strong and diversified industrial economy does not mean that the country should not or need not participate in international trade, both as exporter and importer of industrial goods. This we must continue to do. In fact, the favorable changes that have taken place in our foreign exchange situation and the progress that we have made in the industrial field should now enable us to selectively dispense with import quotas and quantitative restrictions, while retaining the protection given through tariffs. Relaxation of quantitative import controls, must, however, be consistent with our overall Plan priorities. Such relaxation will be in areas where existing quantitative restrictions are hurting rather than helping the future development of high priority industries, for example by unduly delaying the future development of high priority industries, for example by unduly delaying the implementation of critical projects or where indigenous industry is taking advantage of such restrictions for raising costs and prices beyond tolerable limits. Indian industry would, of course, be given all assistance to improve their competitive position and their technology. Many Indian firms are even today in a position to complete successfully International field and, therefore, no longer require the protection through quotas.

Exports of Manufactures

Exports of manufactures are an important and growing segment of our export trade. Government will consider favourable proposals for export-oriented manufacturing capacity in fields where such investment is likely to be internationally competitive after making allowance for the structure of indirect taxation in the form of customs and excise duties and other similar levels. In the case of wholly export-based activities, Government will also be willing to consider exemption from customs/excise duties on inputs, provided there is a substantial net value added in the export product and also such production is likely to generate additional direct and indirect employment.

Compulsory Exports

In many cases, compulsory export obligations have been imposed while approving new industrial capacity because of the need to ensure that import of raw materials and capital goods required by the project are paid for through future exports. Compulsory export obligations, merely for ensuring the foreign exchange balance of the project, would no longer be insisted upon. At the same time, in future, an export commitment for a limited period of five years will not be given the same weightage as before for relaxation of industrial policy. However, in case where a relaxation from industrial Policy has been accorded especially on consideration of export, compulsory export obligations would continue to be imposed and for sufficiently long period. In the past, while export obligations were imposed, equal attention was not paid to ensuring that compulsory export obligations are adhered to in actual practice.

Location of Industries

The Government attaches great importance to balanced regional development of the entire country so that disparities in levels of development between different regions are progressively reduced. Government have noted with concern that most of the industrial development that has taken place in our country since independence has been concentrated around the metropolitan areas and large cities. The result has been a rapid deterioration in the living conditions especially for the working classes in the larger cities and attendant problems of slums and environmental pollution. The Government have decided that no more licences should be issued to new industrial units within certain limits of large metropolitan cities having a population more than 1 million and urban areas with a population of more than 5 lakhs as per the 1971 census. State Government and financial institutions will be requested to deny support to new industries in these areas such as these which do not require an industrial licence. The Government of India would also consider providing assistance to large existing industries which want to shift from congested metropolitan cities to approved locations in backward areas.

Pricing Policy

A sound price policy has to aim at a reasonable degree of price stability and a fair parity between prices of agricultural and industrial products. There has been a tendency to regulate prices of industrial products which are vital to the needs of development in a manner which made their production less attractive than production catering to the needs of the elite. It will be the policy of Government to ensure that in cases where there is price control, the controlled price will include an adequate return to the investor. Provided that the industry is operating at a fairly high utilisation of capacity and is conforming to the technologically attainable norms. It will be permitted to earn a sufficient return to provide for a reasonable dividend to the shareholder and also adequate funds to plough back into business for modernization and growth. By the same time, Government cannot permit exorbitant profits being made by industries, which are operating well below their capacity, or by units, which operate, in a monopolistic environment.

Workers' Participation

The most important single resources of any country is the skill and hard work of its people. We, in India, have an abundant supply of labour which is capable of acquiring new skills very quickly and also an existing reservoir of technical and managerial personnel. These resources can be used effectively only in an environment in which the workers and managers develop as sense of personal involvement in the working of the enterprise. Family control of business particularly in the field of large scale industry is an anachronism, and it will be Government's policy to insist on professionalism in management. At the same time, ways and means have to be found to create amongst workers, both public and private sector industries, a stake in the efficient working of their units. The Government are examining the possibilities of encouraging workers' participation in the equity of industrial units without, in any way, adversely affecting their interests. Such equity participation together with an active association of workers in decision making from the shop floor level to the Broad level will provide the necessary environment for a meaningful participation by workers in the management of industry.

Sickness in Industry

One of the disturbing features of the industrial scene in recent years has been the growing incidence of sickness of both large and small units. In some cases, such as cotton and jute and textiles or sugar, a high proportion of the units in the industry has become sick with the result that in order to protect employment, Government has had to take over a number of such units. While Government cannot ignore the necessity of protecting existing employment, the cost of maintaining such employment has also to be taken into account. In a many case, very large amounts of public funds have been pumped into the sick units which has been taken over but they continue to make losses which have to be financed by the public exchequer. This process cannot continue indefinitely.

In future, the take-over of management of units would be resorted to selectively and only after careful examination of the steps required to revive the units. It would also be the policy of the Government to take quick and effective steps for rehabilitation and reconstruction of the units and to ensure professional management of such units on a continuing basis. The cost of overcoming sickness in industry becomes much more manageable if such sickness can be diagnosed at an early date. For this purpose, Government in cooperation with the Reserve Bank of India have instituted arrangements for monitoring incipient sickness in industrial units so that corrective action can be initiated as soon there is evidence of mismanagement of financial and technological weakness. The Government is also considering measures whereby managers or owners who are responsible for mismanaging and turning their units sick are not permitted to play any further part in the management of other units.

Streamlining of Procedures

Government will continue its effort to remove irritants in the industrial approval procedures which come in the way of accelerating industrial development. Since costs of delay are heavy and our country which is seeking to pull itself by its boost-straps can ill-afford them and swift progress should be our wayward, every effort will made to improve administrative arrangements so as to result not only in further speedy and orderly approval procedures but also in enforcing an expeditious translation of letters of intent and industrial licences into productive capacity on ground. In order to streamline and simplify procedures and policies relating to industrial licensing as well as imports and exports, Government have set up high level committees which will submit their report shortly.

Conclusion

Industrial development is a complex process requiring the effective interaction and cooperation of all sections of society. If the objectives of the new Industrial Policy of accelerating the pace of industrial growth, rapid increase in levels of employment, productivity and income of industrial workers and a wide dispersal of small and village industries have to be achieve, the willing cooperation of industrial worker, trade unions, managers, entrepreneurs, financial institutions and various governmental authorities responsible for implementing schemes of assistance will be essential. The main burnt of the effort has, however, to be borne by our industrial workers and managers who are second to none in their skills and efficiency. The Government earnestly appeals to all these group to work together in a spirit of dedication to the national cause. It is only by our own skills and efforts that we can hope to solve the numerous problems facing the country.

1977 has been a year of historical changes and people's expectations in the political and economic fields are high. It is hoped that the new direction that is being to the industrial policy of the country will help in the creation of a just and equitable society in which, the benefits of industrial development will be shared by all the people.

4. INDUSTRIAL POLICY STATEMENT NEW DELHI JULY, 1980

Industrial Policy Resolution 1956

The Industrial Policy Resolution 1956 has served as the cornerstone of the Congress Government Policy-Frame from the past quarter of a century. The Industrial Policy announcement of 1956 in fact reflects the value system of our country and has shown conclusively the merit of constructive flexibility. In terms of this Resolution the task of raising the pillars of economic infrastructure in the country was entrusted to the public sector for reasons of its great reliability, for very large investments required and the longer gestation periods of the projects crucial for economic development. The 1956 Resolution, therefore, forms the basis of this statement.

Take Off Stage

2. Industrialisation in a developing country has two aspects

viz. optimum utilisation of installed capacity and expansion of industries. The industrial progress of India during the past three decades can be attributed to the policies pursued by the Congress Government. While the country had reached a take of stage towards mid-1970s, both the growth channels-optimum utilisation of installed capacity as well as expansion of industries ere choked off by the 33 months rule of the Janata Party and its successor Government. The runaway of the economy has been damaged by the last two governments and the entire process of development was put in reverse gear.

Revival of the Economic Infrastructure

3. The first task before is the revival of the economy, which is presently inhibited by infrastructural gaps and inadequacies in performance. This put the economy into a vicious cycle of shortages of major industrial inputs like energy, transport and coal. To normalise the situation, Government are working on war-footing to break this vicious circle and to put the economy again on its feet.

Industrialisation and Economic Progress

4. Industrialisation is a *sine quo non* of economic progress. Our Government is committed to rapid and balanced industrialisation of the country with a view to benefiting the common man in the shape of increasing availability of goods at fair prices, larger employment and higher per capita income. A higher standard of living implies that more of industrial goods go into the consumption basket of the people. Industrialisation is also essential to provide the much-needs support for agriculture and for the development of infrastructural facilities like energy and transport. The net economic impact of industrialisation much-needs support for agriculture and for the development of infrastructural facilities like energy and transport. The net economic impact of industrialisation must travel down ultimately to the maximum number of people.

Distribution of Benefits of Industrialisation

5. The pattern of distribution of benefits of industrialisation should be such as to cover as large a segment of the country's population, both rural and urban, while avoiding economic concentration in a few hands. New thrusts need to be made to establish a dynamic industrial economy as indicated in the election manifesto of the Congress Party. Now that the Congress Party has been entrusted with the responsibility of the Government, what is needed above all is a set of pragmatic policies which will remove the lingering constraints to industrial production and, at the same time act as catalysts for faster growth in the coming decades, within the following socio-economic objectives.

Socio-Economic Objectives

- Optimum utilisation of the installed capacity.
- Maximising production and achieving higher productivity.
- Higher employment generation.
- Correction of regional imbalances through a preferential development of industrially backward areas.
- Strengthening of the agricultural base by according a preferential treatment to agro-based industries, and promoting optimum intersectioral relationship.
- Faster promotion of export- oriented and import substitution industries.
- Promoting economic federalism with an equitable spread of investment and the dispersal of returns amongst widely spread over small but growing units in rural as well as urban areas.
- Consumer protection against high prices and bad quality.

Role of Public Sector

6. An unfortunate development during the recent political vacuum in the country has been erosion of faith in the public

sector which has been reflected in its rather poor performance in recent years. Public sector, which was conceived to provide the pitt pillars of the country's economic infrastructure, was rendered hollow. The gigantic task before us, therefore, is to rehabilitate faith in the public sector. We have not only to restorage people's faith in the public sector. But have to evolve effective operational systems of management in the public sector undertakings. The public sector has to be identified as people's and not as "No body's Sector" as was rendered by the last Government. Public Sector constitutes as substantial segment of industrial activity in the country and its contribution in terms of generating surpluses and employment for further growth of the economy needs to be improved.

Unit-by-Unit Examination for Corrective Steps

7. Government has decided to launch a drive to revive the efficiency of public sector undertakings. Industrial undertakings in this sector will be closely examined on a unit-by-unit basis and corrective action will be taken in terms of a time-bound programme wherever necessary. Some of the units were allowed to get into chronic problems and instead of contributing surpluses, tended to put a drain on the public exchequer. Priority will be accorded to convert losing concerns into viable ones through broad restructuring of the system and by providing dynamic and competent management.

Management Cadre

8. On the positive side, public sector will continue playing an increasingly important role. B part of the reason for unsatisfactory performance of some of the units in the public sector has been the absence of proper management cadre. It is proposed to take effective steps to build the public sector undertakings and emphasis will be placed on developing management cadres in functional fields such as operations, finance, marketing and information system.

Role of Private Sector

9. The Government would pursue the goal of a vibrant, self-reliant and modern economy in which all sectors and all segments of the society have a positive role to play. The Industrial Policy Resolution of 1956 assigned a role to play. The Industrial Policy Resolution of 1956 assigned a role for industrial undertakings in the private sector within the framework of socio-economic policy of the State and subject to certain regulations in terms of relevant legislations. Government recognises that it would be, in general, desirable to allow private sector undertakings to develop in consonance with targets and objectives of national plans and policies but shall not permit the growth of monopolistic tendencies or concentration of economic power and wealth in a few hands.

Economic Federalism

10. It will be Government's endeavour to reverse the trends of the last three years towards creating artificial divisions between small and large-scale industry under the misconception that these interests are essentially conflicting. While making all efforts towards integrated industrial development, it is proposed to promote the concept of economic federalism with the setting up of a few nucleus plants in each district identified as industrially backward, to generate as many ancillaries and small and cottage units as possible.

Nucleus Plants

11. A nucleus plant would concentrate on assembling the products of the ancillary units falling within its orbit on producing the inputs needed by a large number of smaller units and making adequate marketing arrangements. The nucleus will also ensure a widely spread pattern of investment and employment and will distribute the benefits of industrialisation to the maximum possible. The nucleus plants would also work for upgrading the technology of small units. Small is beautiful only if it is growing just as the phased manufacturing programme with a view to reducing reliance

on imported components and material structure, a carefully worked out time bound programme for greater ancillarisation in certain industries will contribute considerably towards dispersal of industry and growth of entrepreneurship.

Ancillarisation

11a. The proposed nucleus plans in industrially backward districts would generate a spreadout network of small scale units or existing network of small scale units or existing network of small scale units in an area would acquire a faster growth by the coming up of a nucleus plant in the area. Such two-way traffic would create an ancillarisation effect in terms of large employment, more equitable distribution of the benefits of such an industrialisation in the shape of higher per capita income for the larger number of people in the area.

In between the nucleus large plants and the satellite ancillaries, the Government would promote a system of linkages for an integrated industrial development. The Government would evolve scheme of phased development. The Government would evolve schemes of Phased development of industrially backward areas through ancillarisation.

Re-defining of Small Scale Units

12. In order to boost the development of small scale industries and to ensure their rapid growth, Government have decided:

i. to increase the limit of investment in the case of tiny units from Rs.1 lakh to Rs.2 lakhs;
ii. to increase the limit of investment in the case of small scale units from Rs. 10 lakhs to Rs. 20 lakhs; and
iii. to increase the limit of investment in case of ancillaries from Rs. 15 lakhs to Rs. 25 lakhs.

13. This would eliminate the tendency to circumvent the

present limit by understating the value of machinery and equipment, falsification of accounts or resort to 'benami' units. The enhancement of the limit in terms of investment in plants and machinery will also help genuine small scale units particularly those being set up by young and technically qualified entrepreneurs, to come up. This measure will also facilitate long overdue modernisation of many of the existing small scale units.

Financial Support to Small Units

14. One of the major constraints to the growth of decentralised sector has been the difficulties of finance experienced particularly by industrial entrepreneurs in small, cottage and rural sector. although, there is adequate network of institutional finance, yet here is need for coordinating the flow of capital, both short term and long term. Government would evolve a system of coordination to ensure the flow of credit to the growing units in the decentralised sector at the right time and on appropriate terms. Government proposes to strengthen the existing arrangements and make such changes as may be necessary to facilitate the availability of credit to the growing units in the small scale sector.

Buffer Stocks for Critical Inputs

15. In order to assist the growth of small scale industries it is proposed to introduce a scheme for building up of buffer stocks of essential materials which are often difficult to obtain for this the existing set-up such as Small Industries Development Corporations in the Centre will also be utilised. Special needs of states which rely heavily on a few essential raw materials will receive priority.

Marketing Support and Reservation of Items for Small Scale Industries

16. Policies regarding marketing support to the decentralised sectors and reservation of items for small-scale industries, shall continue to be in force in the interest of growth of the small scale industries.

Village Industries

17. Government is determined to promote such a form of industrialisation in the country as to generate economic viability in the village. Promotion of suitable industries in rural areas will be accelerated to generate higher employment and higher per capita income for the villagers in the country without disturbing the ecological balance. Handlooms, handicrafts, khadi and other village industries will receive greater attention to achieve a faster rate of growth in the village.

Correcting Regional Imbalances

18. Industrialisation will play an important role in correcting the regional imbalances and reviving the industrial growth to lead the economy once again to the take-off stage. For the achievement of this goal, Government have decided to encourage dispersal of industry and setting up of units in industrially backward areas. Special concessions and facilities will be offered for this purpose and these incentives will be growth and performance oriented.

Evaluation of Incentives

19. In the past, numerous incentives had been provided to industries from time to time. It is Government's considered view that all incentives given to industry must be performance oriented. It is therefore, proposed that a regular periodic assessment will be made of the impact of these incentives to see the extent to which they have fulfilled their initial purpose. Unless it is apparent that the purpose is purpose is being served, Government will review the system incentives.

Generation of Employment and Higher Production

20. Industrial development has to be viewed in the broader context of generating higher production and employment. Overcoming the problems of poverty and backwardsness need a multi-pronged approach. An integral part of this approach would be to create new focal points of industrial

growth which have the maximum effect on the quality of life. This will have to be based essentially on the utilisation of local materials and locally available manpower. The ripple effect of substantial investment in backward districts in the past has in many cases not been adequate, mainly because such investment did not have effective linkages with local resources. Government, therefore, propose to encourage investment by public and private sector which will meet these criteria and would also promote a network of spread out ancillaries.

Endorsement of Licences to Reflect Existing Productive Capacity

21. In 1975, Government had taken certain decisions in regard to the recognition of additional capacities as a result of replacement and modernisation of equipment. Liberalisation of investment procedure for stimulating production in a certain selected industries and for endorsement of excess production over licensed capacity on the basis of a simplified procedure. Government feels that in several industries which are important from the point of view of national economy or are engaged in the production of articles of mass consumption, the productive capacity endorsed on the original licences or as amended in terms of the 1975 notification may not reflect the full productive potential of the unit. As a result of increased labour productivity or technological improvements, the productive capacities may have increased.

Government propose to recognise such capacities on a selective basis. It would not be in public interest to permit licensing procedures or a rigid locational policy to stand in the way of maximising production. The necessary notifications listing the industries, and spelling out the simplified procedures for such endorsement will be issued separately.

Provision for Automatic Growth

22. In view of the constraints on resources in a developing country like ours, and also taking into account the considerable

increase in the prices of capital goods, particularly those required to be imported it is necessary to ensure that no avoidable restrictions are placed on the fullest utilisation of the existing industrial capacities. This is particularly true of the core industries, of industries which have direct linkages with the core sector, and industries which have a long term export potential. All these industries are of basic, critical and strategic importance for the growth of the economy. In February, 1973, Government had announced a list of such industries, following the classification of industries, mentioned in the First Schedule to the Industries (Dev. and Reg.) Act, 1951. Later in 1975, Government had permitted the facility for automatic expansion in respect of 15 industries. The extent of increased capacity permitted in respect of these industries was limited to 5% per annum or 25% in a five-year plan period and could be undertaken in one or more stages. This expansion was to be addition to the normal permissible expansion in production by 25% of the approved capacity. Government have now decided that this facility will also be extended to other industries included in Appendix-I. In this behalf, the necessary notifications will be issued separately.

Export-oriented Units

23. Industry must contribute its share in creating a more favourable balance to trade by catering to the ever-increasing foreign markets. Government would sympathetically consider requests for setting up 100% export oriented units, requests for expansion of existing units exclusively for purposes for export and for allowing higher production for explicating fully the emerging export opportunities.

Advanced Technology for Economies of Scale

24. In a number of cases Indian Industry has not been able to compete in markets abroad because the scale of output which is related to the level of domestic demand is too small to give them the advantages of modern technology and economies of scale. In case where a larger production base

would increase the competitiveness of Indian Industry abroad, Government will consider favourably the induction of advanced technology, and will permit creation of capacity large enough to make it competitive in world markets, provided substantial exports are likely. The purpose of introducing such a policy would be not only to encourage exports but also to enable industry tc produce better quality products at lower costs which will ultimately benefit the consumer in terms of price and quality.

Research and Development

25. The Indian Industry must earmark substantial resources for R&D to constantly up-date technologies with a view to optimal utilisation of scarce resources, better service to a consumer and achieving greater exports. We also have to lay greater emphasis on bringing the benefits of the latest R&D to the medium and small units.

Transfer of Technology

26. Government will take active measures to facilitate the transfer of technology from efficiently operating units to new units. Companies which have well established R&D orgnisation, and have demonstrated their ability to absorb, adapt and disseminate modern technology will be permitted to import such technology as will increase their efficiency and cost-effectiveness. This will not only lead to saving of foreign exchange but would also ensure self-sufficiency and higher foreign exchange earnings.

Modernization Packages

27. "Modernisation Packages" will be evolved to suit the requirements of each industry, and will include all aspects i.e. appropriate location and optimum use of energy and the adoption of the right kind of scale and technology in order to minimise costs and improve efficiency in the use of scarce materials, the supply of which come from non-renewable

sources. Government's endeavour to ensure that the process of modernisation percolates down to small units and the villages. As in the case of the large scale modern industry, where new processes and technologies must replace the old and the traditional ones in the decentralised sector also, improved tools and techniques which will contribute to higher productivity and reduce the drudgery are an essential ingredient of the modernisation. Government will review the present arrangements in terms of special facilities and incentives such as soft loans, establishing of proper linkages in the field of marketing and strengthening the credit facilities particularly for the decentralized sector.

Energy Industry Dovetailing

28. Until recently, little effort has been made in dovetailing the industry and energy policies; not has enough attention been paid to the effects of industrial growth on environment and pollution of air and water. Government have decided that such industrial processes and technologies as would aim at optimal utilisation of energy or the exploitation of alternative sources of energy, would be given special assistance, including finance on concessional terms.

Pollution Control

29. Similarly, activities which have a direct bearing on and will contribute to improved environment and reduce the deleterious effects on pollution of air and water would also be made eligible for special assistance on appropriate terms. Government will examine the present scheme for soft loans with a view to including in it activities related to energy conservation, exploitation of non-traditional sources of energy like solar energy and control of water and air pollution and also such other specific industrial activities as are in urgent need of modernisation and upgradation of technology. This will be continuing exercise and the list of industries eligible for soft loans scheme will be reviewed from time to time.

Preserving Ecological Balance

30. Government are committed to the preservation of ecological balance and for improving living conditions in the urban centres of the country. In pursuance of this policy and with a view to encouraging the dispersal of industry, steps have been taken to prevent the growth of industry in the metropolitan cities and the large towns. Setting up of new industrial undertakings within the limits of such urban centres is not permitted.

31. However, in the implementation of this policy, Government propose to remove genuine difficulties, without determent to the basic objectives. It is, therefore, proposed to provide for selective relaxation to enable utilisation of already installed capacities to provide for natural growth and the encourage production for export. The requisite simplification and procedural changes in the application of the present location policy are being announced separately.

Streamlining Licensing Procedures

32. There has already been considerable simplification and streamlining of licensing procedures. Nevertheless, there is scope for further improvement in reducing the period of time taken for disposal of applications for the creation of new capacities, proposals for substantial expansion, and the production of new items. It is proposed to speed up the processes of examination and decision-making and also to examine the possibilities of further rationalisation and simplification of the system of industrial licensing.

Monitoring System and Data Bank

33. It is also proposed that in future, the agencies connected with the issuance of letters of intent / industrial licences will not merely concern themselves with letters of intent / industrial license but would also evolve a comprehensive system of monitoring the implementation of the schemes. For this

purpose, it is proposed to build up a Data Bank of the progress of various licensed / registered investment schemes.

34. The objective of the Data Bank will be to have, in respect of all major investment proposals, information regarding the progress in regard to the import of capital goods, the status in regard to the application for term lending and also the physical implementation of the scheme. The establishment of such a Data Bank will also enable Government to ensure that where parties have willfully failed to implement the letter of intent or have tried to pre-empt capacity are dealt with suitably.

Industrial Sickness: Devising an Early Warning System

35. Government are concerned at the growing problem of sickness in a large number of industrial undertakings. While it is recognised that it would be in the national interest to protect the investments in these undertakings by appropriate remedial action, it is also the view of the Government that deliberate mismanagement and financial improprieties leading to sickness should be death with firmly. Various all-India financial institutions have set up arrangements to detect sickness in undertakings at an early stage with a view to taking necessary corrective action. To ensure this the Government proposes to introduce a checklist to serve as "an early warning system" for identifying symptoms of sickness.

Merger and Amalgamation

36. In the case of existing sick undertakings which show adequate potential for revival, it would be policy of Government to encourage their merger with healthy units which are capable of managing the sick undertakings and restoring their viability. For this purpose, the existing tax concession under Section 72-A of the Income Tax Act will be

made more liberally available to amalgamation proposal, which will serve the purpose of revival of sick units. The existing guidelines will be reviewed with a view to facilitating greater reliance on voluntary mergers of sick units with healthy units which are capable of implementing a viable revival scheme.

Takeover to be in Exceptional Cases

37. It is also Government's policy to ensure that the State Governments, the financing institutions and the labour cooperate effectively for their revival of the sick units. Recourse to take-over of the management under the Industries (Development and Regulation) Act will be taken only in exceptional cases on grounds of public interest where other means for the revival of sick undertakings are not considered feasible. Where such takeover becomes necessary the State Governments will in appropriate cases, be expected to assume responsibility for the financing and management of the undertaking.

Industrial Relations

38. Deteriorating industrial relations in the last three years affected a number of important sectors of economy and let to fall in the industrial production. Government attach great importance to the interests and welfare of labour, but they also consider that the maintenance of constructive and cordial industrial relation in which both labour and management have to cooperate in a responsible manner is essential for the sustained growth of economy. Government have decided to revive the tripartite labour conference and it is hoped that through an attitude of mutual undertakings and constructive cooperation, it will be possible to establish higher standards of productivity and industrial harmony.

Industrial Pricing Policy

39. It is Government's policy that while all reasonable facilities and incentives will be provided to industry, it must recognise and accept its social responsibility particularly in terms of maintaining the price line, avoiding hoarding and speculation, and maximising production on an efficient basis. It is proposed to start dialogue with the industry to ensure that within a stipulated period of time, the prices are rationalised to the benefit of the consumer.

District Industries Centres

40. Government have reviewed the scheme of district industries centres which has not produced benefits commensurate with the expenditure incurred. Government therefore propose to initiate more effective alternatives.

Industrial Investment: An Inter-disciplinary Concept

41. Industrial development is an inter-disciplinary concept. It pertains not only to the manufacturing activity but to all related infrastructural development; licensing and corporate policies; financial, fiscal, trade and pricing policies; industrial relations and management. Scientific and technological development; and broad socio-economic policies. Industrial policy requires close and effective coordination and monitoring at various levels at the Centre as well as between Centre and the States. Its ultimate success will also depend on the extent of cooperation that industry receives from the other sections of society.

42. Government of India trust that the objectives set out in this paper and the measures outlines herein to achieve them will receive the support of all sections of the people to enable the country to attain its larger goals, namely faster economic growth, propriety to its citizens, and the establishment of an egalitarian society.

5. INDUSTRIAL POLICY, 1990
POLICY MEASURES FOR THE PROMOTION OF SMALL SCALE AND AGRO-BASED INDUSTRIES AND CHANGES IN PROCEDURES FOR INDUSTRIAL APPROVALS

Government have been considering the need to take measures for promotion of small scale and agro-based industries and to change procedures for grant of industrial approvals.

2. In pursuance of our policy to reorient industrial growth to serve the objective of employment generation, dispersal of industry in the rural areas, and to enhance the contribution of small scale industries to exports it has been decided to take the measures enumerated below.

3. The investment ceiling in plant & machinery for small scale industries (fixed in 1985) would be raised from the present Rs. 35 lakhs to Rs. 60 lakhs and correspondingly, for ancillary units from Rs. 45 lakhs to Rs. 75 lakhs. In order to enable small scale industries to play an important role in the total export effort, such of the small scale units which undertake to export at least 30 per cent of the annual production by the third year will be permitted to step up their investment in plant & machinery to Rs. 75 lakhs.

4. Investment ceiling in respect of tiny units would also be increased from the present Rs. 2 lakhs to Rs. 5 lakhs. However, with regard to their location, the population limit of 50,000 as per the 1981 census would continue to apply. Steps will be taken to ensure better inflow of credit and other vital inputs and to improve the infrastructure support to the constituents of the Tiny Sector.

5. (i) Presently, 836 items have been reserved for exclusive manufacture in the small-scale sector. Efforts would be made to identify more items amenable to similar reservation. Encroachment and

violation by large-scale units into areas reserved for small-scale sector will be effectively dealt with.

(ii) A new scheme of Central Investment Subsidy exclusively for the small scale sector in rural and backward areas capable of generating higher level of employment at lower capital cost would be implemented.

(iii) With a view to improving the competitiveness of the products manufactured in the small-scale sector, programmes for modernisation and upgradation of technology would be implemented. A number of technology centres, tool rooms, Process and Product Development Centres, testing centres, etc. will be set up under the umbrella of an apex Technology Development Centre in Small Industries Development Organization.

(iv) To ensure adequate and timely flow of credit of the small-scale industries, a new apex bank known as SIDBI has already been established. One of the major tasks of SIDBI and other commercial banks / financial institutions would be to channelise need-based, higher flow of credit, both by way of term loan and working capital, to the tiny and rural industries. A targeted approach will be adopted to ensure implementation and to facilitate monitoring this objective.

(v) The existing regime of fiscal concessions will be reviewed both to provide sustained support to the units in the small-scale sector and to remove the disincentives for their graduation and further growth.

(vi) An exercise will be undertaken to identify locations in rural areas endowed with adequate power supply and intensive campaigns will be launched to attract suitable entrepreneurs, provide all other inputs and foster small scale and tiny industries. Similarly industries which are not energy-intensive will be identified for proliferation in rural areas where power supply is presently a constraint.

(vii) In order to widen the entrepreneurial bases the Government would lay particular emphasis on training of women and youth under the Entrepreneurial Development Programme. A special cell would be established in SIDO and State Directorates of Industries to assist women entrepreneurs.

(viii) One of the persistent complaints of the small scale units is their being subjected to a large number of ACTs / Laws, being required to maintain a number of registers, submit plethora of returns and face an army of Inspectors, particularly in the field of labour legislations. These bureaucracy controls will be reduced so that unnecessary interference is eliminated. Further, procedure will be simplified and paper work cut down.

6. In order to assist the large number of artisans engaged in the rural and cottage industries, the activities of the KVIC and KVI Boards will be expanded, and these organisations will be strengthened to discharge the responsibility more effectively. Special marketing organisations at the Centre and State levels shall be created to assist rural artisans in marketing their products and also in supply of raw materials. Besides, providing concessional credit, training facilities and free consultancy to groups of artisans will also be provided.

7. In agro processing industries greater success has been achieved where growers and processors have been integrated, as in the case of sugar. For the success of other agro-based industries also, close links must be forged between the growers and processor units. Industrial Policy will, therefore, especially promote projects which are organised in close cooperation on the basis of joint ownership. Growers will be encouraged

to set up processing units within the framework of cooperative societies or similar institutional framework. This will also ensure the transmission of better technology for enhanced agricultural production.

8. In sectors where units require licensing, the policy will also encourage location of processing units in rural areas where growers are concentrated. Apart from economic benefits of proximity to raw materials it will help in dispersal of industry and increasing employment in rural areas.

9. Agro processing industry will receive high priority in credit allocation from the Financial Institutions. In appointment of working capital, bank will give higher priority to such industries as compared to the rest of the industrial sector.

10. In order to bring best technology available to these industries, technology approvals will be given 30 days of presentation to the secretariat for Industrial Approvals in the Department of Industrial Development. Government will actively promote the generation, adaptation and adoption of new technologies in the field.

Procedures for Industrial Approvals

11. Indian industry must be made more competitive internationally. It also to be released from unnecessary bureaucratic shackles by reducing the number of clearances required from the Government. While the Government will continue to examine large projects in view of resource constants, decisions in respect of medium sized investments will be left to the entrepreneurs. To achieve these objectives, the following decisions have been taken.

Delicensing

12. All new units upto an investment of Rs. 25 crores in fixed assets in non-backward areas and Rs. 75 crores in Centrally notified backward areas will be exempt from requirement of obtaining licence / registration.

13. For the import of Capital Goods, the entrepreneur would have entitlement to import upto a landed value of 30% of the total value of plant and machinery required for the unit.

Raw Materials and Components

14. For imports of raw materials and components, imports will be permissible upto a landed value of 30% of the ex-factory value of annual production. The ex-factory value of production will exclude the excise duty on the item of production. Raw materials and components on OGL will not be included within this 30 percent limit. For all licensable items of raw materials and components, import licensing procedures will continue to operate.

Foreign Collaboration

15. In respect of transfer of technology, if import of technology is considered necessary by the entrepreneur, he can conclude an agreement with the collaborator, without obtaining any clearance from the Government, provided that royalty payment does not exceed 5% on domestic sales and 8% on exports. If, however, lump-sum payment is involved in the import of technology, the proposal will require Government clearance, but a decision will be communicated to the entrepreneur within a period of 30 days.

Foreign Investment

16. Keeping in view the need to attract effective onflow of technology, investment upto 40% of equity will be allowed on an automatic basis. In such proposals also, the landed value of imported C.G. shall not exceed 30% of value of plant and machinery.

Minimum Economic Size

17. In order to ensure that investment leads to production of goods that attain international competitiveness and that maximum efficiency is ensured the unit would have to conform

to the minimum economic size in cases where such a size has been prescribed.

Expansion

18. The de-regulation suggested above would cover all cases of expansion and would not be restricted only to new units.

Broad-banding

19. The existing broad banding scheme would continue to be in force. In addition, of no extra investment is required, no clearance from the Government would be necessary for production and sale of any new item by existing unit. This would not include those items which are reserved for small scale industries.

Location Policy and Environmental Clearances

20. The location policy would not be applied to such industries by the Centre except for location in and around metropolitan cities with population above 4 million. For these cities location will not be permissible within 20 km calculated from the periphery of the metropolitan area except in prior designed industrial areas and for non-polluting industries such as electronics, computer software and printing. It will be upto State Government to regulate industrial locations keeping in mind local conditions and requirements and their respective special development plans, and zoning and town planning laws. Similarly environmental clearance would have to be obtained from the prescribed authority at the State level. In further should central legislation introduce new provisions, that law would automatically apply to these units as well.

Export Oriented Units

21. 100% export oriented units (UOUs) and units to be set up in export processing zones (EPZs) are also being delicensed under the scheme upto an investment limit of Rs. 75 crores.

Convertibility Clause

22. Such investment shall be exempt from the "Convertibility Clause" applicable to financing the Indian Financial Institutions.

23. It may be clarified that in the application of the proposals listed above, 836 items which are reserved for production the small scale sector will continue to be excluded.

24. The above proposals will be applicable to all manufacturing items in a specified list. The list shall follow the nomenclature of the Indian Trade Classification based on the Harmonised System. In such section of the classification, apart from positive mention of approved items, those not permissible shall be specifically excluded from the benefit of the proposals list above. Approval for excluded items will be as per the existing industrial policy regime and procedures.

25. Units set up by MRTP / FERA companies will be covered by the procedures set out above, but they will continue to need clearances under the provisions and regulations of these two Acts.

26. The existing Delicensed Industries Scheme, Exempted Industries Scheme and DGTD Registration System will stand abolished.

6. STATEMENT OF INDUSTRIAL POLICY NEW DELHI, JULY 24, 1991

Policy Objectives

Pandit Jawaharlal Nehru laid the foundations of modern India. His vision and determination have left a lasting impression on every facet of national endeavour since Independence. It is due to his initiative that India now has a strong and diversified industrial base and is a major industrial nation of the world. The goals and objectives set up for the nation by Pandit Nehru on the eve of Independence, namely, the rapid agricultural and industrial development of our country, rapid expansion of opportunities for gainful employment, progressive reduction of social and economic disparities, removal of poverty and attainment of self-reliance remain as valid today as at the time Pandit Nehru first set them out before the nation. Any industrial policy must contribute to the realisation of these goals and objectives at an accelerated pace. The present statement of industrial policy is inspired by these very concerns, and represents a renewed initiative towards consolidating the gains of national reconstruction at this crucial stage.

2. In 1984, immediately after Independence, Government introduced the Industrial Policy Resolution. This outlined the approach to industrial growth and development. It emphasized the importance to the economy of securing a continuous increase in production and ensuring its equitable distribution. After the adoption of the Constitution and the socio-economic goals, the Industrial Policy was comprehensively revised and adopted in 1956. To meet new challenges, from time, it was modified through statements in 1973, 1977 and 1980.

3. The Industrial Policy Resolution of 1948 was followed by the Industrial Policy Resolution of 1956 which had as its objective the acceleration of the rate of economic growth and the speeding up of industrialization as a means of achieving a socialist pattern of society. In 1956, capital was scarce and the base of entrepreneurship not strong enough. Hence, the 1956 Industrial Policy Resolution gave primacy to the role of the State to assume a predominant and direct responsibility for industrial development.

4. The Industrial Policy Statement of 1973, inter alia, identified high priority industries where investment from large industrial houses and foreign companies would be permitted.

5. The Industrial Policy Statement of 1977 laid emphasis on decentralisation and on the role of small scale, tiny and cottage industries.

6. The Industrial Policy Statement of 1980 focused attention on the need for promoting competition in the domestic market, technological upgradation and modernisation. The policy laid the foundation for an increasingly competitive export base and for encouraging foreign investment in high technology areas. This found expression in the Sixth Five-Year Plan which bore the distinct stamp of Smt. Indira Gandhi. It was Smt. Indira Gandhi who emphasised the need for productivity to be the central concern in all economic and production activities.

7. These policies created a climate for rapid industrial growth in the country. Thus on the eve of the Seventh Five Year Plan, a board-based infrastructure had been built up. Basic industries had been established. A high degree of self-reliance in a large number of items—raw materials, intermediates, finished goods had been achieved. New growth centres of industrial activity had emerged, as had a new generation of entrepreneurs. A large number of engineers, technicians and skilled workers had also been trained.

8. The Seventh Plan recognised the need to consolidate on these strengths and to take initiatives to prepare Indian industry to respond effectively to the emerging challenges. A number of policy and procedural changes were introduced in 1985 and 1986 under the leadership of Shri Rajiv Gandhi aimed at increasing productivity, reducing costs and improving quality. The accent was on opening the domestic market to increased competition and readying our industry to stand on its own in the face of international competition. The public sector was freed from a number of constraints and given a larger measure of autonomy. The technological and managerial modernisation of industry was pursued as the key instrument

for increasing productivity and improving our competitiveness in the world. The net result of all these changes was that Indian industry grew by an impressive average annual growth rate of 8.5% in the Seventh Plan Period.

9. Government is pledged to launching a reinvigorated struggle for social and economic justice, to end poverty and unemployment and to build a modern, democratic, socialist, prosperous and forward-looking India. Such a society can be built if India grows as part of the world economy and not in isolation.

10. While Government will continue to follow the policy of self-reliance, there would be greater emphasis placed on building up our ability to pay for imports through our own foreign exchange earnings. Government is also committed to development and utilisation of indigenous capabilities in technology and manufacturing as well as its upgradation to world standards.

11. Government will continue to pursue a sound policy framework encompassing encouragement of entrepreneurship, development of indigenous technology through investment in research and development, bringing in new technology dismantling of the regulatory system, development of the capital markets and increasing competitiveness for the benefit of the common man. The spread of industrialisation to backward areas of the country will be actively promoted through appropriate incentives, institutions and infrastructure investments.

12. Government will provide enhanced support to the small-scale sector so that it flourishes in an environment of economic efficiency and continuous technological upgradation.

13. Foreign investment and technology collaboration will be welcomed to obtain higher technology, to increase exports and to expand the production base.

14. Government will endeavour to abolish the monopoly of any sector or any individual enterprise in any field of manufacture, except on strategic or military considerations and open all manufacturing activity to competition.

15. The Government will ensure that the public sector plays its rightful role in the evolving socio-economic scenario of the country. Government will ensure that the public sector is run on business lines as envisaged in the Industrial Policy Resolution of 1956 and would continue to innovate and lead in strategic areas of national importance. In the 1950s and 1960s the principal instrument for controlling the commanding heights of the economy was investment in the capital of key industries. Today, the State has other instruments of intervention, particularly fiscal and monetary instruments. The State also commands the bulk of the nation's savings. Banks and financial institutions are under State Control. Where State intervention is necessary, these instruments will prove more effective and decisive.

16. Government will fully protect the interests of labour, enhance their welfare and equip them in all respects to deal with the inevitability of technological change. Government believes that no small section of society can corner the gains of growth, leaving workers to bear its pains. Labour will be made an equal partner in progress and prosperity. Workers participation in management will be promoted. Workers cooperatives will be encouraged to participate in packages designed to turn around sick companies. Intensive training, skill development and upgradation programmes will be launched.

17. Government will continue to visualise new horizons. The major objectives of the new industrial policy package will be to build in the gains already made, correct the distortions or weaknesses that may have crept in, maintain a sustained growth in productivity and gainful employment and attain international competitiveness. The pursuit of these objectives

will be tempered by the need to preserve the environment and ensure the efficient use of available resources. All sectors of industry whether small, medium or large, belonging to the public, private or cooperative sector will be encouraged to grow and improve on their past performance.

18. Government's policy will be continuity with change.

19. In pursuit of the above objectives, Government have decided to take a series of initiatives in respect of the policies relating to the following areas.

A. Industrial Licensing.
B. Foreign Investment.
C. Foreign Technology Agreements.
D. Public Sector Policy.
E. MRTP Act.

A package for the Small and Tiny Sectors of industry is being announced separately.

A. Industrial Licensing Policy

20. Industrial Licensing is governed by the Industries (Development & Regulation) Act, 1951. The Industrial Policy Resolution of 1956 identified the following three categories of industries: those that would be reserved for development in the public sector, those that would be permitted for development through private enterprise with or without State participation, and those in which investment initiatives would ordinarily emanate from private entrepreneurs. Over the years, keeping in view the changing industrial scene in the country, the policy has undergone modifications. Industrial licensing policy and procedures have also been liberalised from time to time. A full realisation of the industrial potential of the country calls for a continuation of this process of change.

21. In order to achieve the objectives of the strategy for the industrial sector for the 191s and beyond it is necessary

to make a number of changes in the system of industrial approvals. Major policy initiates and procedural reforms are called for in order to actively encourage and assist Indian entrepreneurs to exploit and meet the emerging domestic and global opportunities and challenges. The bedrock of any such package of measures must be to let the entrepreneurs make investment decisions on the basis of their own commercial judgement. The attainment of technological dynamism and international competitiveness requires that enterprises must be enabled to swiftly respond to fast changing external conditions that have become characteristic of today's industrial world. Government policy and procedures must be geared to assisting entrepreneurs in their efforts. This can be done only if the role played by the Government were to be changed from that of only exercising control to one of providing help and guidance by making essential procedures fully transparent and by eliminating delays.

22. The winds of change have been with us for some time. The industrial licensing system has been gradually moving away from the concept of capacity licensing. The system of reservations for public sector undertakings has been evolving towards an ethos of greater flexibility and private sector enterprise has been gradually allowed to enter into many of these areas on a case-by-case basis. Further impetus must be provided to these changes which alone can push this country towards the attainment of its entrepreneurial and industrial potential. This calls for bold and imaginative decisions designed to remove restraints on capacity creation, while at the same time, ensuring that over-riding national interests are not jeopardised.

23. In the above context, industrial licensing will henceforth be abolished for all industries, except those specified, irrespective of levels of investment. These specified industries (Annex-II), will continue to be subject to compulsory licensing for reasons related to security and strategic concerns,

social reasons, problems related to safety and over-riding environmental issues, manufacture of products of hazardous nature and articles of elitist consumption. The exemption from licensing will be particularly helpful to the many dynamic small and medium entrepreneurs who have been unnecessarily hampered by the licensing system. As a whole the Indian economy will benefit by becoming more competitive, more efficient and modern and will take its rightful place in the world of industrial progress.

B. Foreign Investment

24. While freeing Indian industry from official controls, opportunities for promoting foreign investment in India should also be fully exploited. In view of the significant development of India's industrial economy in the last 40 years, the general resilience, size and level of sophistication achieved, and the significant changes that have also taken place in the world industrial economy, the relationship between domestic and foreign industry needs to be much more dynamic than it has been in terms of both technology and investment. Foreign investment would bring attendant advantages of technology transfer, marketing expertise, introduction of modern managerial techniques and new possibilities for promotion of exports. This is particularly necessary in the changing global scenario of industrial and economic cooperation marked by mobility of capital. The Government will, therefore, welcome foreign investment which is in the interest of the country's industrial development.

25. In order to invite foreign investment in high priority industries, requiring large investments and advanced technology, it has been decided to provide approval for direct foreign investment upto 51% foreign equity in such industries. There shall be no bottlenecks of any kind in this process. This group of industries has generally been known as the "Appendix-I Industries" and are areas in which FERA companies have already been allowed to invest on a

discretionary basis. This change will go a longway in making Indian policy on foreign investment transparent. Such framework will make it attractive for companies abroad to invest in India.

26. Promotion of exports of Indian products calls for a systematic exploration of world markets possible only through intensive and highly professional marketing activities. To the extent that expertise of this nature is not well developed so far in India. Government will encourage foreign trading companies to assist us in our export activities. Attraction of substantial investment and access to high technology often closely held, and to world markets, involves interaction with some of the world's largest international manufacturing and marketing firms. The Government will appoint a special board to negotiate with such firms so that we can engage in for purposive negotiation with such large firms, and provide the avenues for large investments in the development of industries and technology in the national interest.

C. Foreign Technology Agreements

27. There is a great need for promoting an industrial environment where the acquisition of technological capability receives priority. In the fast changing world of technology the relationship between the suppliers and users of technology must be a continuous one. Such a relationship becomes difficult to achieve when the approval process includes unnecessary governmental interference on a case-to-case basis involving endemic delays and fostering uncertainty. The Indian entrepreneur has now come of age so that he no longer needs such bureaucratic clearance of his commercial technology relationships with foreign technology suppliers. Indian industry can scarcely be competitive with the rest of the world if it is to operate within such a regulatory environment.

28. With a view to injecting the desired level of technological dynamism in Indian industry, Government will

provide automatic approval for technology agreements related to high priority industries within specified parameters. Similar facilities will be available for other industries as well if such agreements do not require the expenditure of free foreign exchange. Indian companies will be free to negotiate the terms of technology transfer with their foreign counterparts according to their own commercial judgement. The predictability and independence of action that this measure is providing to Indian industry will induce them to develop indigenous competence for the efficient absorption of foreign technology. Greater competitive pressure will also induce our industry to invest much more in research and development then they have been doing in the past. In order to help this process, the hiring of foreign technicians and foreign testing of indigenously developed technologies, will also not require prior clearance as prescribed so far, individually or as part of industrial or investment approvals.

D. Public Sector Policy

29. The public sector has been central to philosophy of development. In the pursuit of our development objectives, public ownership and control in critical sectors of the economy has played an important role in preventing the concentration of economic power, reducing regional disparities and ensuring that planned development serves the common goods.

30. The Industrial Policy Resolution of 1956 gave the public sector a strategic role in the economy. Massive investments have been made over the past four decades to build a public sector which has a commanding role in the economy. Today key sectors of the economy are dominated by mature public enterprises that have successfully expanded production, opened up new areas of technology and built up a reserve of technical competence in a number of areas.

31. After the initial exuberance of the public sector entering new areas of industrial and technical competence, a number

of problems have begun to manifest themselves in many of the public enterprises. Serious problems are observed in the insufficient growth in productivity, poor project management, overmanning, lack of continuous technological upgradation, and inadequate attention to R&D and human resource development. In addition, public enterprises have shown a very low rate of return on the capital invested. This has inhabited their ability to regenerate themselves in terms of new investments as become a burden rather than being an asset to the Government. The original concept of the public sector has also undergone considerable dilution. The most striking example is the takeover of sick units from the private sector. This category of public sector units accounts for almost one third of the total losses of central public enterprises. Another category of public enterprises, which does not fit in to the original idea of the public sector being at the commanding heights of the economy, is the plethora of public enterprises which are in the consumer goods services sector.

It is time therefore that the Government adopt a new approach to public enterprises. There must be a great commitment to the support of public enterprises which are essential for the operation of the industrial economy. Measures must be taken to make these enterprises more growth oriented and technically dynamic. Units which may be faltering at present but are potentially viable must be structured and given a new lease of life. The priority areas for growth of public enterprises in the future will be the followings:

- Essential infrastructure goods and services.
- Exploration and exploitation of oil and mineral resources.
- Technology development and building of manufacturing capabilities in areas which are crucial in the long term development of the economy and where private sector investment is inadequate

- Manufacture of products where strategic considerations predominate such as defence equipment

At the same time the public sector will not be barred from entering areas not specifically reserved for it.

33. In view of these considerations, Government will review the existing portfolio of public investments with greater realism. This review will be in respect of industries based on low technology, small scale and non-strategic areas, inefficient and unproductive areas, areas with low or nil social considerations or public purpose, and areas where the private sector has developed sufficient expertise and resources.

Government will strengthen those public enterprises which fall in the reserved areas of operation or are in high priority areas or are generating good or reasonable profits. Such enterprises will be provided a much greater degree of management autonomy through the system of memoranda of understanding. Competition will also be induced in these areas by inviting private sector participation. In the case of selected enterprises, part of Government holdings in the equity share capital of these enterprises will be disinvested in order to provide further market discipline to the performance of public enterprises. There are a large number of chronically sick public enterprises incurring heavy losses, operating in a competitive market and serve little or no public purpose. These needed to be attended to. The country must be proud of the public sector that it owns and its must operate in the public interest.

E. Monopolies and Restrictive Trade Practices Act (MRTP Act)

35. The principal objectives sought to be achieved through the MRTP Act are as follows:-

i) Prevention of concentration of economic power to the common detriment, control of monopolies.

ii) Prohibition of monopolies and restrictive and unfair trade practices.

36. The MRTP Act became effective in June 1970. With the emphasis placed on productivity in the Sixth Plan, major amendments to the MRTP Act were carried out in 1982 and 1984 in order to remove impediments to industrial growth and expansion. This process of change was given a new momentum in 1985 by an increase of the threshold limit of assets.

37. With the growing complexity of industrial structure and the need for achieving economies of scale for ensuring higher productivity and competitive advantage in the international market, the interference of the Government through the MRTP Act in investment decision of large companies has become deleterious in its effects on Indian industrial growth. The pre-entry scrutiny of investment decisions by so-called MRTP companies will no longer be required. Instead, emphasis will be on controlling and regulating monopolistic, restrictive and unfair trade practices rather than making it expansion, establishment of new undertakings, merger, amalgamation and takeover and appointment of certain directors. The thrust of policy will be more on controlling unfair or restrictive business practices. The MRTP Act will be restructured by eliminating the legal requirement for prior governmental approval for expansions relating to merger, amalgamation, and takeover will also be repealed, the provisions regarding restrictions on acquisition of and transfer of share will be appropriately incorporated in the Companies Act.

38. Simultaneously, provisions of the MRTP Act will be strengthened in order to enable the MRTP Commission to take appropriate action in respect of the monopolistic, restrictive and unfair trade practices. The newly empowered MRTP Commission will be encouraged to require investigation suo moto or on complaints received from individual consumers or classes of consumers.

F. Decisions of Government

39. In view of the consideration outlined above Government have decided to take a series of measures to unshackle the Indian industrial economy from the cobwebs of unnecessary bureaucratic control. These measures complement the other series of measures being taken by Govt. in the areas of trade policy, exchange rate management, fiscal policy, financial sector reform and overall macro economic management.

A. Industrial Licensing Policy

i) Industrial Licensing will be abolished for all projects except for a short list of industries related to security and strategic concerns, social reasons, hazardous chemicals and over-riding environmental reasons, and items of elitist consumption (list attached as Annexure II). Industries reserved for the small-scale sector will continue to be so reserved.

ii) Areas where security and strategic concerns predominate, will continue to be reserved for the public sector. (List attached as Annexure I).

iii) In projects where imported capital goods are required, automatic clearance will be given.

   a) In case where foreign exchange availability is ensured through foreign equity.

   b) If the CIF value of imported capital goods required is less than 25% of total value (net of taxes) of plant and equipment, upto a maximum value of Rs.2 crore. In view of the current difficult foreign exchange situation, this scheme (e.r.(iii) b) will come into force from April, 1992.

   In other case, imports of capital goods will require clearance from the Secretariat of Industrial Approvals (SIA) in the Department of Industrial Development according to availability of foreign exchange resources.

iv) In locations other than cities of more than 1 million populations, there will be no requirement of obtaining industrials from the Central Government except for industries subject to compulsory licensing. In respect of cities with population greater than 1 million, industries other than those of a non-polluting nature such as electronics, computer software and printing will be located outside 25 kms. of the periphery, except in prior designated industrial areas.

A flexible location policy would be adopted in respect of such cities (with population greater than 1 million) which require industrial regeneration.

Zoning and Land Use Regulation and Environmental legislation will continue to regulate industrial locations.

Appropriate incentives and the design of investments in infrastructure development will be used to promote the dispersal of industry particularly to rural and backward areas and to reduce congestion in cities.

v) The system of phased manufacturing programmes run on an administrative case by case basis will not be applicable to new project. Existing projects with such programmes will continue to be governed by them.

vi) Existing units will be provided a new broad banding facility to enable them to produce any article without additional investment.

vii) The exemption from licensing will apply to all substantial expansions of existing units.

viii) The mandatory convertibility clause will no linger be applicable for term loans from the financial institutions for new projects and substantial expansions.

Procedural Consequences

ix) All existing registration schemes (Delicensed Registration, Exempted Industries Registration, DGTD Registration) will be abolished.

x) Entrepreneurs will henceforth only be required to file an information memorandum on new projects and substantial expansions.

xi) The lists at Annexure II and Annexure III will be notified in the Indian Trade Classification (Harmonised System).

B. Foreign Investment

i) Approval will be given for direct foreign investment upto 51 per cent foreign equity in high priority industries (Annexure III). There shall be no bottlenecks of any kind in the process. Such Clearance will be available if foreign equity covers the foreign exchange requirement for imported capital goods. Consequential amendments to the Foreign Exchange Regulation Act (1973) shall be carried out.

ii) While the import of components, raw materials and intermediate goods, and payment of know-how fees and royalties will be governed by the general policy applicable to other domestic units, the payment of dividends would be monitored through the Reserve Bank of India so as to ensure that outflows on accounts of dividend payments are balanced by export earnings over a period of time.

iii) Other foreign equity proposals, including proposals involving 51% foreign equity which do not meet the criteria under (ii) above will continue to need prior clearance. Foreign equity proposals needs not necessarily be accompanied by foreign technology agreements.

iv) To provide access to international markets, majority foreign equity holding upto 51% equity will be allowed for trading companies primarily engaged in export activities. While the thrust would be on export activities, such trading houses shall be at par with domestic trading and export houses in accordance with the Import-Export Policy.

v) A special Empowered Board would be constituted to negotiate with a number of large international fines and approved direct foreign investment in select areas. This would be a special programme to attract substantial investment that would provide access to high technology and world markets. The investment programmes of such firms would be considered in totality, free from pre-determined parameters or procedures.

C. Foreign Technology Agreements

i) Automatic permission will be given for foreign technology agreements in high priority industries (Annexure III) upto a lumpsum payment of Rs. 1 crore 5% royalty for modestic sales and 8% for exports subject to total payments of 8% of sales over a 10 year period from date of agreement or 7 years from commencement of production. The prescribed royalty rates are net of taxes and will be calculated according to standard procedures.

ii) In respect of industries other than those in Annexure III, automatic permission will be given subject to the same guidelines as above if no free foreign exchange is required for any payments.

iii) All other proposals will need specific approval under the general procedures in force.

iv) No permission will be necessary for hiring of foreign technicians, foreign testing of Indigenously developed technologies, Payment may be made from blanket permits or free foreign exchanges according to RBI guidelines.

D. Public Sector

i) Portfolio of public sector investments will be reviewed with a view to focus the public sector on strategic, high-tech and essential infrastructure. Whereas some reservation for the public sector is being retained there would be no bar for areas of exclusivity to be opened up to the private sector selectively. Similarly the public sector will also be allowed entry in areas not reserved for it.

ii) Public enterprises which are chronically sick and which are unlikely to be turned around will, for the formulation of revival / rehabilitation schemes, be referred to the Board for Industrial and financial Reconstruction (BIFR), or other similar high level institutions created to protect the interests of workers likely to be affected by such rehabilitation packages.

iii) In order to raise resources and encourage wider public participation, a part of the government's shareholding in the public sector would be offered to mutual funds, financial institutions, general public and workers.

iv) Boards of public sector companies would be made more professional and given greater powers.

v) There will be a greater thrust on performance improvement through the Memoranda of Understanding (MOU) system through which management's would be granted greater autonomy and will be held accountable. Technical expertise on the part of the Government would be upgraded to make the MOU negotiations and implementation more effective.

vi) To facilitate in a fuller discussion on performance,

the MOU signed between Government and the public enterprise would be placed in Parliament. While focussing on major management issues, this would also help place matters on day-to-day operations of public enterprises in their correct perspective.

E. MRTP Act

i) The MRTP Act will be amended to remove the threshold limits of assets in respect of MRTP companies and dominant undertakings. This eliminates the requirement of prior approval of Central Government for establishment of new undertakings, expansion of undertakings, merger, amalgamation and takeover and appointment of Directors under certain circumstances.

ii) Emphasis will be placed on controlling and regulating monopolistic restrictive and unfair trade practices. Simultaneously, the newly empowered MRTP Commission will be authorized to initiate investigations suo moto or on complaints received from individual consumers or classes of consumers in regard to monopolistic, restrictive and unfair trade practices.

iii) Necessary comprehensive amendments will be made in the MRTP Act in this regard and for enabling the MRTP Commission to exercise punitive and compensatory powers.

ANNEXURE TO INDUSTRIAL POLICIES OF GOVT. OF INDIA
LIST OF INDUSTRIES RESERVED FOR THE PUBLIC SECTOR

1. Arms and ammunition and allied items of defence equipment, Defence aircraft and warships.
2. Atomic energy.
3. Coal and lignite.

4. Mineral oils.
5. Mining of iron ore, manganese ore, chrome ore, gypsum, sulphur, gold and diamond.
6. Mining of copper, lead, zinc, tin, molybdenum and wolfram.
7. Minerals specified in the Schedule to the Atomic Energy (Control of Production and Use) Order, 1953.
8. Railway transport.

Source:- www.laghu-udyog.com/policies

APPENDIX-III (B)

KHADI & VILLAGE INDUSTRIES

1. With the liberalization and globalization of the economy and the removal of quantitative restrictions, the smaller units of the khadi and village industry sector are facing stiff competition. A large portion of India's population lives in the villages where illiteracy still prevails and large industry is not in a position to absorb the work force from rural areas. In view of this, it is necessary to create more employment opportunities in villages by utilizing local resources and skills so that rural people can get work in the villages itself.

2. This would also reduce the migration of unemployed rural youths to urban areas in search of jobs. Only a few of them get absorbed in urban areas and this constant flow of people to urban areas has put the existing civic infrastructure under severe pressure. As a result, the number of jhuggi-jhonpari clusters and slum dwellers in urban areas is steadily increasing. The khadi and village industry sector has got the potential to create new jobs in rural areas. During the Ninth Plan period, new policy measures were provided to the sector for enhancing production and employment.

TABLE 1

Performance of the Khadi & Village Industries Sector Production, Employment and Exports

(Rs. in Crores)

Sl. No.	*Sub Sector (Scheme)*	*Unit*	*Ninth Plan Actual Achievement*				*2001-02 (Anti.)*	*Tenth Plan Target*	
			1997-98	*1998-99*	*1999-2000*	*2000-2001*		*2002-03*	*2006-07 Terminal year*
(A)	Production								
1	Khadi cloth	Rs.crore	624	636	552	432	444	457	750
2	Village Industries	Rs.crore	3,895	4,477	5,613	5,914	6,607	6,810	12,500
(B)	Employment								
1	Khadi & Village Industries	Persons million	5.65	5.82	5.92	6.0	6.6	7.02	8.95

TABLE 2

Plan Outlay/Expenditure of the Khadi and Village Industries

Sl. No.	Sub-Sector (Scheme)	Ninth Plan Actual					Nitnth Plan (Expdr.)	Tenth Plan	
		1997-98	1998-99	1999-2000	2000-2001	2001-2002 (Anti.)		2002-2003	2002-2007
M/o. Agro & Rural Industries									
1	Khadi & Village Industries	440.78	346.23	201.93	261.48	330.00	1,580.42	392.00	2,080.00
2	NPRI							1.00	5.00
	Total	440.78	346.23	201.93	261.48	330.00	1,580.42	393.00	2,085.00

3. A committee on strengthening of the khadi and village industries sector was set up under the chairmanship of Shri K.C. Pant, Deputy Chairman, Planning Commission. The report of the Pant Committee, submitted in November 2001, recommended a special package for the development of the sector. The Ministry of Agro and Rural Industries, which is the nodal ministry for the khadi and village industry sector, is implementing this package. The package includes:

> (i) providing the option of market development assistance (MDA) or rebate for khadi cloth; (ii) continuity of rebate/MDA for five years; (iii) creation of a database for the sector; and (iv) intensive marketing support so that the sector may fulfil the objectives of generating rural employment and improving the quality of life of the rural people.

4. The performance of the khadi and village industries is in Table-1 while the Ninth Plan expenditure and outlay for the Tenth Plan and Annual Plan 2002-03 are indicated in Table 5.4.2. The Scheme-wise break up of Tenth Plan outlay is given in the Appendix. The export of village industry products, which was Rs. 13.83 crore in 1994-95 reached Rs.29.66 crore by 1999-2000 and is expected to touch Rs. 35 crore by the terminal year of the Tenth Plan.

5. In the areas of research and development (R&D), various sponsored projects were taken up and funded by the Khadi and Village Industries Commission (KVIC) from the science and technology grant from the Department of Science and Technology. The Jamnalal Bajaj Central Research Institute (JBCRI), Wardha, one of the prominent R&D institutes under the KVIC, is in the process of being revamped. It is proposed to upgrade JBCRI to the National Institute of Rural Industrialisation (NIRI), involving an estimated expenditure of Rs. 8 crore.

6. Some of the technologies developed by the R&D institutions under the KVIC are:

- High productive 6, 8 and 12 spindle all steel new model charkha (NMC).
- Development of semi-automatic and Nepali looms for weaving.
- Development of nine spindle charkhas for muslin khadi.
- Production system for 500 and 600 counts muslin khadi.
- New shades of herbal dyes.
- Suitable and modern Jacquard looms for weaving.
- Improvement in loom for northeastern states.
- Production of portable Ghani for vegetable oil extraction.
- Isolation and naturalising of bitter aspect from neem.
- Isolation of various components from sunflower cake.
- Development of LYMPO bricks from ash of rice husk and broken brick lumps.
- Formulation of new herbal formulations and herbal soaps.
- Development of bio-manure, bio pesticides and bioinsecticides.
- Use of non-edible oils in soap formulations.
- Use of cashew nut liquid in rubber manufacturing.
- Use of different fibres in hand-made paper.
- Decorticators for oilseeds and pulses.
- Development of paddy dehuskers and rice polishers
- Improvement of the potter wheel.
- New technology for tile making.
- Neera preservation.

- Value added products of honey, bakery and fruit products.
- Curing of bee diseases and artificial insemination of bees.

7. Over the years, the production of khadi cloth has been on the decline. Hence employment in this area is also falling. However, production and employment in village industries have grown from Rs. 3,895 crore in 1997-98 to Rs. 6,607 crore in 2001-02 (anticipated) and new job creation has been reported. The main reasons for the poor performance in khadi production were (a) uncertainty over the continuation of the rebate policy for khadi, which upset the production schedule and output of khadi producers; (b) high stock of unsold khadi and mismatch in khadi production; (c) the project finance approach adopted in place of existing pattern approach for village industries units took the rural entrepreneurs some time to get used to; and (d) there was a shortfall in availing funds from banks and budgetary resources.

8. In a major initiative during the Ninth Plan, the marketing of a select range of village industry products was launched under the brand name 'Sarvodaya', with a focus on quality. The National Institute of Design (NID), Ahmedabad, has been entrusted with a project to introduce new and trendy designs in khadi. New designs developed by the National Institute of Fashion Technology (NIFT), New Delhi, would be taken up for production by khadi industries. These initiatives are expected to improve the demand for khadi and to boost production and employment.

9. Apart from announcing the khadi package in line with the recommendations of the Pant Committee, the Government would emphasize on the concept of 'No Loss' against the earlier concept of 'No Profit' in order to strengthen the khadi and village industries and to make the sector viable and vibrant.

10. In 1994, the High Powered Committee to examine and suggest appropriate policy support to strengthen the khadi and village industry sector under the then Prime Minister had envisaged the creation of two million jobs in the khadi and village industries sector during the Eighth Plan. This was to be done by the Rural Employment Generation Programme (REGP) and the KVIC was to be the implementing agency. Taking into account the progress of job creation, the target for REGP has been revised and a total of 1.5 million jobs were envisaged to be created by the end of the Ninth Plan. Till 31 March 2001, one million jobs had been created in the sector under REGP. During the Tenth Plan period, two million new jobs would be created in the khadi and village industries sector. The targets for khadi and village industries for the terminal year of the Tenth Plan are given in Table-1.

11. Since 1995-96, under the REGP, 25 per cent of the project cost is provided as margin money for projects that cost upto Rs. 10 lakh. For projects costing between Rs. 10 and 25 lakh, an additional 10 per cent of the remaining cost of the projects is also provided as margin money. For the northeastern region, Sikkim, Andaman & Nicobar Islands, Lakshadweep, hill areas, border areas, tribal areas and for weaker sections (scheduled castes, scheduled tribes, other backward classes, women/physically handicapped/ex-servicemen and minority community beneficiary/institution), margin money is provided at 30 per cent of the project cost. Initially, institutional financing was made available to KVIC in the form of a line of credit of Rs. 1,000 crore, popularly known as Consortium Bank Credit (CBC). Till 31 March 2002, the KVIC had utilised Rs. 738.14 crore for the creation of new jobs in the khadi and village industries sector.

12. In order to extend the quality control network of the sector, 17 national level laboratories have been identified. These laboratories have been accorded accreditation for testing and standardization of khadi and village industries products

and will cater to the needs of local artisans as well as institutions.

13. Marketing is the key to the success of any product. KVIC is providing the necessary marketing inputs to the khadi and village industries sector for both domestic as well as export marketing. Its main focus, however, is on domestic marketing. Financial assistance is provided to directly aided institutions, State/Union Territory KVI Boards and their aided organisations for setting up sales outlets, renovation or expansion of existing sales outlets, purchase of mobile vans and organising exhibitions to create awareness about khadi and village industries products. KVIC has been participating in international exhibitions being organized by the India Trade Promotion Organization (ITPO). Representatives of non-government organizations (NGOs) and KVI Boards are provided financial assistance for ITPO exhibitions. Khadi Gramodyog Bhawans are proposed to be opened in countries like the United States, the United Kingdom, Germany, South Africa, etc. for export promotion. Accordingly Export Promotion Council (EPC) status for khadi and village industry product exports is being envisaged.

14. An 8 per cent per annum growth in khadi cloth production has been envisaged during the Tenth Plan period. Employment in khadi industries is expected to increase at 3 per cent per annum and major efforts would be made up to improve the quality and value of khadi production by focusing upon design inputs and improving the quality of khadi cloth. Anti-crease treatment for khadi cloth would be achieved by technology tie-up with renowned laboratories and research institutions. Khadi institutions would be strengthened to become economically viable by developing backward and forward linkages.

15. In order to increase the earnings of khadi artisans attention would need to be given on ensuring higher productivity by introducing improved tools and equipments.

Programmes to upgrade skills through training for khadi artisans would be taken up. Use of improved tools and techniques would encourage artisans to produce value-added khadi cloth items, decoratives, etc. With an eye on developing a niche market for khadi, it is proposed to restructure and strengthen the marketing strategy.

16. For village industries efforts would be made to provide adequate finance, tax exemptions, particularly in sales tax, octroi, purchase tax, etc. Awareness would be generated in village industries about the Margin Money Scheme of the KVIC and to prepare economically viable and bankable projects by village industries entrepreneurs. Efforts would be made to increase full time employment in village industries and enable the artisans to produce items round the year. Special quality assurance and product development programmes would need to be taken up for village industries to increase their marketability. Cluster development of village industries need to be undertaken in a way that makes all inputs available at one place and provides marketing inputs to increase sales of village industries units.

17. Technology interfaces are proposed to be established in the Tenth Plan to disseminate information as well as function as technology adoption centres. One-time financial assistance would be provided to such technology interfaces. The technologists/scientists and experts attached to these interfaces will interact with the local institutions, individuals and artisans for on-the-spot assessment of their technology-related or technical problems. NIRI would act as the coordinating agency for all such technology interfaces.

MAIN STRATEGIES OF THE KHADI AND VILLAGE INDUSTRIES SECTOR FOR THE TENTH PLAN

- Provide employment to rural people in villages.
- Produce saleable/marketable products

- Creating self-reliance amongst people and building up of a strong rural community
- More emphasis on 'No Loss' instead of 'No Profit' by khadi and village industries organizations/ institutions.

18. In the Tenth Plan, it is proposed to set up rural industrial estates and artisan clusters to provide necessary infrastructure and support services to the village industries. Developed land, power, water, common facility centres, training and skill upgradation centres, design and quality inputs and common packaging facilities would be provided at such clusters. The Common Facility Centres would be managed by the implementing agency for the industrial estate. Financial assistance would be provided to Common Facility Centres by KVIC or by agencies like the National Bank for Agriculture and Rural Development (NABARD), Small Industries Development Bank of India (SIDBI), Council for the Advancement of People's Action and Rural Technology (CAPART), etc.

National Programme for Rural Industrialization

19. Under the National Programme for Rural Industrialization (NPRI), 50 clusters have been identified by the KVIC for cluster development. Twelve clusters were taken up in 1999-2000, out of which five have commenced production. Further work on the promotion of clusters for increasing rural employment and establishment of backward and forward linkages, setting up of Common Facility Centres, common service network support for satellite cluster units, etc, have been taken up by the KVIC.

The Path Ahead

20. The Tenth Plan strategies for the khadi and village industries sector would include: (a) generation of additional employment in rural areas; (b) adoption of market-oriented production plan; (c) creation of self-employment in rural

areas and building up of rural communities by fully utilizing local resources, raw materials and manpower; and (d) adoption of 'no loss' practice by khadi and village industries units instead of the present 'no profit' policy.

21. Rural industrial estates are proposed to be set up in the Tenth Plan to provide the required infrastructure and support services to village industries and artisan units. Growth of khadi cloth is expected to be 8 per cent in value terms and the sector is expected to see a 3 per cent growth in employment generation. Khadi producing institutions would need to be strengthened to become economically viable by developing backward and forward linkages. Cluster development approach would be adopted for the growth of village industries to achieve the Tenth Plan targets. A network of quality control laboratories would be necessary to provide testing facilities and standardization of quality for village industries. Setting up of technology interfaces to serve as information dissemination and technology adoption centres would also be required for village industries.

22. More rural/village industry clusters would be taken up under the NPRI for higher production and employment generation in these clusters. The cluster development programme would envisage the establishment of backward and forward linkages, setting up of common facility centres and common service network support for satellite cluster units.

SOURCE

10th Five-Year Plan, Khadi & Village Industries, V-2, Chapter-5, Govt. of India.

www.plaiiningcommission.nic.in/plans/planrel/fiveyr/10th/volume2/v2_ch5_4.pdf

APPENDIX-IV

SCHEMES FOR WOMEN ENTREPRENEURS OFFERED BY GOVERNMENT OF INDIA & STATE GOVERNMENTS AND GOVERNMENTAL AGENCIES

SMALL INDUSTRIES DEVELOPMENT BANK OF INDIA (SIDBI) - MAHILA UDYAM NIDHI SCHEME FOR WOMEN ENTREPRENEURS

Purpose: To meet gap in equity

Eligible Borrowers

Women entrepreneurs for setting up new projects in tiny/small-scale sector and rehabilitation of viable sick SSI units. Existing tiny and small scale industrial units & service enterprises [tiny enterprises would include all industrial units and service industries (except Road Transport Operators) satisfying the investment ceiling prescribed for tiny enterprises] undertaking expansion, modernization technology upgradation and diversification can also be considered.

Norms

- Scheme operated through SFCs / twin function SIDCs / Scheduled Commercial Banks / Scheduled Urban Cooperative Banks
- Cost of Project - Not to exceed Rs. 1 million
- Soft Loan limit - 25% of cost of Project subject to a maximum of Rs. 2,50,000 per project
- Service charges - 1% p.a. on soft loan

ANDHRA PRADESH STATE FINANCIAL CORPORATION (APSFC) - MAHILA UDYAM NIDHI SCHEME

All new industrial projects with project cost not exceeding Rs. 10.00 lacs promoted by women entrepreneurs with minimum of 51% share in equity are eligible for equity type of assistance under the scheme along with regular term loan. The cost of project should not exceed Rs. 10.00 lacs. Under the scheme, SIDBI seed capital assistance by way of soft loan at 1% p.a. service charges is considered up to a maximum of 15% of project cost to meet the gap in equity. Minimum promoters contribution should be 10% of the project cost. The soft loan repayment period can be a maximum of 10 years with a minimum period up to 5 years. Service activities like hospitals/nursing homes, hotels/restaurants and professional services in Medicine, dentistry, architecture, etc. are also covered under the scheme.

DELHI FINANCIAL CORPORATION (DFC) - MAHILA UDYAM NIDHI SCHEME (MUN)

Delhi Financial Corporation has been operating a special scheme viz. Mahila Udyam Nidhi Scheme (MUN) for providing, inter-alia, equity type assistance to women entrepreneurs for setting up industrial units in the small scale and tiny sector and undertaking service activities eligible for assistance under its Refinance Scheme.

Eligibility Criteria

- New projects in tiny and small-scale sectors for manufacture, preservation or processing of goods. [Tiny enterprises would include all industrial units and service industries (except Road Transport Operators) satisfying the investment ceiling prescribed for tiny enterprises viz. Rs. 5 lakh].
- Existing tiny and small-scale industrial units and service enterprises as mentioned above [including those which have availed of MUN assistance earlier], undertaking expansion, modernization, technology upgradation and diversification.
- Sick units in the tiny and small-scale sectors including, service enterprises as mentioned above, which are considered potentially viable.

- All industrial activities and service activities [except Road Transport Operators] in the SSI sector.
- Projects which avail of any margin money or seed/ special capital assistance under the Schemes of Central/State Governments, State Financial Corporations and other state level institutions or banks [except State investment subsidy] are not eligible for assistance under the Scheme.

1. WOMEN ENTREPRENEURS OWNING AND MANAGING ENTERPRISES WITH MINIMUM FINANCIAL STAKE OF 51% OF THE EQUITY

Project Cost

Project cost [including margin money for working capital should not exceed Rs. 10 lakh in the case of new projects. In the case of existing units and service enterprises, the outlay on expansion/ modernisation/ technology upgradation, or diversification or rehabilitation should not exceed Rs. 10 lakh per project.

Nature and Extent of Assistance

There would be no change in the existing level of promoters' contribution at 10% of the project cost. However, the ceiling of soft loan assistance under the Scheme has been enhanced from the present level of 15% of the project cost subject to a maximum of Rs. 1.5 lakh per project to 25% of the project cost subject to a maximum of Rs. 2.5 lakh per project. The DER will, therefore, be 1.857:1 [excluding State subsidy which may be retained for meeting working capital].

Interest Rate

a) Upto Rs. 25000 - 12%
b) Above Rs. 25000 and upto Rs. 2 lacs - 13.5%
c) Above Rs. 2 lacs - 16%

Maximum Quantum of Loan

Rs. 6.5 term loan and Rs. 2.5 seed capital.

Promoter's Contribution

10% (DER 1.857:1).

Service Charge

Service charge on the soft loan assistance under MUN would be @ 1% p.a.

2. WOMEN ENTREPRENEURS INDEPENDENTLY OR WITH MORE THAN 60% SHARE HELD AS MANAGING PARTNER IN JOINT VENTURE WITH OTHERS

Project Cost

The total project cost should not exceed Rs.15 lakh.

Maximum Quantum of Loan

Rs. 7.5 lakhs Term Loan

Promoter's Contribution

15% (DER 3:1) Term Loan.

ECONOMIC DEVELOPMENT CORPORATION OF GOA, DAMAN & DIU, DADRA & NAGAR HAVELI LTD. (EDC) - MAHILA UDYAM NIDHI SCHEME (MUN)

The Corporation has been operating a special scheme viz. Mahila Udyam Nidhi Scheme (MUN) for providing, inter-alia, equity type assistance to women entrepreneurs for setting up industrial units in the small scale and tiny sector and undertaking service activities eligible for assistance under its Refinance Scheme.

Eligibility Criteria

- New projects in tiny and small-scale sectors for

manufacture, preservation or processing of goods. [Tiny enterprises would include all industrial units and service industries (except Road Transport Operators) satisfying the investment ceiling prescribed for tiny enterprises viz. Rs. 5 lakh].

- Existing tiny and small-scale industrial units and service enterprises as mentioned above [including those which have availed of MUN assistance earlier], undertaking expansion, modernisation, technology upgradation and diversification.
- Sick units in the tiny and small-scale sectors including, service enterprises as mentioned above, which are considered potentially viable.
- All industrial activities and service activities [except Road Transport Operators] in the SSI sector.

Projects which avail of any margin money or seed/special capital assistance under the Schemes of Central/State Governments, State Financial Corporations and other state level institutions or banks [except State investment subsidy] are not eligible for assistance under the Scheme.

GUJARAT STATE FINANCIAL CORPORATION (GSFC) - MAHILA UDYAM NIDHI SCHEME (MUN)

The Corporation has been operating a special scheme viz. Mahila Udyam Nidhi Scheme (MUN) for providing, inter-alia, equity type assistance to women entrepreneurs for setting up industrial units in the small scale and tiny sector and undertaking service activities eligible for assistance under its Refinance Scheme.

Eligibility Criteria

- New projects in tiny and small-scale sectors for manufacture, preservation or processing of goods. [Tiny enterprises would include all industrial units and service industries (except Road Transport

Operators) satisfying the investment ceiling prescribed for tiny enterprises viz. Rs. 5 lakh].

- Existing tiny and small-scale industrial units and service enterprises as mentioned above [including those which have availed of MUN assistance earlier], undertaking expansion, modernisation, technology upgradation and diversification.
- Sick units in the tiny and small-scale sectors including, service enterprises as mentioned above, which are considered potentially viable.
- All industrial activities and service activities [except Road Transport Operators] in the SSI sector.
- Projects which avail of any margin money or seed/special capital assistance under the Schemes of Central/State Governments, State Financial Corporations and other state level institutions or banks [except State investment subsidy] are not eligible for assistance under the Scheme.

HARYANA FINANCIAL CORPORATION (HFC) – MAHILA DHYAM NIDHI SCHEME

New Industrial projects in the small sector upto project cost of Rs. 10.00 lakhs which are covered for refinance and set up by new women entrepreneurs are eligible for financial assistance with minimum promoters contribution of 10%. Soft loan upto 15% of project cost, at annual service charge of 1% is available to meet the gap in equity after providing promoters contribution.

HIMACHAL PRADESH FINANCIAL CORPORATION (HPFC) - SCHEME FOR WOMEN ENTREPRENEURS

Scheme was formulated with twin objectives of providing training and extension service support to women entrepreneurs through a comprehensive package suited to their other skills and socioeconomic status and extending financial assistance on concessional terms to enable them to set up industrial units in SSI sector. Amount sanctioned for the scheme during 1997-98 Rs. 220 lakhs.

JAMMU & KASHMIR STATE FINANCIAL CORPORATION (JK SFC) - MAHILA UDYAM NIDHI SCHEME (MUN)

The corporation has been operating a special scheme viz. Mahila Udyam Nidhi Scheme (MUN) for providing, inter-alia, equity type assistance to women entrepreneurs for setting up industrial units in the small scale and tiny sector and undertaking service activities eligible for assistance under its Refinance Scheme.

Eligibility Criteria

- New projects in tiny and small-scale sectors for manufacture, preservation or processing of goods. [Tiny enterprises would include all industrial units and service industries (except Road Transport Operators) satisfying the investment ceiling prescribed for tiny enterprises viz. Rs. 5 lakh].
- Existing tiny and small-scale industrial units and service enterprises as mentioned above [including those which have availed of MUN assistance earlier], undertaking expansion, modernization, technology upgradation and diversification.
- Sick units in the tiny and small-scale sectors including, service enterprises as mentioned above, which are considered potentially viable.
- All industrial activities and service activities [except Road Transport Operators] in the SSI sector.
- Projects which avail of any margin money or seed/special capital assistance under the Schemes of Central/State Governments, State Financial Corporations and other state level institutions or banks [except State investment subsidy] are not eligible for assistance under the scheme.

KARNATAKA STATE FINANCIAL CORPORATION (KSFC) - MAHILA UDHYAM NIDHI SCHEME

This scheme is meant for extending financial assistance to first generation women entrepreneurs to set up new SSI units. This scheme provides equity type of assistance along with term loan. Existing tiny/SSI and service units are also eligible for assistance for expansion/ diversification/ modernization costing upto Rs. 10.00 lakhs. The ceiling on project cost is Rs. 10.00 lakhs and the maximum equity assistance is Rs. 2.50 lakhs at 25% of the project cost. The Women entrepreneurs who seek assistance under this scheme should possess managerial and technical skill to run the unit and they shall be the chief promoter of the proposed unit. The equity type of assistance is termed as soft seed capital, which carries interest at 1% p.a. The term loan component carries the normal rate of interest.

MAHARASHTRA STATE FINANCIAL CORPORATION (MSFC) - SCHEME FOR WOMEN ENTREPRENEURS

The scheme has been formulated by IDBI to [1] provide training and extension services support to women entrepreneurs through a comprehensive package suited to their skills and socio-economic status and (2) extending financial assistance on promoter's contribution @ 12.5% to 15% of the project cost, depending on the location to enable them to set up industrial units in the SSI Sector.

The programme of training and extension services is organized by IDBI through designated approved agencies independently and or in association with other development agencies.

The assistance in the form of term loans is granted for all projects in the SSI Sectors including cottage, village and tiny industry promoted and managed by women entrepreneurs. In case of partnership/ Pvt. Ltd. Co., women entrepreneurs should have major share-minimum 51%. DER required to be maintained is 2: 1. Repayment period 8 years including 2 years moratorium. DER 2:1

Maximum Quantum of Financial Assistance: Upto Rs. 90 lakhs depending upon constitution.

MAHARASHTRA STATE FINANCIAL CORPORATION (MSFC) - MAHILA UDYAM NIDHI SCHEME

In order to give further boost to women entrepreneurs to take up industrial activity, apart from providing them term loan assistance and training assistance through IDBI, the Corporation now operates Mahila Udyam Nidhi Scheme. Under the scheme, the Corporation provides equity type assistance to Women Entrepreneurs to set up new industrial projects upto 15% of project cost (for project cost upto Rs. 10 lakhs) by way of Seed Capital. The women entrepreneurs will be required to bring in promoter's contribution to the extent of 10% of project cost. The soft loan assistance is repayable within a period of 10 years including initial moratorium of 5 years. In case of Partnership/Pvt. Ltd. Co., the women promoter should have major share (say 51%). For term loan, repayment period is 8 years including 2 years moratorium.

Debt Equity Ratio: 2 : 1

ORISSA STATE FINANCIAL CORPORAITON (OSFC) - MAHILA UDHYAM NIDHI SCHEME

This scheme is meant for extending financial assistance to first generation women entrepreneurs to set up new SSI units. This scheme provides equity type of assistance along with term loan. Existing tiny/SSI and service units are also eligible for assistance for expansion/ diversification/ modernisation costing upto Rs. 10.00 lakhs. The ceiling on project cost is Rs. 10.00 lakhs and the maximum equity assistance is Rs. 2.50 lakhs at 25% of the project cost. The

Women entrepreneurs who seek assistance under this scheme should possess managerial and technical skill to run the unit and they shall be the chief promoter of the proposed unit. The equity type of assistance is termed as soft seed capital, which carries interest at 1% p.a. The term loan component carries the normal rate of interest.

PONDICHERRY INDUSTRIAL PROMOTION DEVELOPMENT & INVESTMENT CORPORATION (PIPDIC) - MAHILA UDAYAM NIDHI SCHEME

Eligibility : Women entrepreneurs for setting up new projects.

Purpose : To set up new SSI Units / Service activities.

Remarks

Cost of project - Not to exceed Rs. 10 lakhs.

Soft Loan Limit -25% of cost of project subject to a maximum of Rs. 2.5 lakh per project.

Service charges - 1% p.a. on soft loan.

PONDICHERRY INDUSTIRAL PROMOTION DEVELOPMENT & INVESTMENT CORPORATION (PIPDIC) - MAGALIR UDAVI SCHEME FOR WOMEN ENTREPRENEURS

Eligibility: For women entrepreneurs.

Purpose: To set up new SSI Units / Tiny projects.

REMARKS

Cost of the project - up to Rs. 20 lakhs.

Term Loan -75% of the project cost.

Interest Concessional - 2% less than the normal interest rate.

PUNJAB FINANCIAL CORPORATION (PFC) - MAHILA UDYAM NIDHI SCHEME

All new industrial projects in the small scale eligible for refinance assistance and set up by new women entrepreneurs where the cost of project does not exceed Rs. 10.00 lakhs would be eligible for assistance under the scheme. Minimum promoters' contribution shall be 10% of the project cost. Seed Capital Assistance by way of soft loan is given upto maximum of 25% of the project cost to meet the gap in equity after taking into account the promoters' own contribution. A service charge of one per cent per annum is levied on this loan.

Index

A

Abed, F.H., 39
Adilabad, 216
Administrators, 89
Afghanistan-Vietnam, 89
Agrarian Sector, 103
Agricultural and Industrial Sector, 326
Agricultural, 105
  Fairs, 86
  Labour, 34
  Marketing, 65, 71, 79
  Production, 326
  Resources, 27
  Revolution, 4
  Sector, 33, 94, 332
Agro-Based
  Enterprises, 32
  Industries, 21, 113, 358
  Rural Industries, 32
Agro-Enterprises, 19, 26, 28, 30, 31
Agro-Forest Based and Food Preservation, 301
Agro-Industrial Development, 26
Aid Agencies, 21
Aircraft Manufacture, 308
Aizwal, 6, 23
All India Small Scale Industrial Board, 130, 139
All India Term Lending Institutions, 135-136
America, 309
Amul Complex, 209
Anantpur, 255
Ancient Hindu Varnas, 164
Andhra Pradesh, 142, 171, 213, 214, 216, 218, 227, 234, 236, 246-249
AP Mahila Udyam Nidhi Scheme, 394
AP Mutually Aided Coop. Society
  Act, 1995, 227, 232
Arms and Ammunition, 319
Asia, 3, 23, 24, 28, 39, 88, 89, 90, 96, 99, 107
Asian Countries, 23, 24, 27, 89, 90, 93, 96, 97, 98, 99
Asian Region, 99
Asian Villages, 99
Assam, 181
Association of Small Scale Industrial Entrepreneurs, 138
Atomic Energy, 319

B

Baichitola Village, 53
Bangladesh, 38-41, 47
Bangladesh Society, 50

Banking System, 60
Banks, 58-60, 62-64, 85, 254, 329
  Nationalization, 60
  Role of, 60, 62
Boards for
  Coir, 110
  Handicraft, 110
  Handloom, 110
  Khadi and Village Industry, 110
  Sericulture, 110
BRAC (Bangladesh Rural Advanced Committee), 40-47, 49, 52, 53, 54, 55, 57
  Activities, 42, 44
  Institutions Building, 45
  Poultry Development Program, 41
  Socio-Economic Program, 46
British Education System, 210
Brunei, 89
Business and Trade, 6, 23

C

Capital Goods Industries, 332
Caste
  Council, 179
  Groups, 165
  System, 164
Central Advisory Council, 313
Central Investment Subsidy, 114
Chemical/Plastic/Rubber Product, 302
Child Marriage, 52
Chilli Processing Unit, 235-237
  Profile, 238-239
China, Mobile Industry Coop Unit, 312
Chinese, 19, 89
Chittoor, 257
Christian Missionaries, 176
Christianity, 170
Civilization, 67
Cluster Association, 254
Constitution of India, 110
Cooperative Movement, 209
Cottage and Small Industries, 110,112
Cottage and Small Scale Industries,, 310, 311
Cottage and Village Industries, 110
Cottage Industries, 19, 21, 65, 88, 91, 100, 112, 117, 328, 330
Cuddapah, 255
Cultural and Socio-economic Data, 31
Cultural Traditions, 16
Cultural Values, 65

D

Dairy Industry, 209
Damodar Valley Scheme, 309
Data Bank, 354, 355
Decision Making, 7, 20, 170, 244, 340
Deep Tube Wells, 46
Delhi-Nidhi Scheme, 395
Delicensed Industries Scheme, 364
Developing Countries Economy, 97
Developing Countries in Asia, 165
Developing Countries, 19, 24, 27, 34, 73, 76, 86, 88, 93, 94, 97, 100, 101, 102, 103, 105, 107, 214, 267, 336, 350

Development Entreneurship, 12, 24
Development Strategy, 119
DIC (District Industrial Centre), 15, 59, 60, 62, 63, 111, 112, 141, 183, 328, 329, 357
Differential Interest Scheme, 254
Directive Principles of State Policy, 110
Districts of Narsingdi, (BD), 49
Districts of Natore (BD), 49
Districts of Pabna (BD), 49, 53
Divisioin of Labour, 4
DRDA, 217, 218, 233, 234, 235, 237
DWCRA (Development of Women and Children in Rural Areas), 225, 226, 244, 246

E

Economic Independence, 19
Economic Information Service, 142-144
Economic System, 100
ED Promotional Agencies, 17
EDP (Entrepreneurship Development Programme), 2759, 60, 62, 121, 199
EDP Among Women, 8, 12, 14
EDTP (Entrepreneurship Development Training Program), 268-271
Education, 13, ,15, 22, 41, 45, 52, 93, 165, 175, 178, 179, 207, 208, 247
  Extention, 65, 66, 86
  Functional, 49
  Consciousness Raising, 47
Educational Institutes, 15, 16
Eighth Plan, 389
Electronic and Electrical Products, 304
Empowerment of Women, 1, 8
EMT (Entrepreneur Motivation Development Lab), 271, 272
Enterprises Categories, 13
Entreneurship Among Women, 3, 6
Entrepreneur Development Program, 272, 274, 276, 278
Entrepreneurial
  Activity, 2, 3, 5, 6, 8, 9, 10, 11, 15-19, 28, 58, 59, 61, ,62, 94, 173, 179, 180, 234
  Characteristics, 189-191
  Development Organisation, 183
  Development Phases, 193-199
  Development Program, 7
  Problems, 177-178
  Role Requirement, 191
  Group, 177
  Individual, 177
  Institution, 178
Entrepreneurship 1, 2
  Development Institute of India, Ahmedabad, 145
  Development Program, 360
Entrepreneurship Development, 3, 14-19, 34, ,38, 58, 59, 89, 144, 146, 149, 162, 163, 166, 169, 174-176, 178, 180, 189, 201, 267
EPI (Expanded Program on Immunization), 41
EPZ (Export Processing Zone), 116
Equity Fund Scheme, 62

ESCAP Document, 204
Export Oriented Industries, 113
Export Promotion Council, 390
Exports Markets, 88
Extension Functionaries, 87
Extension Methods in Agriculture Marketing, 71

F

Factories Act, 122
Fair Price Shops, 222
Family Planning, 20, 41
FERA, 363, 371
Fertilizers-Petrochemicals, 333
Financial Institutions, 58-60, 63, 96, 115, 121, 134, 139, 145, 339, 342
First Five Year Plan, 110, 111, 316
Fisheries, 105
Five Year Plan, 121
FMCG, 247
Food and Agricultural Organization (India), 21
Foreign Exchange Regulation Act, 335, 336, 379
Foreign Technology Agreement, 380
Free Market Policies, 95

G

Gandhi, Indira, 117, 367
Gandhi, Rajiv, 117
Gram Sevak, 47
Grameen Bank (Bangladesh), 38, 46, 245, 247, 248
Green Revolution, 211
Gujarat, 246
Guntur Dist., 222

H

Handicraft (Tribal), 181
Handicraft Industries, 91, 104, 105, 108
Handicrafts, 92, 161
Handloom, 92
Handloom Industry, 311
Handloom Sector, 331
Harmonised System, 116, 363, 379
Heavy Industries, 317
High Technology Industries, 332
Hindu Jajmani System, 10, 164, 165
Hirakund Dam, 309
HLL (Hindustan Liver Ltd), 245-248
Hong Kong, 89
Hosiery and Textiles, 305

I

IDBI (Industrial Development Bank of India), 329
Imphal, 6, 23
Import Export Policy, 380
India, Indonesia and Philippines, 88
Indian Economy, 122, 210
  Industry, 117, 118, 314
  Planners, 211
  Small Scale Industry Board, 128
  Trade Classification, 116, 363
Indonesia, 23
Industrial and Economic Policy, 336

Industrial Development, 62, 65, 88, 96, 106, 107, 112, 162, 168, 173, 179, 182, 183, 267, 341, 349, 361, 377

Industrial Corporation of Artisans, 128

Industrial
- Development Agencies, 8, 192
- Development Policies, 109, 185
- Development Program, 96
- Disputes Relations, 313
- Economy, 337, 344
- Estates, 321
- Licensing, 369
- Policy, 369, 377
- Licensing System, 370
- Machinery, 313
- Measures, 109
- Peace, 323
- Policies (India), 88, 306
- Policy Resolution (1948), 110, 116, 306-315, 323, 365
- Policy Resolution (1956), 111, 116, 315-325, 346, 369, 373
- Policy Resolution (1973), 111
- Policy Resolution (1977), 325-342
- Policy Resolution (1980), 342-358
- Policy Resolution (1990), 358-364
- Policy Resolution (1991), 364-393
- Policy Resolution, 365
- Policy Statement, 365, 366
- Policy Statement (1973), 116
- Policy Statement (1977), 116
- Policy Statement (1980), 117
- Policy, 109-113, 116, 121, 324, 326, 327, 338, 341, 342, 357, 360, 365
- Promotion, 9
- Relations, 323; 357
- Resources, 182
- Revolution, 4
- Sector, 113, 326
- Strategy, 337
- Technology and Knowledge, 314
- Truce Resolution, 314

Industrialization, 5, 10, 97, 98, 100, 103-105, 116, 118, 127, 144, 162, 165, 166, 182, 145, 204, 245, 314, 317, 342-344, 346, 349, 367

Industries (Development and Regulation) Act, 323, 351, 269

Industries and Khadi and Village Industries Commission, 15

Industry and Trade, 323

Infant Mortaility, 42

International
- Economy, 337
- Trade, 337

International Women Year Conference, Mexico City, 20

IRD (Integrated Rural Development), 104, 106

IRDP (Bangladesh), 21

Iron and Steel, 308

ITPO, 390

J

Janta Party, 343

Japan and Switzerland, 182

Japan, 96, 103, 166

JKSFC, 400

K

Kaira Dist.(Guj), 209

Karnataka, 246, 247

Kerala, 181

Kerala Economy, 181
Khadi and Village and Cottage Industry Board, 360
Khadi and Village Industries Commission (KVIC), 84, 330
Khadi and Village Industries, 92, 383, 386, 387, 389, 390, 391
Khadi and Village Industry Commission, 92, 128, 129
Korea, 23
Kosi Reservoir, 309
KSFC, 401
Kurnool, 257

L

Labour Resources, 75, 168
Laos, 22
Large Scale Industries, 89, 94, 95, 101, 100, 103, 311, 312, 321, 331, 333, 336
  Role of, 331
Leather Products, 302
Legislation, 112
List of Technical Development under KVIC, 387
List of Agro-Based Industries, 299-300
List of Products, 218-221
Literacy and Education Level, 10

M

MACT, 226-228, 234, 240, 248, 249
  Act, 1995, 227
  Objectives, 228-231
  Organizational Setup, 239-240
Madhya Pradesh, 13, 246
Maheshpur, 53
Mahila Banks (AP), 221, 228
Mahila Udyam Nidhi Scheme for Women Enterprise, 394
Management Development Institute, New Delhi, 145
Management Development Program, 40
Managerial Skills, 11
Margin Money Scheme, 391
Market Economy, 204
Marketing and Information System, 345
Marketing Strategies, 79, 95
Marketing System, 79, 82
MART (Marketing and Research Team), 246, 248
Mass Communication, 86, 87
MC (Management Committee), 47, 55
Mechanical Engineering Industries, 303
Media, 85, 86, 87, 212
Medium Industry, 95, 100, 103, 108
Medium Sectors, 112
Mineral Oils, 308
Ministry of Education, 41
Ministry of Fisheries and Livestock, 41
Ministry of Health and Family Planning, 41
Ministry of Industry, 34, 90, 109, 119, 130, 139, 145
Ministry of Relief and Rehabilitation, 41
Mizoram, 181
Modern Sector, 92

Modern Economy, 346
Mohd. Younis, 38
MRTP, 363, 369, 375
ACT (Monopolies and Restrictive Trade Practices), 332, 375, 376, 384
Objective Achieved, 375-376
MSFC, 401, 402
Mutual Adided Coop. Society Act, 1995, 217
Mynamar-Chinese Border, 22

N

NABARD, 237
Nalgonda, 216, 222, 246, 247, 248
National
Economy, 100, 110, 111, 310, 350
Institute of Design, 388
Institute of Fashion Technology (NIFT), 388
Planning Commission, 306
Nationalized Banks, 329
Nationalized Banks, 61
Nehru, JL, 364, 365
Neo-Economic Environment, 1
Nepal, 22, 23
New Farm Technologies, 25
NGO (Non-Governmental Organization), 34, 35, 40, 213, 218, 236, 240, 243, 244, 245, 246, 254, 390
Case Study, 253
NIESBUD (Nat. Inst. For Entrepreneurship and Small Business Dev.), 145, 149
Ninth Five Year Plan, 383
NIRI, 391
NISIET, 143-147, 149
Non-Formal Primary Education Program, 42
North East Region, 139
NSIC (National Small Industries Corp), 130, 139, 140
Nuclear Families, 5, 204

O

Ongole, 216
OSFC, 402
OTEP (Oral Therapist Extension Program), 42
Other Financial Institutions, 137-138

P

Padmavathi Rashtriya Seva Samiti (PRSS), 213
Pant Committee, 388
Pant, KC, 386
Parvathagiri, 236, 238
Percy Amendment, 20
Personal Profiles of Women Beneficiaries, 249-253
Philippines, 22, 23
Physical/Economic Structure, 185, 186
Plan Outlays, 121
Plan Outlays Table, 123
Planners, 24, 28, 89
Planning Commission, 130, 139, 211, 318, 386
Planning Schemes, 104
Planning, 69, 70
Policy Initiative, 222-224
Policy Makers, 89
Political Emancipation, 1
Political Structure, 172

Politico-Social Movement, 5
Polygamy and Divorce, 50
Powerloom Sector, 331
Powerlooms, 92
Preamble to Industrial Constitution, 316-317
Price Data Tools, 87
Price Policy, 339
Private Sector, 318, 320, 334, 346
Production Commission, 313
Project Shakti, 213, 245, 246, 247, 249
Public Sector, 40, 117, 119, 317, 318, 320, 321, 322, 334, 342, 344, ,345, 368, 370, 377, 381
  Banks, 61
  Policy, 369
  Undetakings, 330
  Policy, 373
  Sector, Role, 344, 346
Public/Private Sector Industries, 340
Punt Service, 222

R

Railways and Air Transport, 319
Rayalseema, 258
Research Laboratories, 138
Resolution of Industrial Conference, 311
River Krishna, 222
Rural
  Communities of India, 25
  Credit Project, 42
  Development, 26, 105, 210, 233
  Economy, 23, 24, 26, 32, 92, 94
  Employment Generation Program, 389
  Industrialization (India), 109
  Industrialization in Asia, 97
  Industrialization, 12, 88, 89, 93, 94, 96, 97, 106-108, 127, 161, 162
  Industries Program, 106
  Industries, 32, 90, 95
  Industrialization, 3
  Industry Schemes, 99
  Industry, 98-100
  Poverty, 24
Rural-Tribal Community, 169
Rural-Urban Migration, 95

S

Sarvodaya, 388
Schedule A, 324
Schedule B, 324
Science and Technology, 66, 165, 334
Second Five Year Plan, 316
Self Help Movements, 218
SENDCO (Small Enterprises National Documentation Centre), 144
Sericulture, 41, 50, 92
Seventh Five Year Plan, 113, 117, 129, 366
Seventh Plan Period, 118
SHGs (Self-Help Groups), 214, 216, 217, 218, 222, 224, 227, 228, 234, 236, 238, 240, 242, 244-249, 258
  Growth and Performance, 258-260
  Practices, 216
SIDBI, 115, 255,. 359
SIDCO (Small Scale Industrial Development Organization), 120, 130, 139, 140, 141, 143, 145, 148, 360

Sierra Leone, 73

Singapore, 89

Sixth Five Year Plan, 112, 117, 120, 129

Sixth Plan, 210

Small
- Cottage Industries, 92
- Industrial Service Institute, (SISI), 13, 59, 329
- Industry Development Corp., 348
- Scale and Cottage Industries, 104, 107, 109, 161, 162, 332
- Scale and Village Industries, 111
- Scale Enterprise, 92
- Scale Enterprises Development, 34
- Scale Industrial Development, 58, 88
- Scale Industrial Development Industries, 122
- Scale Industries, 34, 59, 90, 91, 94, 95, 96, 100, 101, 102, 109, 110, 112-115, 119, 120, 139
- Scale Industry Board and Development Commission, 92
- Scale Industry Development (India), 130
- Scale Industry Sector, 120, 139
- Scale Industry, 122, 127, 140, 141, 145, 267, 321, 322, 327, 332, 347, 348, 359, 363
- Scale Sector, 115, 119, 120, 140, 141, 184

Small Scale and Cottage Industries, 90, 101, 102, 107, 108

Social and
- Cultural Barriers, 9
- Economic Development, 18, 201
- Economic Justice, 118
- Economic Policy, 316, 317
- Occupational Mobility, 5
- Codes of Behaviour, 201
- Cultural Factors, 3

Social
- Employment Program, 39
- Equality, 1
- Infrastructure, 185-186
- Justice, 103
- Mobilization, 41
- Order, 306
- Sanctions, 4, 16, 203
- Status, 201, 232
- Stratification (Caste System), 4, 203
- Structure, 169

Society(ies), 1, 24, 6, 10, 23, 38, 40, 102, 118, 157, 167, 174, 201, 203, 204, 209, 211, 217, 233, 267, 317, 346, 357, 368
- Agrarian, 166, 267
- Caste Society in India, 6, 23
- Cooperative and Thrift--, 224
- Cooperatives, 217, 227, 232
- Development of -, 40
- Egalitarian, 357
- Hindu, 164
- Industrial, 166
- Japanese, 165
- Modern Economic, 105
- Socialist Pattern of -, 116, 316, 318, 365
- Traditional Developing , 5, 19
- Tribal, 6, 23
- Weaker Sections of -, 61
- Women and , 4, 203

Socio-Economic
- Development, 109
- Development Programmes, 7
- Level of Family, 22
- Objectives, 344

Policy, 346
Problem, 90
Surveys, 45

South Asia, 89

South East Asia, 22, 89

South Korea, 89

Special Institutions, 131, 132, 152

Special Institutions at State Level, 132, 134

Spices Board, Kochi, 242

Sri Lanka, 22

SSID (Small Scale Industrial Development Program), 27

State Bank of India, 62

State Khadi and Village Industry, 128

Status of DWCRA, 218

Status of Women, 1

Storage Facility, 79

Swayam Krishi, 213

T

Taiwan, 89

Tariff Policy, 315

Techno-Economic Survey, 106, 143, 168

Technology Development Centre in Small Industrial Development Org., 115

Technology, 100, 101, 113, 115, 117, 118, 162, 166, 245, 334, 335, 346, 350, 359, 361, 367, 391
Foreign, 331, 372
Indigenous, 95, 334
Modern, 95, 326
Productions, 95

Telephone-etc., 308

Tenth Plan, 386, 390, 391

Thailand, 23

Third World Countries, 98

Tirupati, 254

Traditional
Artisans, 93
Cultivation, 23
Industries, 98, 127
Occupations, 10, 11
Sector, 92
Small Industries, 92

Training Methodology, 277

Training Modules, 277

Transfer of Technology, 140, 207, 352, 362

Tribal
Council, 173
Women in Manipur, 23
Women in Meghalaya, 23
Women in Mizoram, 23
Women in Nagaland, 23

U

UNDP, 21, 208, 210

UNICEF, 213

United Nations, 20

Urbanization, 5

US Foreign Assistance Act, 20

V

Village and Small Scale Industries, 121-123

Village Industries Subjects, 129, 129

Visvesaraya, Sir M, 97

VO (Village Organization), Status, 48

VO (Village Organization), 43, 45-47, 49-55
Activities, 56

Vyasya Community, 164

W

War and
  Liberation (Bangladesh), 39
Warangal, 234, 235, 237
West Bengal, 21
Westernization, 5, 204
Women Coop. Thrift Societies, 227, 228
Women Development Mutual Aided Coop. Society, 261
Women Entrepreneurs, 12-15, 33, 34
Women Health and Developmet Program, 42
Women, 1, 2,
  Asian, 23
  Biological and Social Roles, 203
  Categorization, 5
  Domestic Roles, 206
  Economic Activities, 204
  Economic and Social Development, 2
  Economic and Social Role, 210
  Economic Conditions, 2
  Education, 5
  Entrepreneurs, 3, 4, 5, 7
  Exploitation, 52
  In Agriculture, 206, 210
  In Industry, 206
  Indian, 210
  Labour, 207
  Lower Caste, 208
  Manipur, 6
  Meghalaya, 6
  Mizoram, 6
  Nagaland, 6
  Participation in Development, 204
  Resources and Skills, 207
  Role in Development, 208
    Rural, 213
  SHG, 247
  Social and Cultural Sanctions, 6
  Social Roles, 4
  Socio-Economic Status of
  Rural--,218
  Status, 209
  Traditional Status, 204
  Tribal, 6
  Welfare Agencies, 14
  Welfare Workers, 14
Works Committee, 313
World Bank (India), 21

Y

YCO (Youth Charitable Org.) 261, 262, 264
Yigi Kamera, 73

Z

Zoning and Land Use Regulation, 378

□□□